Bronze Age, Roman and Later Occupation at Chieveley, West Berkshire

The archaeology of the A34 / M4 Road Junction Improvement

Andrew Mudd

with contributions from

Alex Thorne, Jane Timby, Tora Hylton, Ian Meadows,
Val Fryer, Rowena Gale and Karen Deighton

BAR British Series 433
2007

Published in 2016 by
BAR Publishing, Oxford

BAR British Series 433

Bronze Age, Roman and Later Occupation at Chieveley, West Berkshire

ISBN 978 1 4073 0038 2

© Northamptonshire Archaeology and the Publisher 2007

The authors' moral rights under the 1988 UK Copyright,
Designs and Patents Act are hereby expressly asserted.

All rights reserved. No part of this work may be copied, reproduced, stored,
sold, distributed, scanned, saved in any form of digital format or transmitted
in any form digitally, without the written permission of the Publisher.

BAR Publishing is the trading name of British Archaeological Reports (Oxford) Ltd.
British Archaeological Reports was first incorporated in 1974 to publish the BAR
Series, International and British. In 1992 Hadrian Books Ltd became part of the BAR
group. This volume was originally published by Archaeopress in conjunction with
British Archaeological Reports (Oxford) Ltd / Hadrian Books Ltd, the Series principal
publisher, in 2007. This present volume is published by BAR Publishing, 2016.

PUBLISHING

BAR titles are available from:

	BAR Publishing
	122 Banbury Rd, Oxford, OX2 7BP, UK
EMAIL	info@barpublishing.com
PHONE	+44 (0)1865 310431
FAX	+44 (0)1865 316916
	www.barpublishing.com

CONTENTS

Summary

Chapter 1: Introduction — page 1
- Background and location — 1
- Details of construction — 1
- Site areas — 1
- Contract protocol — 1
- Archive — 2

Chapter 2: Archaeological Background — 4
- Scope of project investigations — 4
- Archaeology of the area — 4
- Project-based information — 4

Chapter 3: Summary of Investigation and Results — 9
- Mitigation measures — 9
- Summary of results — 9

Chapter 4: Prehistoric Features — 17
- Area E: Later prehistoric pits and gullies in Trench 11 — 17
- Area E: Trenches 13 - 29: possible prehistoric features — 26
- Area A: Isolated Iron Age pit — 28

Chapter 5: Roman Features — 34
- Introduction — 34
- Early Roman features in Trial Pit 139 — 34
- Possible Roman features in Trench 28 — 34
- Earlier Roman features at the northern end of Trench 29 — 34
- Late Roman pits at the northern end of Trench 29 — 34
- Trench 11: Linear ditches and related features — 35
- Area D Trench 1: miscellaneous Iron Age and Roman pottery — 38

Chapter 6: Saxon Features — 40
- Introduction — 40
- Area E: Pit 29248 — 40
- Area C Trench 10: group of pits — 41

Chapter 7: Post-medieval Features — 42
- Area A Trench 16: Hollow-way and other features — 42
- Area B: Field boundaries — 44
- Area C Trench 10: Timber structure and field boundary ditches — 44
- Area E trench 11: Ditch and related features — 44
- Area E: Other linear features — 45
- Area D: Field boundaries — 45

Chapter 8: Worked and Burnt Flint — 48
by Alex Thorne
- Worked flint: Introduction — 48
- Burnt flint — 61

Chapter 9: The Pottery — 65
by Jane Timby
- Introduction — 65
- Methodology — 65
- Bronze Age — 65
- Iron Age — 67
- Roman — 67
- Discussion — 70
- Saxon — 70
- Pottery from Snelsmore Farm site — 71

Chapter 10: Metal and other finds — 73
by Tora Hylton with Ian Meadows
- Introduction — 73
- Roman finds — 73
- 'Saxon' Lava Quern — 74
- Post-medieval finds — 74
- Coins *by Ian Meadows* — 75

Chapter 11: Environmental Evidence — 76
- Charred plant remains *by Val Fryer* — 76
- The wood charcoals *by Rowena Gale* — 82
- The animal bone *by Karen Deighton* — 83
- Soil tests *by Karen Deighton* — 83

Chapter 12: Radiocarbon Dating — 84

Chapter 13: Discussion — 85
- Pre-Bronze Age activity — 85
- Bronze Age occupation — 85
- Iron Age, Roman and Saxon — 89
- Post-medieval features — 90
- Conclusions — 91

Bibliography — 94

Figures

1.1	Project location	page 2
1.2	Areas of archaeological works	3
2.1	Known and potential archaeological features and finds before present fieldwork	5
2.2	Summary results of surface collection survey	6
2.3	Interpretation of geophysical survey results (Stratascan 2002)	7
3.1	Locations of all trenches	10
3.2	Trenches north of M4 motorway	11
3.3	Trenches south of M4 motorway	12
4.1	Bronze Age pits and other features in Area E Trench 11	18
4.2	Pit Groups 11047 and 11138	19
4.3	Sections of Pit Groups 11047 and 11138 (with projected sections of peripheral pits)	23
4.4	Pits 11090 and 11024	27
4.5	Pits 11090, 11024, 11110, 11195 and 11033 (sections)	29
4.6	Pit Groups 11174, 11155 and 11213 (sections)	31
4.7	Bronze Age features in Area E	33
5.1	Trial Pit 139 (from Oxford Archaeology 2002); Trench 28. Area E	36
5.2	Roman and early Saxon features in Area E	37
5.3	Late Roman 'cremation' pits, Group 29247. Area E	38
6.1	Probable early-mid Saxon pit 29248	39
6.2	Trench 10, Area C, showing early-mid Saxon pits, post-medieval ditches and undated post-built structure	40
6.3	Sections of early-mid Saxon pits	41
7.1	Plan of post-medieval hollow-way and other features, Trench 16, Area A	43
7.2	Section through post-medieval hollow-way, Trench 16, Area A	45
7.3	Post-medieval features in Areas A, B and C	46
7.4	Post-medieval features in Areas D and E	47
8.1	Length and breadth dimensions of flint artefacts, Northamptonshire Archaeology collection	53
8.2	Length and breadth dimensions of flint artefacts, Gifford collection	54
8.3	Length and breadth dimensions of flint artefacts, Oxford Archaeology collection	55
8.4	Worked flint distribution from surface collection (from GGP 2000 archive)	56
8.5	Worked flint distribution from trial pits (from OA 2002 archive)	57
8.6	Worked flint distribution from excavations (NA 2003)	58
8.7	Burnt flint distribution by weight from surface collection	59
8.8	Burnt flint distribution by weight from trial pits	60
8.9	Burnt flint distribution by weight from excavations	63
8.10	Flint artefacts from all stages of fieldwork. See catalogue for details	64
9.1	Bronze Age pottery (1-3) and Roman pottery (4-8) from excavations	68
9.2	Roman pottery (9-15) from excavations	69
9.3	Roman pottery (16-18) and late Saxon / medieval pottery (19) from excavations	71
10.1	Roman spoon from layer 29014	74
12.1	Radiocarbon calibration plot from charcoal in Pit 11090 (SUERC-4148), using OxCal v3.8 calibration software	84
13.1	Copy of part of Tithe Map for Snelsmore 1840 (Berkshire Record Office Ref. D/D1 34/3, by kind permission)	92
13.2	Copy of part of John Rocque's map of Berkshire c. 1761 (Berkshire Record Office, by kind permission)	93

Please note that larger versions of Figures 4.3, 4.5 and 4.6 are available to download from www.barpublishing.com/additional-downloads.html

Colour Plates

1	Area E Trench 11 looking south. Bronze Age pit 11047 being excavated	page 15
2	Area A Trench 16 looking north. Hollow-way is visible as a silty band	15
3	Central shaft of Pit Group 11047 recorded in the watching brief. Area E Trench 11	16
4	Bronze Age pit 11065 (part of Group 11047) under excavation. Area E Trench 11	16
5	Bronze Age Pit Group 11138 under excavation. Area E Trench 11	16
6	Selection of Roman pottery from Pit Group 29247. Flask (lower left) from Layer 29014, miniature jar (top right) from Pit 29229, rest from Pit 29018	16

Plates

1	Photograph of Snelsmore Farm showing soil marks in Area A. (NMR Ref. OS/79119. Crown copyright. Northamptonshire County Council: Licence No. 100019331)	8
2	Bronze Age pit 11077 (part of Group 11138). Area E Trench 11	20
3	Bronze Age pits 11066 and 11068 (part of Group 11138). Area E Trench 11	21
4	Bronze Age pit 11090, showing lenses of burnt flint. Area E Trench 11	21
5	?Bronze Age gully 29021. Area E Trench 29	28
6	Late Roman pit 29018 (part of Group 29247). Area E Trench 29	35
7	Late Roman quernstone, overlying a patch of burnt clay, base of Layer 29014 (part of Group 29247). Area E Trench 29	35

Tables

1.1	Summary of mitigation measures	9
8.1	General composition of the Chieveley flint assemblages. Percentages are given as a proportion of the entire collection	48
8.2	Composition of the flint group excavated from CHRF Trench 11 middle/late Bronze Age and other contexts. Percentages relate to the stratified assemblage from the pits	49
8.3	Composition of the Northamptonshire Archaeology flint assemblage	50
8.4	Gifford flint categories per field	51
8.5	Oxford Archaeology flint categories	51
8.6	Categories of raw material	52
8.7	Total weight of burnt flint recovered by Area	61
8.8	Quantities of hand-retrieved flint from excavated features (Northamptonshire Archaeology 2003)	61
8.9	Quantity of burnt flint recovered from bulk soil samples (Northamptonshire Archaeology 2003)	62
9.1	Pottery fabrics and quantifications	66
10.1	Catalogue of coins	75
11.1	Charred plant macrofossils and other remains from Bronze Age pit 11090 (Area E)	77
11.2	Charred plant macrofossils and other remains from Bronze Age pit 11033 (Area E)	77
11.3	Charred plant and other remains from late Bronze Age/early Iron Age pit 11053, Group 11047 (Area E)	78
11.4	Charred plant macrofossils and other remains from Bronze Age/Iron Age pit group 11138 (Area E)	78
11.5	Charred plant macrofossils and other remains from possible Bronze Age gullies in Trench 29 (Area E)	79
11.6	Charred plant macrofossils and other remains from late Roman and Saxon features in Trench 29 (Area E)	79
11.7	Charred plant remains and other material from Saxon pits in Area C Trench 10	80
11.8	Charred plant macrofossils, supplementary sample assessment (Area E)	81
11.9	The wood charcoals	82
11.10	Animal bone, summary of species present	83
11.11	Result of soil pH tests	83
12.1	Radiocarbon dates (calibration using OxCal v.3.8)	84

Contributors

Andrew Mudd BA MIFA,
Northamptonshire Archaeology, 2 Bolton House, Wootton Hall Park, Northampton NN4 8BE

Alex Thorne BSc AIFA,
Northamptonshire Archaeology

Val Fryer BA MIFA,
Church Farm, Sisland, Loddon, Norfolk NR14 6EF

Tora Hylton,
Northamptonshire Archaeology

Ian Meadows BA,
Northamptonshire Archaeology

Rowena Gale,
Honorary Research Associate, Royal Botanic Gardens, Kew

Jane Timby BA PhD MIFA,
Sister Mary's Cottage, High Street, Chalford, Glos GL6 8DH

Karen Deighton MSc
Northamptonshire Archaeology

Acknowledgements

Northamptonshire Archaeology is particularly grateful to Costain Ltd who funded the archaeological work. With a project of this nature, closely tied to the construction programme, co-ordination of all works was vital and thanks in particular are due to Darren James, Project Manager, and Lee Davies, Construction Manager, for making this possible. Jim Keyte of Gifford WSP oversaw the archaeological work on behalf of the Highways Agency, and offered valuable comments on a draft of this publication. Northamptonshire Archaeology is also grateful to Professor Richard Bradley of Reading University for reviewing this report.

Northamptonshire Archaeology also wishes to thank the many members of its staff who undertook the work. The fieldwork was supervised by Barry Lewis and Jim Brown, while Adrian Butler managed and carried out the geophysical surveys, with the help of Ian Fisher and Jim Brown. The illustrations for this publication were produced by Jacqueline Harding, Leeanne Whitelaw and Drew Smith. Cover illustration by Alex Thorne. The publication was edited by Charlotte Walker. Typesetting is by Drew Smith.

Digital mapping and the copy of the aerial photograph shown as Plate 1 are reproduced under licence from the Ordnance Survey (Northamptonshire County Council Licence No. 100019331).

Summary

Archaeological surveys and excavations ahead of the construction of the new A34 / M4 interchange at Chieveley, West Berkshire, resulted in the investigation of a scatter of Bronze Age, Roman, Saxon and post-medieval features in the areas of the road cutting and soil disposal. Another discrete area of features, probably representing a Roman farmstead, was left to be preserved in situ.

The Middle to Late Bronze Age features comprised a group of pits containing small quantities of pottery, flintwork and charred plant remains, and a relatively high concentration of burnt flint. Some of these pits appeared to have originated as natural solution holes.

Peripheral to the site of the Roman farmstead, a group of pits contained an unusual assemblage of late Roman pottery and other finds. It is thought these may be associated with funerary activity. There was also some early-middle Saxon material from this area, and a group of pits of this date in an apparently isolated location south of the M4. The chief post-medieval feature was a probable hollow-way south of the M4, and there was a scatter of former field boundaries and other minor features.

This report describes the results of the evaluations and excavations and discusses the combined evidence from superficial and subsurface finds. While the results were fragmentary, it is concluded that there was a significant intensification of activity in the area starting in the Middle Bronze Age following a sporadic earlier prehistoric presence. This continued into the Late Bronze Age. The lack of Iron Age material is noted and there seems to have been a re-intensification of occupation in the late Iron Age or early Roman period. The few early-middle Saxon pits were divorced from a settlement context and remain enigmatic.

Chapter 1: Introduction

Background and location

Northamptonshire Archaeology undertook a programme of archaeological work in advance of and during works associated with the construction of the A34 / M4 Junction 13 Road Improvement at Chieveley in West Berkshire (Fig. 1.1). The work comprised a staged series of geophysical surveys, evaluation trenches, area excavations and, subsequently, a watching brief during earth moving. It was undertaken on behalf of the constructor, Costain Ltd, as part of the construction contract in order to mitigate the effects of construction upon archaeological remains. The fieldwork to which this report mainly relates took place between March and July 2003, but this followed on from earlier stages of archaeological survey undertaken by Gifford Graham and Partners in 2000 and Oxford Archaeology in 2002 before the award of contract.

The village of Chieveley lies about 5km north of Newbury within the drainage basin of the River Lambourn. The present A34 follows a dry valley running south to the Lambourn at Newbury. The rolling countryside of the area is formed on the mixed sands, clays and gravels of the Reading Beds, with the underlying Upper Chalk outcropping just north of Chieveley. The more pronounced landforms in the field immediately north of the motorway (south of Radnall Farm) were shown to have been caused by quarrying and recent made ground. The soils developed on the Reading Beds are naturally acidic and not favourable to the preservation of archaeological material, particularly bone. The ground was found to be free-draining in some places, but surprisingly impermeable in others. There is no natural permanent watercourse in the immediate vicinity. Several wells and ponds are shown on maps of the area.

This geological complexity is relevant to the archaeology of the site, particularly with regard to the definition and interpretation of features, which was occasionally problematic.

Details of construction

The site of archaeological works covered about 48ha on both the northern and southern sides of the M4 motorway and on the western side of the existing A34 and motorway junction (Fig. 1.2). All this land, apart from the site compound, was within the boundary of compulsory purchase or lease at the time of the contract.

From the south, the new road construction departed from the pre-existing A34 just north of the Curridge Road Overbridge (SU 473714), passing under the M4 in a deep cutting, running east of Radnall Farm, and rejoining the A34 just south of Chieveley Crossroads Bridge (SU 480738). The total linear distance is about 2.3km. Within this length of road a number of junctions linked the new road to the pre-existing A34, local roads, farms and bridleways. These included a new access to Radnall Farm from Graces Lane (Chieveley). Soil disposal and landscaping areas lay immediately west of the road cutting on both sides of the M4 motorway. A smaller area lay on the eastern side, south of Chalky Lane. The site compound lay to the west of the construction area between Snelsmore Farm and Green Lane.

Site Areas

The site was divided in to several areas (Fig. 1.2; A-F) continuing the terminology of earlier mitigation work (below) for ease of reference. They are as follows:

Area A: principally taken by cuttings for the new A34 and local Oxford Road, together with Gantry 3 for the equestrian bridge and adjacent landscaping.

Area B: a small part taken by Gantry 3, the rest designated for soil disposal although, in the event, only part was used.

Area C: almost all taken by the new A34 cutting and M4 slip road.

Area D: partly taken by road cutting, but most for soil disposal.

Area E: eastern margin taken by road cutting, the western side by Radnall Farm Access Road. The rest used for soil disposal.

Area F: largely designated for road cutting and balancing pond.

Contract protocol

This report has been undertaken in accordance with the Highways Agency's ('Employer's') Requirements, issued as part of the tender (Section 11 Archaeological Interest [Tender Amendment 7], Annex 11/1 & references), which stated the Contractor's responsibilities for the detailed design, implementation and publication of the Archaeological Work. It represents, along with the deposition of the finds and paper archive with Berkshire Museums Service, the final stage of the archaeological programme.

The specification of work was detailed in the overall *Archaeological Design and Mitigation Strategy* (NA 2003) submitted by Costain Ltd / Northamptonshire Archaeology prior to site works in fulfilment of the Employer's Requirements, and approved by the Employer's Agent, Gifford WSP. The *Archaeological Design and Mitigation Strategy* included an overview of pre-existing archaeological information, the project research design, and methods statements for all the investigations to be undertaken. It also included an outline of the scope of the later *Assessment and Updated Project Design* (NA 2004), which was undertaken in line with

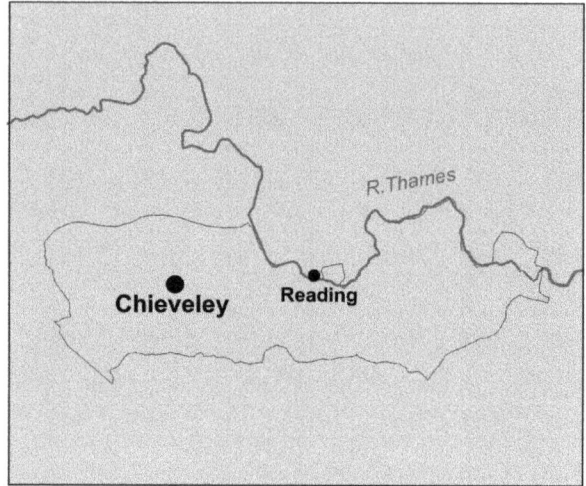

Fig 1.1 Project location

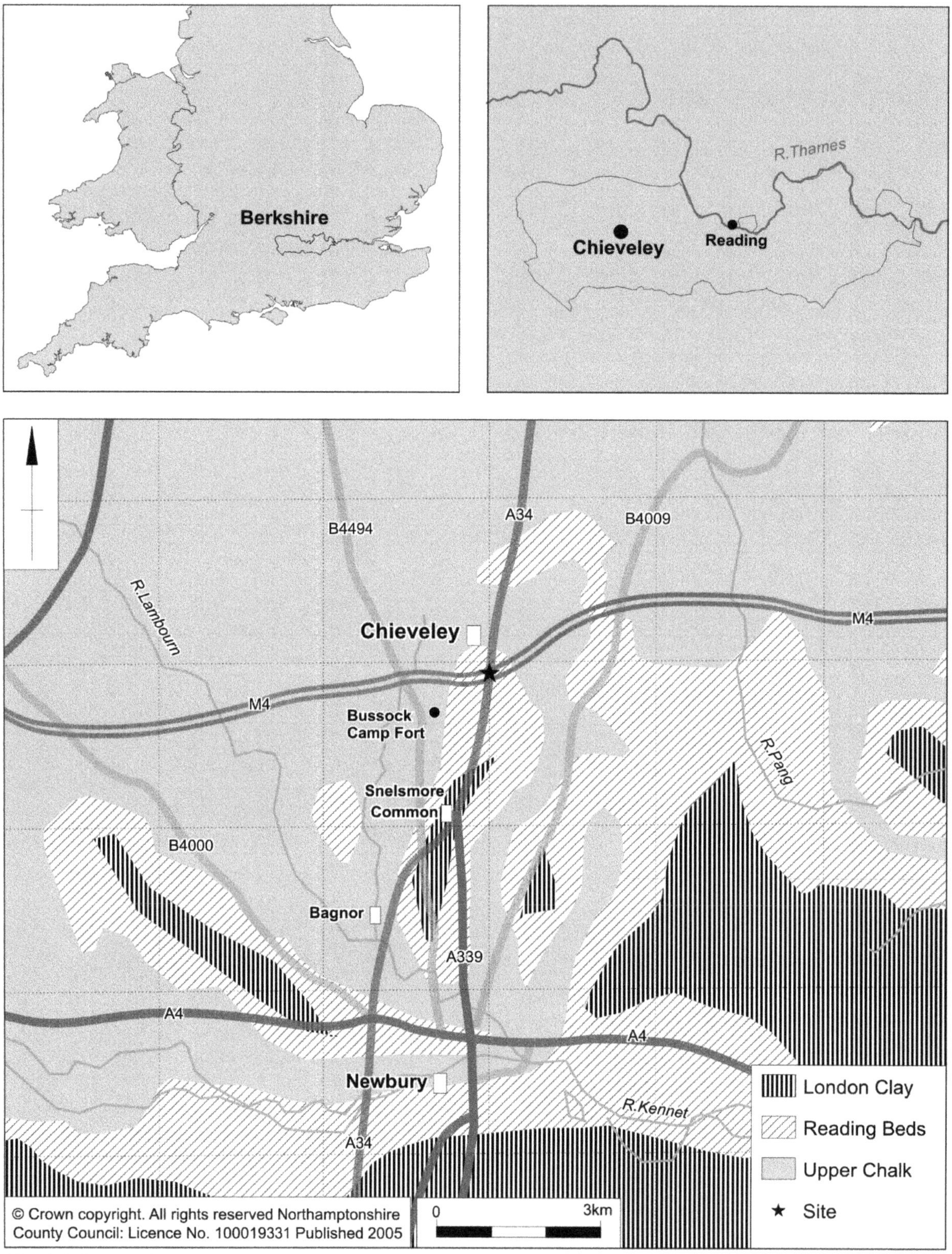

English Heritage's procedural document *Management of Archaeological Projects* (1991).

All designs, proposals and deliveries were subject to the procedure of certification which formed part of the contract and was undertaken by Gifford WSP for the Highways Agency.

Archive

All the finds and paper and digital archives have been, or are to be, stored in the West Berkshire Museum, Newbury, with Accession Numbers NEBYM: 2000.5 (Gifford archive), NEBYM 2002.5 (Oxford Archaeology archive), and NEBYM: 2003.1 and NEBYM:2003.2 (Northamptonshire Archaeology). The archaeological community is grateful to the landowner, Mr C Povey of Great Shefford (Hungerford), for donating the material.

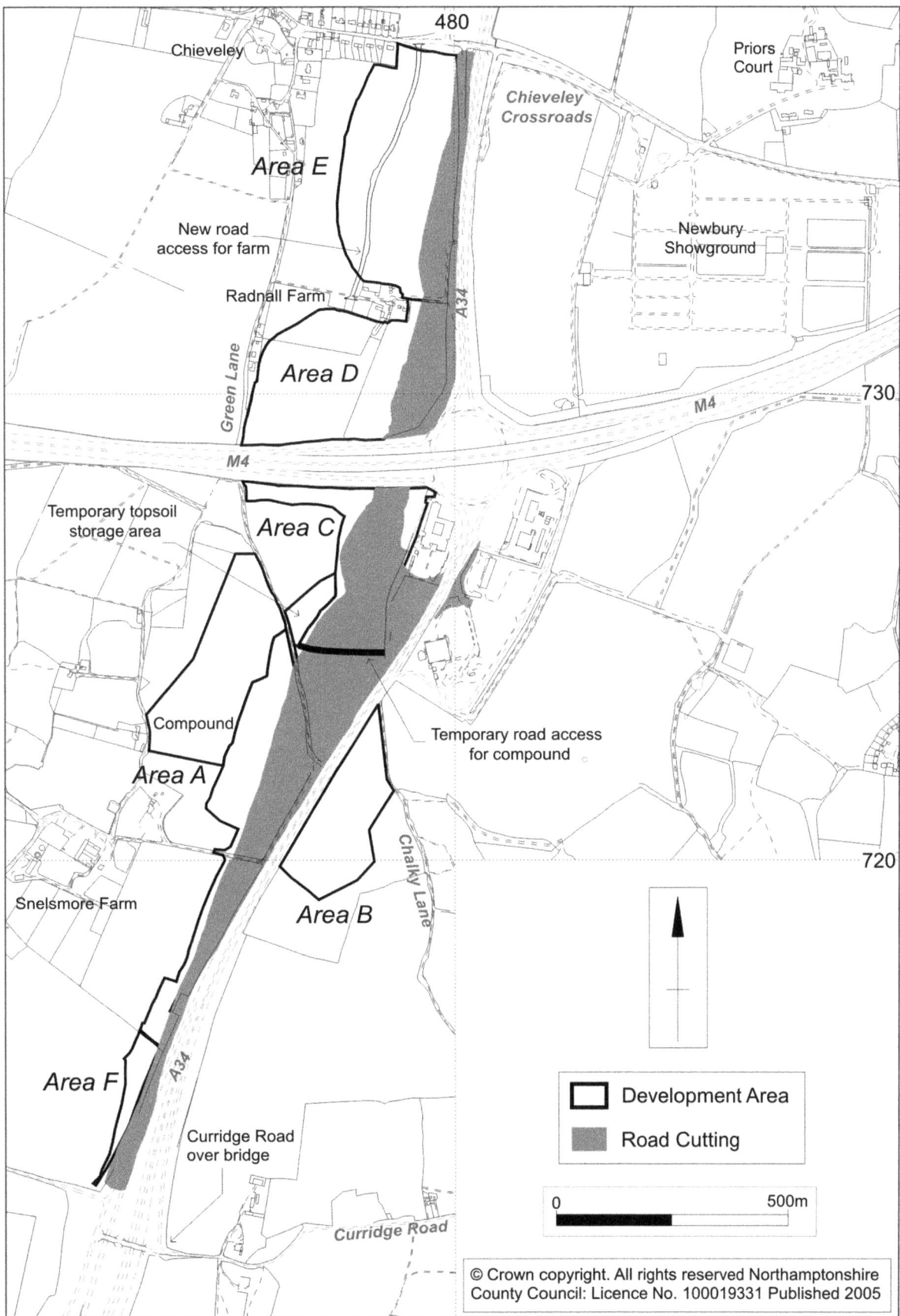

Fig 1.2 Areas of archaeological works

Chapter 2: Archaeological Background

Scope of project investigations

The archaeological fieldwork undertaken by Northamptonshire Archaeology represented a stage in a programme of mitigation measures carried out over the course of several years before and after the award of the construction contract. The earlier work included an archaeological desk-based assessment by Gifford Graham and Partners (GGP 1999), a field-walking survey, also by Gifford Graham and Partners (GGP 2000), detailed magnetometer surveys over parts of the site (Stratascan 2002), and a systematic test-pitting survey (Oxford Archaeology 2002). The work undertaken by Northamptonshire Archaeology essentially completed the evaluation of the site (further geophysical survey and trial trenching), followed by area excavations where archaeological features would be unavoidably destroyed.

In combination these desk-based and field investigations provide a body of information which has been summarised and in some cases re-analysed for this report. Northamptonshire Archaeology's remit for the final stages of mitigation included a review and re-examination of existing records, which resulted in a certain amount of new information (below). Subsequently, and following standard English Heritage post-excavation procedures, the 'assessment report' recommended integrating the material from the earlier stages of fieldwork with the excavation results (NA 2004). This retrospective on the mitigation strategy has enabled some critical assessment of archaeological interpretations of the various types of evidence gathered. This is of some interest and relevance for any type of survey work which endeavours to predict the nature of subsurface archaeological deposits from limited or 'non-intrusive' investigations.

Archaeology of the area

Known archaeological remains are not common in this part of West Berkshire. Searches of the county Historical Environment Record (formerly Sites and Monuments Record) were undertaken in 1999 and 2003 (GGP 1999; NA 2003) in an area within a 1km radius of the site. The records included several buildings and chance finds of medieval and later material, but significant earlier sites were sparse.

There is an Iron Age hillfort at Bussock Camp, c. 1km to the south-west (Fig. 1.1), which is a Scheduled Monument. This was the only Iron Age settlement recorded in the data capture area. Perhaps more surprisingly, there were only three occurrences of Roman material before the current fieldwork, two being metalwork finds (coins and a brooch), both possibly from the same site north of Chieveley village. Five 'Iron Age-Roman' sherds were recovered during fieldwalking by Mr D H King around Snelsmore Farm, but, like the medieval and later material also found, these may well be stray finds.

The earlier prehistoric sites in the immediate area are shown on Figure 2.1 and comprised the cropmark of a probable ring-ditch to the east of the A34 and west of Prior's Court, a collection of flintwork from an adjacent field recovered during fieldwalking, and a 'Type B' Beaker discovered in 1932 on the site of the present Newbury Showground. It is possible that the latter represents the site of a barrow, although this has not been verified.

Project-based information

Desk-Based Assessment
(Gifford Graham and Partners, August 1999)

The desk-based assessment involved a consultation of the West Berkshire Historical Environment Record and historical maps, together with an extensive review of published information on the region and the, then unpublished, reports on the archaeology of the A34 Newbury Bypass (GGP 1999). No sites were identified within the development area itself, the small quantity of medieval and later artefacts being interpreted as 'chance finds' of little archaeological significance. The cartographic evidence showed 'little change in the landscape between 1761 (the date of Speed's map of the county) and the late nineteenth century' (GGP 1999, 8.2), the major impact being the construction of the M4 motorway and the widening of the A34 since the early 1970s.

Surface collection (field-walking) survey
(Gifford Graham and Partners, August 2000

The surface collection survey was undertaken on three ploughed fields within the development area. These comprised most of Areas A and F, Area C (with the exception of the proposed planting strip along the edge of the M4), a marginal strip of Area B, and Area E (Fig. 2.2).

The survey found:

1. Significant quantities of prehistoric (mostly Bronze Age) pottery in the northern part of Area E, suggesting the possible presence of a Bronze Age site (GGP 2000, 4.1.2).

2. Statistically significant quantities of worked and burnt flint in Area E, suggesting other Bronze Age or later Neolithic activity.

3. A high density of worked and burnt flint in Area A, possibly the ploughed remains of a burnt mound.

Chapter 2: Archaeological Background

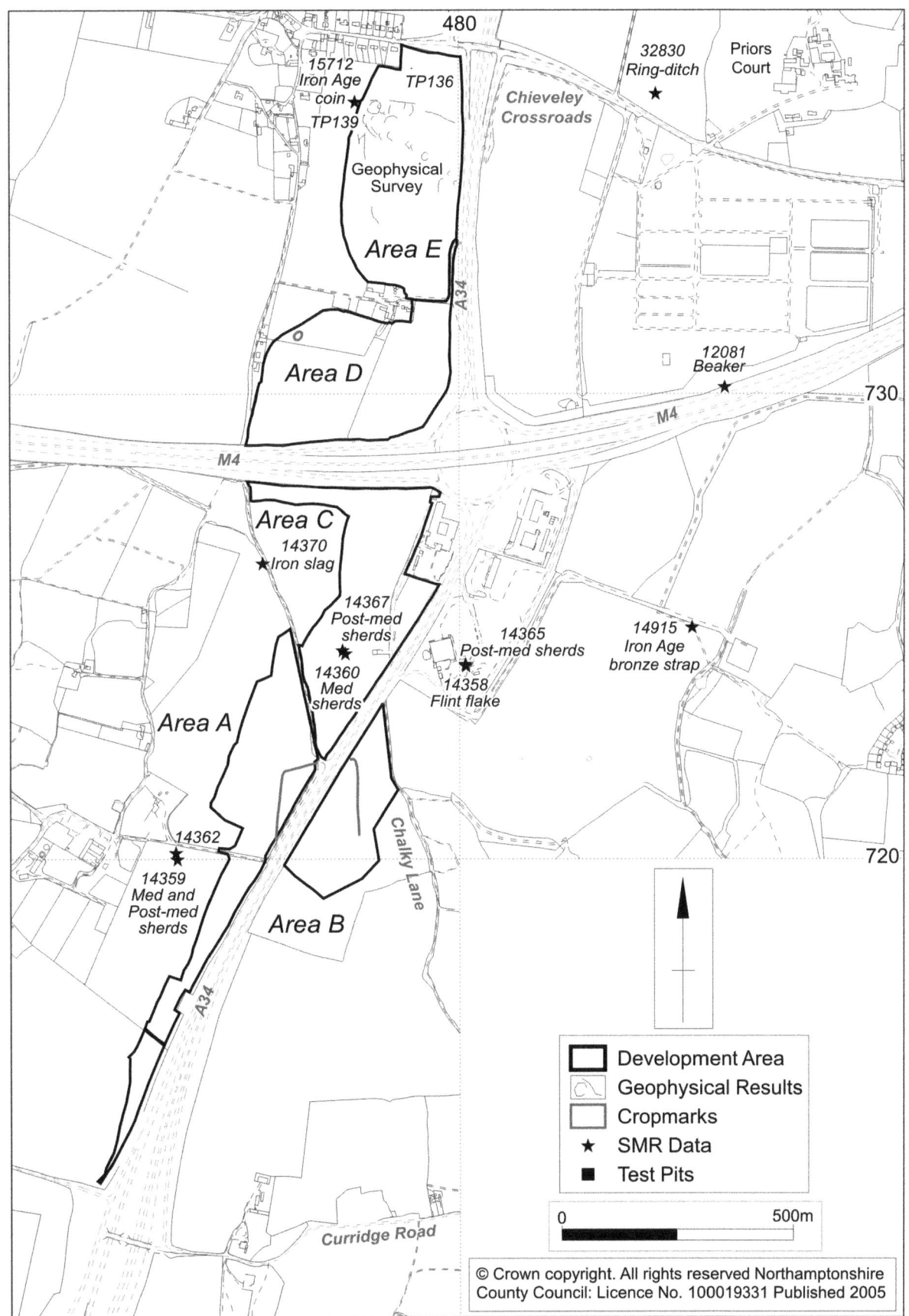

Fig 2.1 Known and potential archaeological features and finds before present fieldwork

4. A small scatter of worked flint on the margin of Area B, described as 'potentially significant' (GGP 2000, 3.1.8)

5. A concentration of post-medieval tile and pottery in Area E, thought to be related to a house demolished ahead of the widening of the A34 (GGP 2000, 3.5.3).

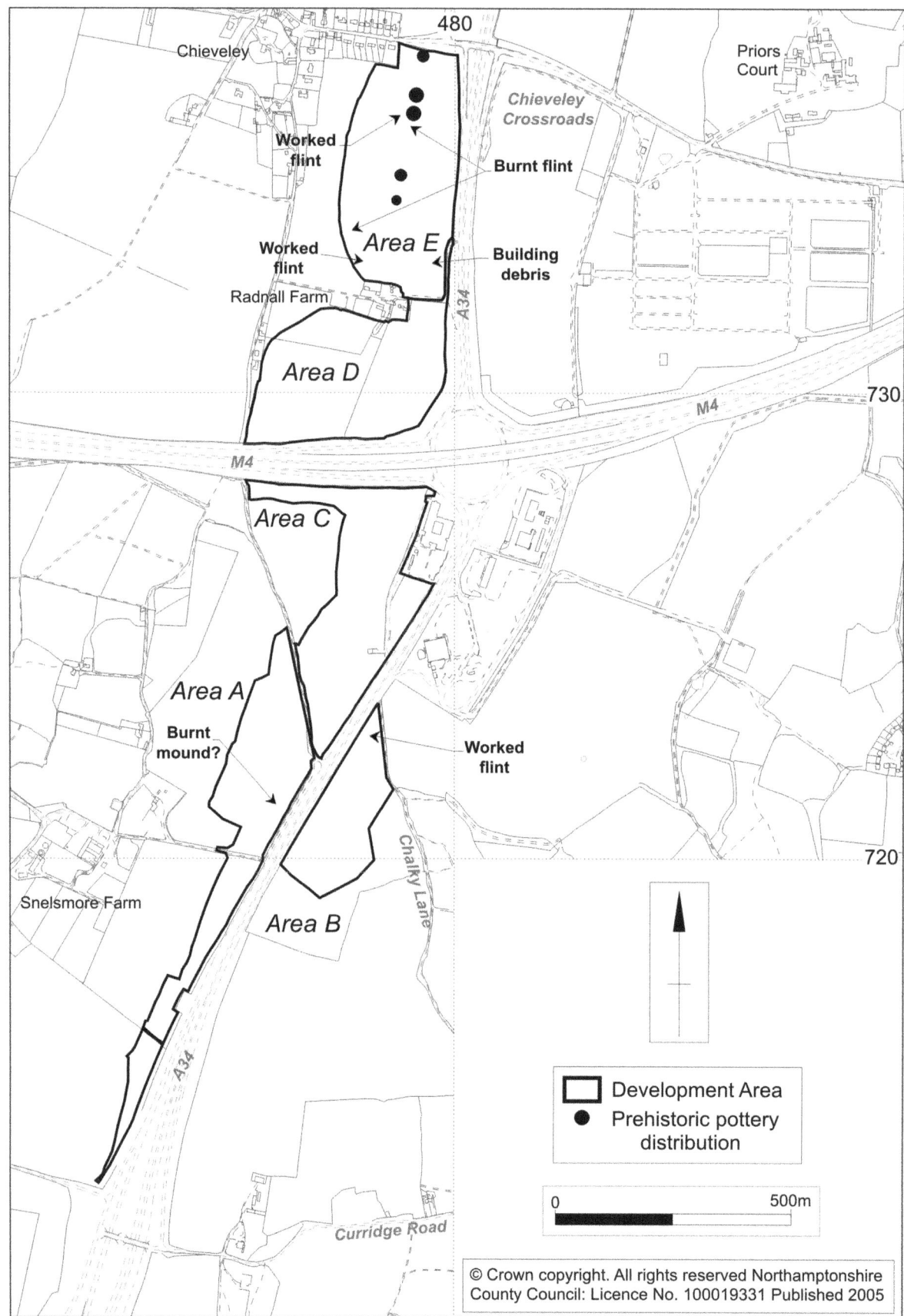

Fig 2.2 Summary results of surface collection survey

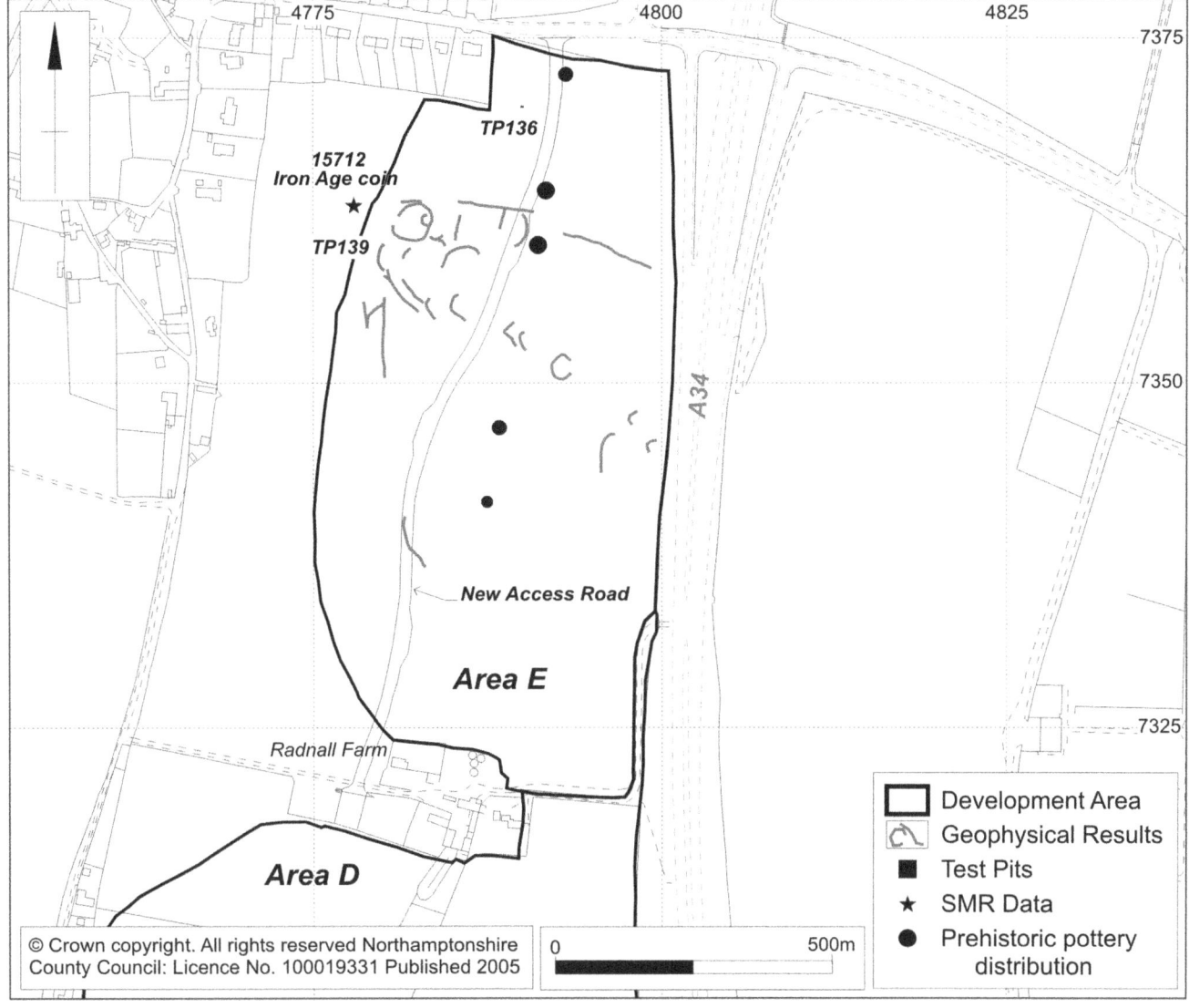

Fig 2.3 Interpretation of geophysical survey results (Stratascan 2002)

Geophysical Survey
(Stratascan, May – September 2002)

The geophysical survey comprised a magnetic susceptibility survey over the entire development area, followed by detailed magnetometer surveys in Areas D and E.

The magnetic susceptibility survey indicated the following areas of interest:

1. A broad strip about 50m in width in the central part of Area A.
2. A possibly corresponding enhancement in the southern part of Area B.
3. Several areas of enhancement in Area C.
4. A strong enhancement in the north-east corner of Area D; and in a central band running north-south.
5. The south-east corner of Area E, corresponding to Area D; the north-west corner of Area E, corresponding to the results of the fieldwalking; and the central eastern border of Area E.

The detailed magnetometer survey in Area D was undertaken in six sample blocks. No features of archaeological interest were discovered. A number of magnetic anomalies of modern origin were recorded.

The detailed magnetometer survey covered the entire extent of Area E (Fig. 2.3). This survey located ditches and possible pits in the north-west corner of the site which were interpreted as evidence of a settlement. Other linear features were recorded in other parts of Area E, some of which may be archaeologically significant. Modern disturbances caused by pipelines in the south-east corner of the field, and by a trackway on the eastern side, were also recorded.

Trial-Pitting Survey
(Oxford Archaeology, September 2002)

A total of 159 1m by 1m trial pits were excavated, covering, as far as was practicable, the entire development area. These were located in a systematic manner on a 50m grid which was the same as used for the geophysical surveys.

The results can be summarised as follows:

1. In TP136, on the northern part of Area E (Fig. 2.3), a large number of pot sherds, representing two Middle Bronze Age vessels, were recovered from the topsoil and its interface with the natural clay and flint. This indicated Bronze Age occupation on the site.
2. In TP139, in the north-west part of Area E (Fig. 2.3), two inter-cutting ditches containing 1st century AD pottery were discovered. These features lay just west of the area of ditches and pits found in the geophysical survey and together provided evidence of a late Iron Age/early Roman enclosure settlement (OA 2002, 6.2.6).
3. Small quantities of prehistoric finds from the trial pits south of the M4 (Areas A, B, C and F), suggest occupation or activity in this period in the vicinity of the development area. It was not possible to ascertain the location or nature of this activity or occupation on available information.
4. Area D showed modern made ground in all the trial pits (OA 2002, 4.1.4). The area includes a recent quarry pit.

Updated data
(Northamptonshire Archaeology 2003)

A new search of the Historical Environment Record resulted in a single new relevant entry – the find of a late Iron Age coin close to the north-west corner of Area E (Fig. 2.1). This lay within the area identified as a late Iron Age/early Roman settlement to which it is undoubtedly related. The coin was identified as a gold quarter stater, probably of the Atrebates tribe.

A search of aerial photographs from the National Monuments Record yielded two photographs showing possible new archaeological features in the development area. One photograph shows a soil mark in Area A appearing as the angle of a bank and ditch, which may have formed two sides of an enclosure (Fig. 2.1; Plate 1). This was later investigated in an open area excavation (Trench 16).

The overlapping photograph in the same flight run shows a possible circular or rectangular mound in Area D to the west of Radnall Farm. Trial trenching later showed this feature to have been spurious.

Plate 1.
Photograph of Snelsmore Farm showing soil marks in Area A.
(NMR Ref OS/79119. Crown copyright. Northamptonshire County Council:Licence No. 100019331)

Chapter 3: Summary of investigations and results

Mitigation measures

The various archaeological works were closely linked to the construction programme to ensure minimum adverse effect on the construction itself. As a consequence, several stages of work were undertaken more or less simultaneously in different areas of the site. For ease of reference, the mitigation measures for each area are summarised in tabular form (Table 1.1) while their locations are shown on Figures 3.1-3.3. Reports on the archaeological works follow below.

For practical recording purposes the area of investigation was divided into two 'sites' which were investigated concurrently for much of the time, those north of the M4 being given the site code CHRF and those to the south SNEL.

The works are shown in the order in which they were started, reflecting the logic of the construction programme. The areas of most archaeological activity, Area E Trench 11 and the Radnall Farm Access Road, were the last areas to be cleared.

Area	Geo.	TT	S & R	Exc.	Pres.	Significant finds
Site Compound	*	*				None
Temporary compound access			*			None
Area D Soil Disposal		*				None
Area D Cutting		*	*			None
Area E Soil Disposal (NW of Radnall Farm Access)					*	Late Iron Age/early Roman settlement
Area E Soil Disposal & Cutting		*		*		Bronze Age pits (Trench 11)
Radnall Farm Access			*	*		?Bronze Age features Roman pits & ditches Saxon pit
Area C	*		*	*		Saxon pits Undated structure
Area A (N)	*			*		Post-medieval trackway Iron Age pit
Areas A (S) & F		*				None
Area B	*	*				None

Table 1.1: Summary of mitigation measures

Geo. geophysical survey; *TT* trial trenching; *S & R* strip and record; *Exc.* excavation; *Pres.* preservation in situ

A watching brief was also maintained during topsoil removal, and during the excavation of the road cutting in Area E, Trench 11, where additional pits were discovered and examined.

Summary of results

The following is a brief summary of the results of the investigations. Full descriptive accounts of the main features of archaeological interest are given in Chapters 4-7. The detailed results of the other mitigation measures, which yielded little of significance, have been presented in the assessment report (NA 2003) and are not reiterated here.

Site Compound Geophysical Survey

Detailed magnetometer survey over the entire 5.1ha produced no identifiable archaeological features. A single pit-like anomaly may have been an archaeological feature, but its isolation suggested that it may have represented debris in the ploughsoil.

Site Compound Trial Trenching

Nine trenches with combined length of *c.* 500m were excavated. No archaeological features were discovered. Three small pits, without finds, are likely to have been natural features.

Bronze Age, Roman and later occupation at Chieveley, West Berkshire

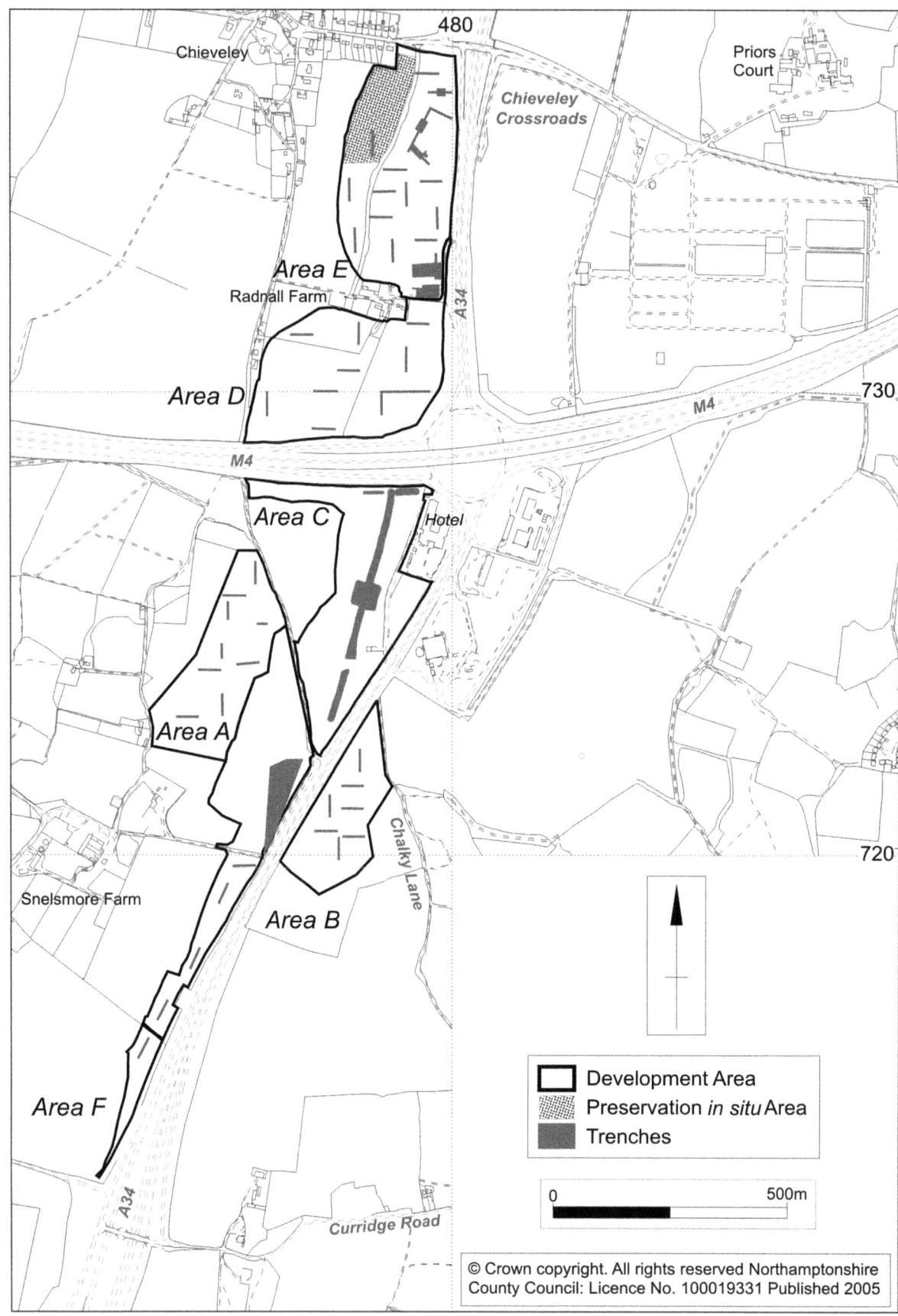

Fig 3.1 Locations of all trenches

Chapter 3: Summary of investigations and results

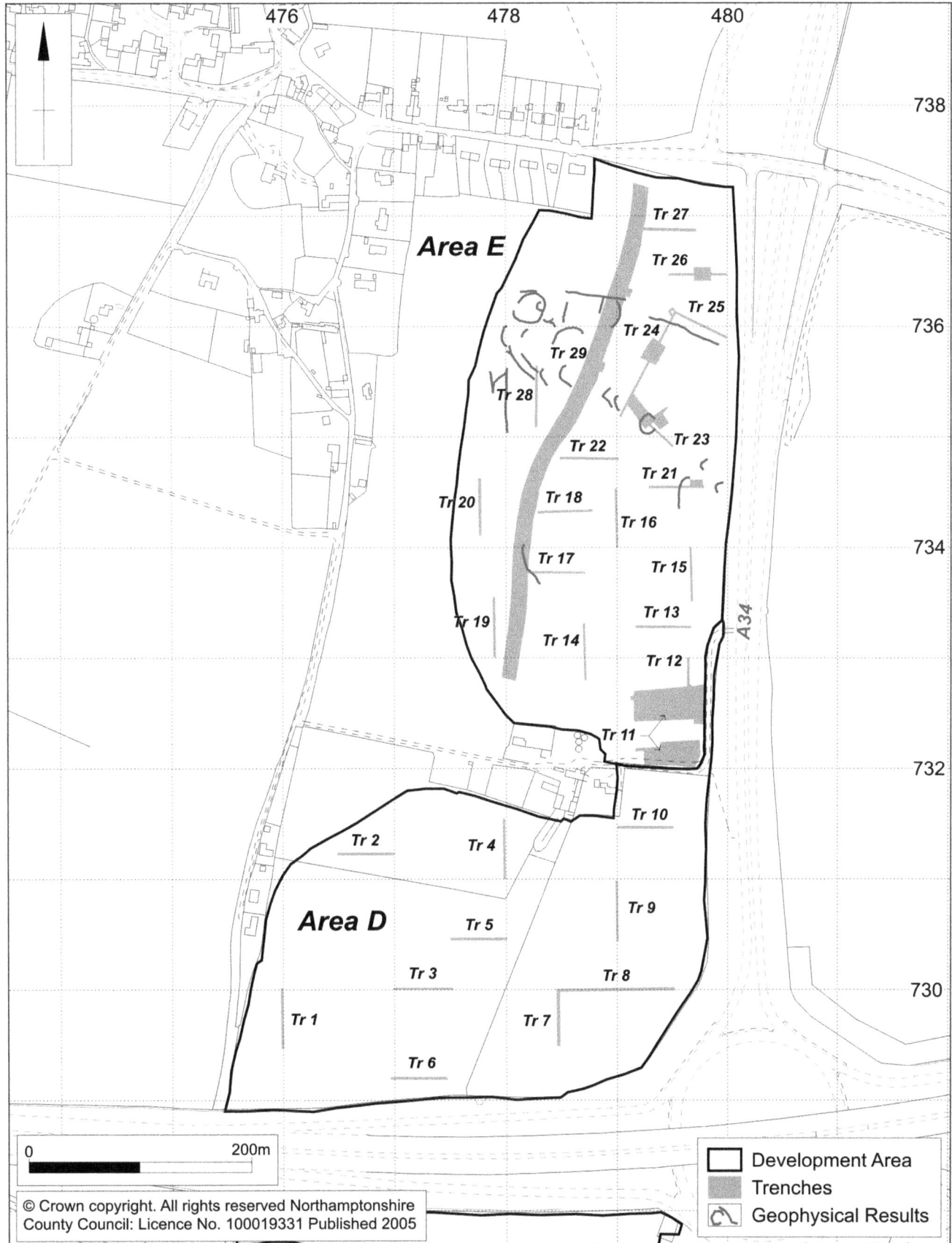

Fig 3.2 Trenches north of M4 motorway

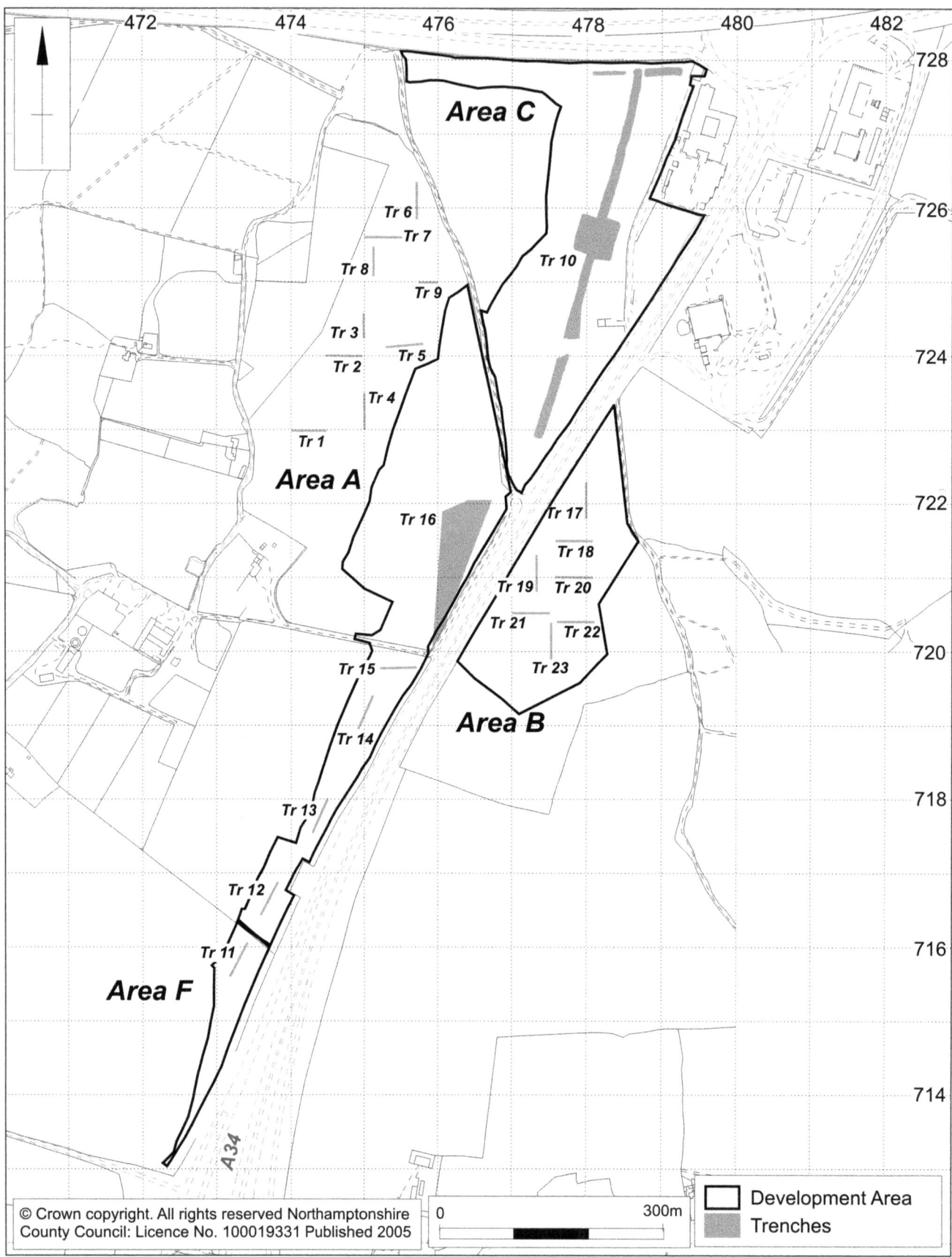

Fig 3.3 Trenches south of M4 motorway

Area D Trial Trenching

Ten trenches with a combined length of *c*. 800m were excavated (Fig. 3.2). No significant archaeological features were discovered. Two large post-medieval quarry pits were revealed in the lowest part of the field (Trenches 5 and 6). In the northern area (Trenches 2 and 4) there was a considerable depth of made ground. There was no trace of the potential cropmark feature (targeted in Trench 2). A gully in Trench 3 was undoubtedly a post-enclosure field boundary, while possible post-holes in Trench 5 are likely to have been post-medieval disturbances, perhaps related to the quarry. East-west gullies in Trenches 7 and 9 are of unknown date but also likely to have been post-medieval. Small, eroded sherds of Iron Age and Roman pottery came from colluvium in Trench 1, perhaps indicating a site to the west of this trench.

Area E (except Trench 11) Trial Trenching

Seventeen trenches (Nos. 12-28) with a combined length of *c*. 900m were excavated (Figs 4.7, 5.2 and 7.4 show the features located). Trenches 17, 21, 23, 24, 25 and 28 were intended to examine features identified from the geophysical survey. Trenches 21, 23, 24, 26 and 28 were enlarged to examine areas surrounding potential archaeological features.

Trench 28, which was targeted to examine the southern limit of the Iron Age/early Roman settlement, revealed three ditches at the northern end of the trench. Pits of possible prehistoric date were examined toward the southern end.

In Trench 27, close to the site where the middle Bronze Age vessels were found in Test Pit 136, a ditch and a pit were found. It remains unclear whether these features are of the same date, but they are regarded as possibly Bronze Age (Chapter 4). Pits of possible prehistoric date were examined in Trenches 20, 23 and 24. Other features examined were considered likely to be natural, including the penannular geophysical anomaly in Trench 23, which appears to have been a tree-throw hole.

Radnall Farm Access Road (Area E Trench 29) Strip and Record

This area was 15m wide and 450m long, passing the eastern margin of the late Iron Age/early Roman features identified in the magnetometer and trial pitting surveys (Figs 4.7, 5.2 and 7.4). A number of pits and ditches of prehistoric, Roman and post-medieval date were examined, as well as a large pit which contained early-middle Saxon pottery (Chapters 4, 5 & 6). Other linear and pit-like features were of uncertain significance. Of particular interest was a shallow depression, 5.2m by 3.8m in size, which contained a large quantity of pottery and other finds of mainly late Roman date. The layer sealed two pits, both sub-rectangular in shape and a little over 1 metre long, which contained larger sherds of pottery and a number of complete and semi-complete vessels. There was also an area of scorched earth overlain by a quernstone fragment. The pottery assemblage bears some resemblance to a funerary group (Timby, Chapter 9). The pits themselves were too small to be conventional graves for adult inhumations and the *in situ* evidence for burning, and the traces of cremated bone in the soil samples, suggested that there might have been a cremation rite practised here.

Area E, Trench 11 Excavation

A group of ten prehistoric pits and a few later features were examined at the southern end of Area E (Chapter 4; Figs 3.2 and 4.1). Trench 11 was expanded to include two separate excavation areas either side of an overhead power cable (Colour Plate 1). The pits were generally up to about 2m deep and filled with soils which included finds of burnt and worked flint, charcoal and small quantities of prehistoric pottery, but little else. The pottery tended to be of mid to late Bronze Age date, with some earlier Iron Age material. There were two exceptionally large pits, each around 10-15m across. These were cut by groups of smaller pits (some of which may have been post-holes) around the edge. They each also included a deeper central shaft which appears to have been a natural solution hole. Other pits were smaller and showed little or no re-cutting. Some may also have originated as natural features, but others appeared entirely man-made. The purpose of these pits and the nature of the prehistoric activity in this area are discussed below.

Areas C and A, Geophysical Survey

These areas were examined with 15.6ha of detailed magnetometer survey. Few features were revealed, several positive anomalies in Area C being probably due to geological or soil variations. A ditch at the southern end of Area C proved to be only anomaly of potential archaeological significance. In Area A the soilmark showed as a very weak linear anomaly. There were a small number of other linear features interpreted from the plot.

Area C, Trench 10 Strip and Record

The strip and record strategy in Area C included the temporary and aborted compound access roads, the M4 slip road diversion, and the main strip down the centre of the road line (520m long by 10m wide). An additional area of 20m by 30m either side of the main trench was opened up in response to the discovery of ditches and post-holes (Fig 6.2). Two ditches were investigated in the expanded excavation area and a third toward the southern end of the trench. They all appeared to be post-medieval (Chapter 7). Five small pits were also examined. One of these yielded early-mid Saxon pottery and lava quern fragments, and another, lava quern fragments on their own. It is possible that all these pits are Saxon in date.

The traces of a post-built timber structure, 17m long and 5m wide, were examined but its date remains unknown.

Area A, Trench 16 Strip and Record

This trench was opened to investigate the soil mark features visible on aerial photographs (Chapter 7; Fig. 7.1; Plate 1; Colour Plate 2). The soilmarks were shown to have been formed by a group of three main ditches and a broad hollow running south-west from the Green Lane access point for about 100m, and then sweeping south-east for the remaining length of the excavated area. The feature appeared to be a hollow-way of post-medieval date, but it was not shown on the Ordnance Survey mapping and the reason for its course remains enigmatic. Two large circular modern pits were discovered. A scatter of other features included a pit containing the base of an Iron Age vessel (Chapter 4).

Area A/F, Trial Trenching

The excavation of five trial trenches in the southern part of Area A and in Area F (SNEL Trenches 11-15) did not reveal features or finds of archaeological significance (Fig. 3.3). Three ditches running on east-west alignments were without dating evidence, but the nature of the fills of two of them suggested that they were field boundaries of relatively recent origin. The third is also likely to have been a field boundary of medieval or later date.

Area B, Geophysical Survey

Detailed magnetometer survey over the entire area (3.6ha) detected only faint anomalies which were thought to represent curvilinear features in the southern part of the site. A small number of other anomalies were also detected. It was uncertain whether any were of archaeological origin.

Area B, Trial Trenching

Seven trial trenches (SNEL Nos 17-23), with a total length of 350m, were excavated. There was one shallow ditch on a NW-SE alignment which was encountered in Trenches 18, 20 and 22. This was undated but appears likely to have been a field boundary (Fig. 7.3). A large pit was found in Trench 23. This was also without finds and its significance is uncertain. The redesign of the area of works here meant that it was not necessary to investigate the feature further.

Colour plate 2
Area A Trench 16 looking north. Hollow-way is visible as a silty band

Colour plate 1
Area E Trench 11 looking south. Bronze Age pit 11047 being excavated

*Above. Colour plate 3
Central shaft of Pit Group 11047
recorded in the watching brief.
Area E Trench 11*

*Below. Colour plate 4
Bronze Age pit 11065 (part of Group 11047)
under excavation. Area E Trench 11*

*Above. Colour plate 5
Bronze Age Pit Group 11138
under excavation. Area E Trench 11*

*Below. Colour plate 6
Selection of Roman pottery from Pit Group 29247.
Flask (lower left) from Layer 29014, miniature jar
(top right) from Pit 29229, rest from Pit 29018*

Chapter 4: Prehistoric features

Area E: later prehistoric pits and gullies in Trench 11

Trench 11 was located toward the southern side of Area E on a natural ridge (Fig 3.2; Colour Plate 1). The discovery of prehistoric features in the trial trench led to an open area excavation around it. Due to the presence of overhead cables the excavation was divided into two parts. The southern part covered 50m by 22m, while the northern area, lying 20m away, covered 54m by 30m. For convenience, similar archaeological features discovered to the north of Trench 11 during the watching brief are also included in this site (Fig. 4.1).

It was the discovery during the watching brief of a deep shaft under the principal pit in Pit Group 11047 that led to the interpretations presented here. Before this, the true character of these features was unclear, both in the difficulty of determining whether they were actually present, and if so, whether they were man-made or natural. This situation was aggravated by a certain amount of variation in the substrate, which included pale, almost white sand, and a range of brown and orange sands and silts. The scarcity of cultural material also added to this problem. A retrospective consideration of these features leaves little doubt that deep shafts with largely sterile fills are natural phenomena here. While wells were dug nearby in historical times, it is most unlikely that any could have been achieved without being shuttered all the way through the sandy geology. Moreover, the exposure of the underlying Upper Chalk during road cutting in other areas of the site showed it to be pitted with silty hollows. This form of chemical weathering must be regarded as common in this type of geological configuration.

Pit Group 11047 (Fig. 4.2)

This feature comprised a wide but comparatively shallow sub-circular pit (11060 - about 10m across) with two smaller, but still substantial pits (11065 and 11056) on the margin. The discovery of a deep central shaft under Pit 11060, which was traced to a depth of 5m without the base being reached, indicates the pit originated as a natural solution pipe (Colour Plate 3). The hollow remaining on the surface became a focus of prehistoric activity.

The north-west and south-east quarters of this group were hand excavated to the base of Pit 11060. The remaining quarters were then machine excavated to expose the complete plan of the feature and the central shaft was machine sectioned to an eventual depth of about 5m.

The central shaft (11225) showed an earlier phase (11226) which had been largely truncated by the shaft to the south (Fig. 4.3). Its northern edge showed a main fill (11148) of patchy brown and yellowish/orange/white sand with thinner, more silty edge silts (11149, 11150, 11151). These were without inclusions and represent the edge slippage of sterile sand.

The later main shaft 11225 was 4m wide at the top of the weathering cone with slopes of 45 degrees. This was filled with a series of loose, layered sands and sandy silts with some small pieces and flecks of charcoal (11143-11146). At a depth of about 2m below the stripped surface, the profile then broke to a 2.5m wide vertical shaft descending a further 3m. The fill for this lower 3m was a more homogeneous loose light reddish brown sand (11147). The base of the shaft was not reached within the formation level of the road cutting.

The large pit 11060 can be interpreted as the natural weathering cone situated over the shaft (11225). It was approximately circular in shape, but the south-eastern quarter was irregular. It had a slightly irregular steepish slope with a wide flat base at a depth of 0.9 m. Over a thin clean silty sand (11075) the main fills (11059, 11058, 11057) consisted of greyish silty sand, with burnt flint, charcoal flecks, flint flakes and a few sherds of prehistoric pottery. Near the base, there was a thin layer containing 10% burnt flint in the north-east quadrant (11074). The pottery from 11058 included several fragments of probable Middle Bronze Age (MBA) urn (fabric FL3). The upper fill, 11057, contained a few sherds of probable Late Bronze Age / Early Iron Age (LBA/EIA) pottery in a sandy fabric (SA4) and there were other miscellaneous sherds from both these layers.

There were two narrower but deeper pits on the margin of 11060, both appeared to cut through its fills. The western pit (11065) was 1.6m wide with steep, partly undercut, sides (Colour Plate 4). Its excavated depth was 1.75m, at which point the excavation was curtailed due to unstable sides. The pit may not have been much deeper than this, but it is impossible to be sure. At this level the fill was a friable bluish grey silty sand (11099) which contained a small utilised flint blade. The later fill (11064), a bluish grey silty sand with trace charcoal flecks and a few burnt flint pieces, contained a prehistoric pottery sherd of probable MBA date. Later re-cuts were recorded towards the top. The first re-cut (11097) had steep edges, undercut in the west to a concave rounded base at a depth of 1.2m. The second re-cut (11098) had a regular profile with steep edges to a concave base at a depth of 1.0m and contained a fill of hard sandy loam with occasional burnt flint, and small trace charcoal flecks (11063). A sherd of probable LBA/EIA pottery in a sandy fabric (SA1) and a flint core/hammerstone (Fig. 8.10.11) came from this fill.

In the top of these group of pits were two shallow scoops; 11093 with a depth of 0.25m, and 1162, the latest feature in the sequence, cut to a similar depth. The sherd of grog-tempered Bronze Age urn from the later scoop (Fill 11061) is likely to be residual.

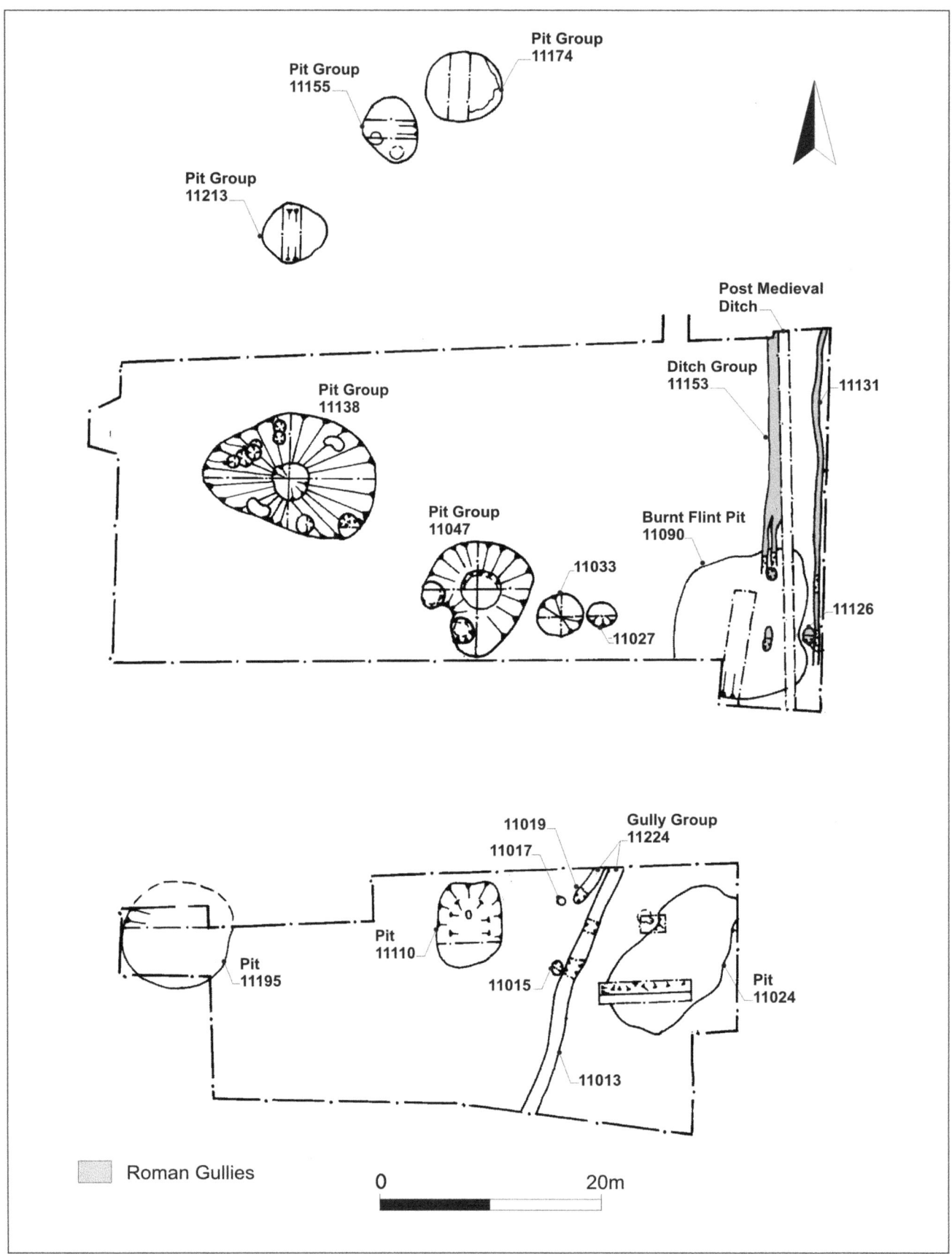

Fig 4.1 Bronze Age pits and other features in Area E Trench 11

To the south was another circular pit (11056) 1.8m wide with steep slopes falling to a concave base at a depth of 1.3m. It appeared to cut all the fills of Pit 11060 and itself was filled with a series of generally loamy sandy fills containing burnt flint and charcoal flecks in varying degrees and a few prehistoric pottery sherds (Fills 1148-1152). A possible re-cut (11053) was recorded towards the base of the pit, the basal fill of which (11052) contained a rim of a thin-walled LBA vessel.

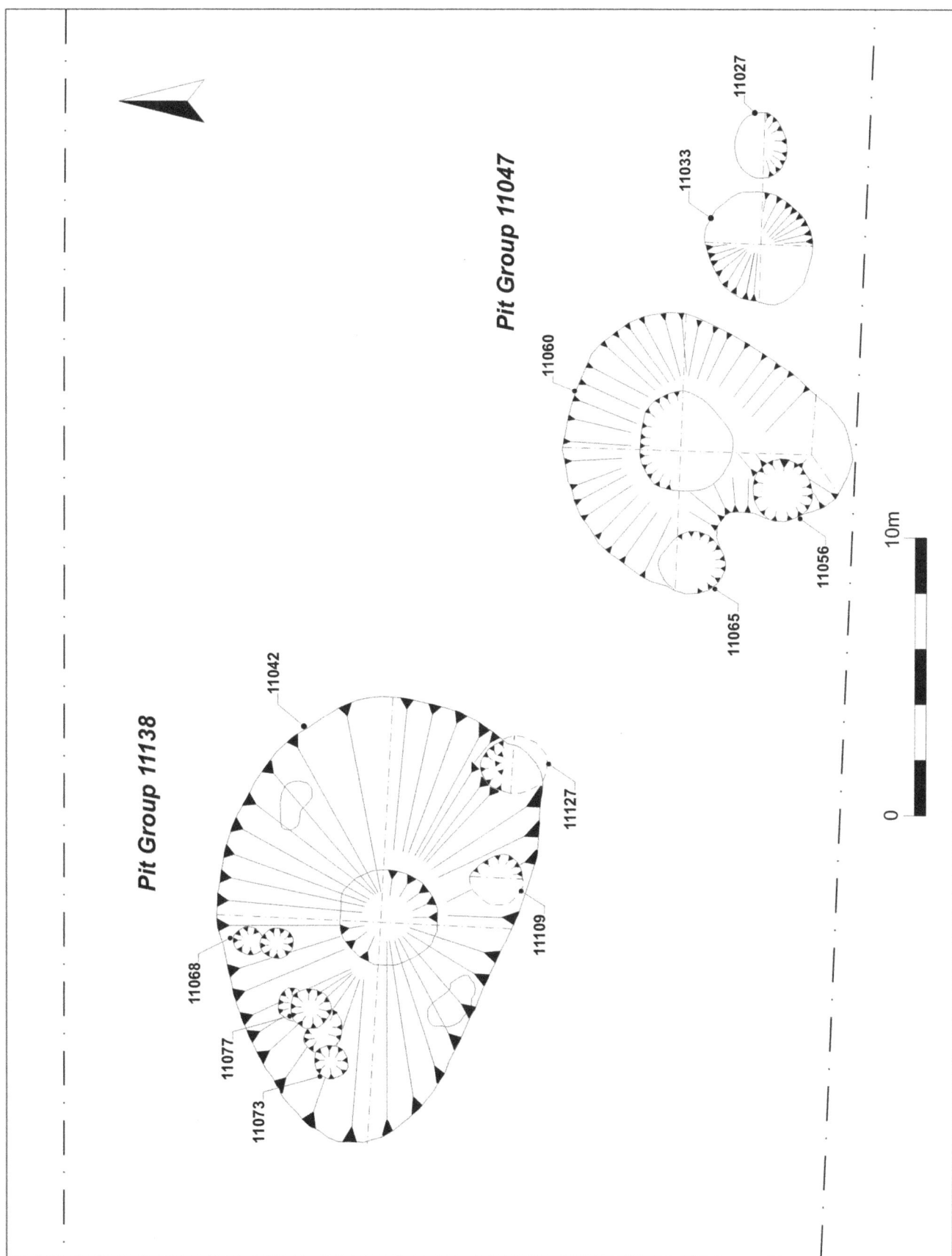

Fig 4.2 Pit Groups 11047 and 11138

Pit Group 11138 (Fig. 4.2; Colour Plate 5)

This group included the largest pit in the trench, Pit 11042 (11 x 16 m), which had a number of smaller pits cut into its base. The presence of a large circular pit (11215) occupying the central 4m of Pit 11042 suggests that, like Pit Group 11047, the feature had its origin as a solution pipe into which the surrounding sediment had collapsed, leaving a hollow on the surface.

The solution pipe was not, however, observed in this case. The lowest fill recorded in Pit 11215 was a loose, pale sand with flecks and a few small lumps of oak charcoal (11102, Sample 75) overlying a clean sand at a depth of about 1.7m below the stripped surface (Fig. 4.3). This was overlain by a loose, whitish sterile sand (11101), overlain in turn by another relatively charcoal-rich lens (11100). Although 11102 was thought to be the lowest fill of a pit, the deposits beneath this are likely to represent redeposited sterile sand rather than the undisturbed substrate. These three deposits can therefore be interpreted as the accumulated upper layers of the solution hollow derived from the slumping of its upper edges, before a period of stability had set in. The charcoal may have been deposited during the accumulation of sediment (i.e. there was some activity involving burning while the hollow was stabilising), or it might have been older material derived from the surrounding soil.

The overlying layer (11043), which filled the base of Pit 11042, was a compact orange-brown silty sand containing moderate amounts of charcoal, but no burnt flint or artefacts (Sample 35). This would appear to represent a relatively stable horizon of accumulation and soil development. The first human activity is represented by several pits of varying dimensions towards the margins of Pit 11042, together with artefacts and burnt flint in the soil which accumulated and filled the hollow. The marginal pits were all sealed by the accumulated layers in Pit 11042 (Fills 11044, 11045 and 11046), but it is not clear whether there was a general episode of pit digging, followed by the infilling of 11042, or whether pit digging and general accumulation occurred together, spread out over a period of time.

Pit 11042 was emptied completely, two quarters by hand, and the remaining quarters by machine in order to establish whether there was any pattern to the distribution of internal pits. Overall, while the pits were found towards the margins of the hollow, there was no regularity to their distribution or form. Their purpose is still enigmatic.

Pit 11109 may have been one of the earliest features since it was largely devoid of finds other than a low presence of charcoal (Samples 84-86), and it may therefore have predated any significant occupation on the site. It was not clear whether it had any relationship with Fill 11043, but it was sealed by Fill 11044. The pit was about 1.5m in diameter with steep sides and was excavated to a depth of 1.2m, although the base did not seem to have been reached. The lowest and principal fill was a soft pale sand (11108) which had probably derived from edge collapse. This was overlain by a mid grey-brown silty sand (11107) and a paler greyish silty sand (11106). Both appeared to be natural accumulations, the greyer cast to 11107 indicating a certain amount of anthropogenic influence, probably redeposited from surrounding sediments.

Nearby, a similar sequence of fills was evident in Pit 11127. This pit had a general diameter of 1.2 -1.3m and steep edges. It was a little over 2m deep. The main fill was a pale sand (11120) with a moderate amount of charcoal flecks and occasional burnt flints (Samples 81-83). This was overlain by siltier and browner deposits (11119 and 11118), also containing charcoal. Fill 11120 would seem to be mostly redeposited sterile sand. The profile suggests that the upper fills may have filled a void formed by the removal of a post, although there was no variation in the composition or compaction of the lower fill to suggest that it represented post-packing that had slumped in upon the removal of the post.

In the north-west quadrant, Pit 11077 was dug to a similar depth, although apparently the base had not quite been reached (Plate 2). This was a narrower pit with vertical sides at depth (the upper profile having been truncated). The lowest fill (11096) was a 'dirty' yellow sand with charcoal (Sample 72). This was overlain by a darker, siltier sand (11076), with charcoal and some burnt flint. A flint-tempered LBA pottery sherd was also recovered.

The upper part of Pit 11077 had been truncated by a shallower 'kidney-shaped' pit, 11079, which was 3 by 1.4 m in size and 0.8 m deep with a steep-sided profile. It was filled with grey-brown sandy silt containing charcoal, the upper fill being equivalent to 11045 of Pit 11042. The southern end of 11079 was apparently cut by a shallow pit 11073, although this may rather have been a natural feature such as a root hole. The nature of Pit 11079 and its purpose, if man-made, are not clear.

Towards the northern edge of Pit 11042 were two shallower inter-cutting pits, 11066 and 11068, which were sealed by 11044 (Plate 3). These were filled with single homogeneous mid to light brown sandy loams (11067 and 11069) containing burnt and worked flints. The two flint flakes from 11067 may have been struck from the same nodule of flint, suggesting that flint knapping took place nearby. The same is true of the flints in 11069, although these were a different sort of flint. Pit 11068 also contained six sherds of LBA/EIA pottery. The relationship between the pits was not clear. Both pits were flat-based and 1168 had an undercut northern

Plate 2 Bronze Age pit 11077 (part of Group 11138). Area E Trench 11

Plate 3 Bronze Age pits 11066 and 11068 (part of Group 11138). Area E Trench 11

edge. It seems likely that they were man-made but their purpose is not known.

In the eastern area another sub-circular pit (11141) was excavated to a depth of 0.5m. It had relatively dark silty upper fills (11139 and 11140) but the feature was substantially destroyed by flood damage during excavation and was not excavated further. Two other pits or groups of inter-cutting pits (11216 and 11219) were planned following machine excavation of the north-east and south-west quadrants. These were not excavated.

All the pits appeared to be sealed by one or more of the upper fills of Pit 11042. Fill 11044 was an orange-brown silty sand with a generally low density of burnt flint, and one small flint flake. The pottery comprised small sherds of flint-tempered MBA pottery and sandy LBA/EIA sherds. It is not clear whether this might indicate a stratified sequence spanning this period. In view of the later dating from the sparse remains elsewhere, it is perhaps more probable that the MBA pottery is residual.

Fill 11045 was a darker brown silty sand with burnt flint and sparse charcoal including indeterminate cereal grains (Sample 37). There were also a few sherds of flint-tempered and grog-tempered pottery of probable LBA date. A small Roman greyware sherd is undoubtedly intrusive. The flintwork included three very rough shattered cores of LBA character and two flakes. The accumulation of this layer appears to correspond to the main period of activity around this pit in the later Bronze Age. It is possible that the peripheral pit-digging also mainly took place at this time, judging by the pottery from Pits 11077 and 11068.

The upper layer (11046) was a brown silty sand with occasional charcoal and burnt flint inclusions (Sample 38). This undoubtedly represents slow accumulation in the top of the hollow. Three sherds of probable Late Iron Age (LIA) pottery, with a beaded rim and burnished finish, show that there was some activity nearby at this time, but this seems unlikely to be related to the pit-based activity of earlier times. The sparse burnt flint is probably residual.

Burnt flint pit 11090
(Figs 4.4 and 4.5; Plate 4)

A very large sub-rectangular prehistoric pit (11090), 13.2m by 12.8m in area, was initially machine-excavated within a 10m by 1m sondage to a depth of 0.7m (Fig. 4.5, S. 115). Within this sondage the eastern third was further hand-excavated to a total depth of 1.4m. The pit had a gradual upper slope, dropping sharply before easing to a gradual slope at the base. The base was later recorded during the watching brief at a depth of 1.5m across the full width of the feature. This part of the site had a clayey silt substrate. There was no sign of a central shaft.

The pit was initially filled up to a height of 0.85m with several layers of compact silts (11089 to 11085) which became sandier higher up and generally contained, to varying degrees, occasional burnt flint and charcoal flecks. The primary fill, 11089, contained several small sherds of flint-tempered pottery (Fabric FL4) which may date to the LBA or EIA (Timby, Chapter 9). The predominant fill (11087) included several large pieces of oak charcoal and burnt flints, both up to 100mm in size, and MBA pottery sherds. A radiocarbon date on charcoal from this context is calibrated to *c.* 1200-1400 BC (SUERC-4148 GU-12338) confirming the MBA date for the material. This appears to be incompatible with the later date of the pottery from 11089 unless the stratigraphy became inverted through redeposition. The possible implications of this are discussed below (Chapter 13).

Overlying these sandy clay/clay fills was a distinct compact tip-line (11083) consisting almost entirely of burnt flint. In the excavated region the tip-line was 3m in

Plate 4 Bronze Age pit 11090, showing lenses of burnt flint. Area E Trench 11

length and 0.10-0.25m thick. Most flints were moderately sized lumps between 3mm and 30mm in size. The flint was in a soil matrix of dark grey silty sand with charcoal, some of which could be identified as hazel, willow and hawthorne. This silty sand formed an overlying layer (11082) below another very similar tip-line (11081) of burnt flint over 5m in length. The uppermost fill was a more friable orange-brown silty sand with sparser burnt flints (11080).

No other feature in any of the areas excavated was found with such dense amounts of burnt flint. The flint was concentrated in two layers also generally visible on the surface in the southern parts of the pit covering an area of 3m x 4m. They clearly formed tip-lines and there is no suggestion of *in situ* burning, the burnt flints presumably having been disposed of from areas of use nearby.

The disposal of burnt waste may have been one of the purposes of the pit. Above the initial thin silting layers (11089 and 11088) the main fill of the pit (11087) contained a moderate density of burnt flint and charcoal, which included some quite large pieces. It would seem that they were deposited deliberately, rather than being the result of long-term natural accumulation. There are two lines of evidence that indicate that the main period of activity involving burning was in the MBA - the pottery from 11087 and the radiocarbon date from the same context. There is a case for arguing that the MBA pottery may be residual, and the radiocarbon sample may have been from oak heartwood, thereby shifting the date of activity towards 1000 BC rather than earlier. This is supported by the identification of LBA or EIA pottery from the primary fill, suggesting that the infilling of the pit, and therefore probably also its excavation, took place later. It is therefore possible that the pit was dug to bury midden material, either simply to clear debris or as some more formalised act of burial.

Pit 11033 (Figs 4.4 and 4.5)

This circular pit (11033) was 4.0m across with initially shallow sides dropping sharply before easing to a small flat base at a depth of 1.5m (Fig. 4.5, S. 103). Its fills (11035-11038) were brown, compact clayey silts, becoming sandier toward the top of the sequence. There was charcoal and occasional burnt flint throughout. It is likely that the fills were all natural accumulations over time, with the occasional admixture of background cultural material. A single sherd of LBA/EIA pottery came from 11036, and a group of four waste flakes and one utilised flake came from the pit as a whole. The flints are technologically typical of the LBA. The fragmentary charred material included cereal, indicating some crop processing or consumption in the area.

Pit 11027 (Fig. 4.4)

Nearby was a small oval pit (11027) 1.5m by 2.0m in plan with a gentle slope to a flat base at a depth of 0.3m.

It had a primary fill of mottled grey/brown silt with a large quantity of burnt flint and charcoal traces (11029), and a loamier upper fill (11028) with similar inclusions.

Pit 11024 (Fig. 4.4)

A large ovoid pit (11024) in the south-eastern corner of the trench was 15m long and 8m wide. It was hand-excavated within a 2m by 7m sondage to a depth of 1.25m. This established an irregular western edge and base, but further east there appeared to be a substantial layer of re-deposited natural clayey silt which was not completely removed. It is probable, therefore that the full depth of the feature was not established.

The lower fill (11023) was a clean orange sandy silt with occasional charcoal flecks (Fig. 4.5, S. 60). The upper fills (11022, 11021 and 11020 [=11005]) were varying mottled sandy deposits with occasional burnt flints and relatively large quantities of charred plant remains, which the assessment showed to be wood charcoal. There was a relatively large group of 30 sherds (267 g) of flint-tempered MBA pottery from the excavated part of this feature, including recognisable bucket urn fragments. The worked flint assemblage comprised a retouched and utilised flake, and a waste flake (from 11005); and from 11022 four waste flakes. All were in sharp condition suggesting discard close to their place of manufacture.

An interpretation of this feature is unclear although it may well have been of natural origin, and appears to have silted up naturally with the admixture of cultural material from time to time from intermittent activities involving heated stones.

Pit 11110 (Fig. 4.1)

This was a large pit 7.4m by 6.0m in area and sub-rectangular in shape. It reached a depth of 1.3m deep below the stripped surface. It was initially partly examined with a machine-excavated sondage, and later half the remainder of the feature was hand-excavated.

It had a gentle, slightly irregular, slope to a flat base, although this was not entirely exposed (Fig. 4.5, S. 126). At the base of the pit was a small depression [11116]. It was 0.20m in diameter, with straight sides to a V-shaped base at a depth of 0.14m. The earliest fills were an orange clayey silt (11114) and dark orange sand with charcoal flecks (11115). Above this was a thin but clear iron-panning horizon, and upper layers of mottled sandy silts with some charcoal flecks (11113, 11112 and 11111). The fills were generally an orange brown colour with some greying toward the top of the sequence (11111). The pit was largely devoid of cultural material except for a core rejuvenation flake (Fig. 8.10.9) and a utilised blade. These are not diagnostically earlier than the Bronze Age material from the site, but the absence of burnt flint suggests that they may be, and the lithic material is not characteristically late.

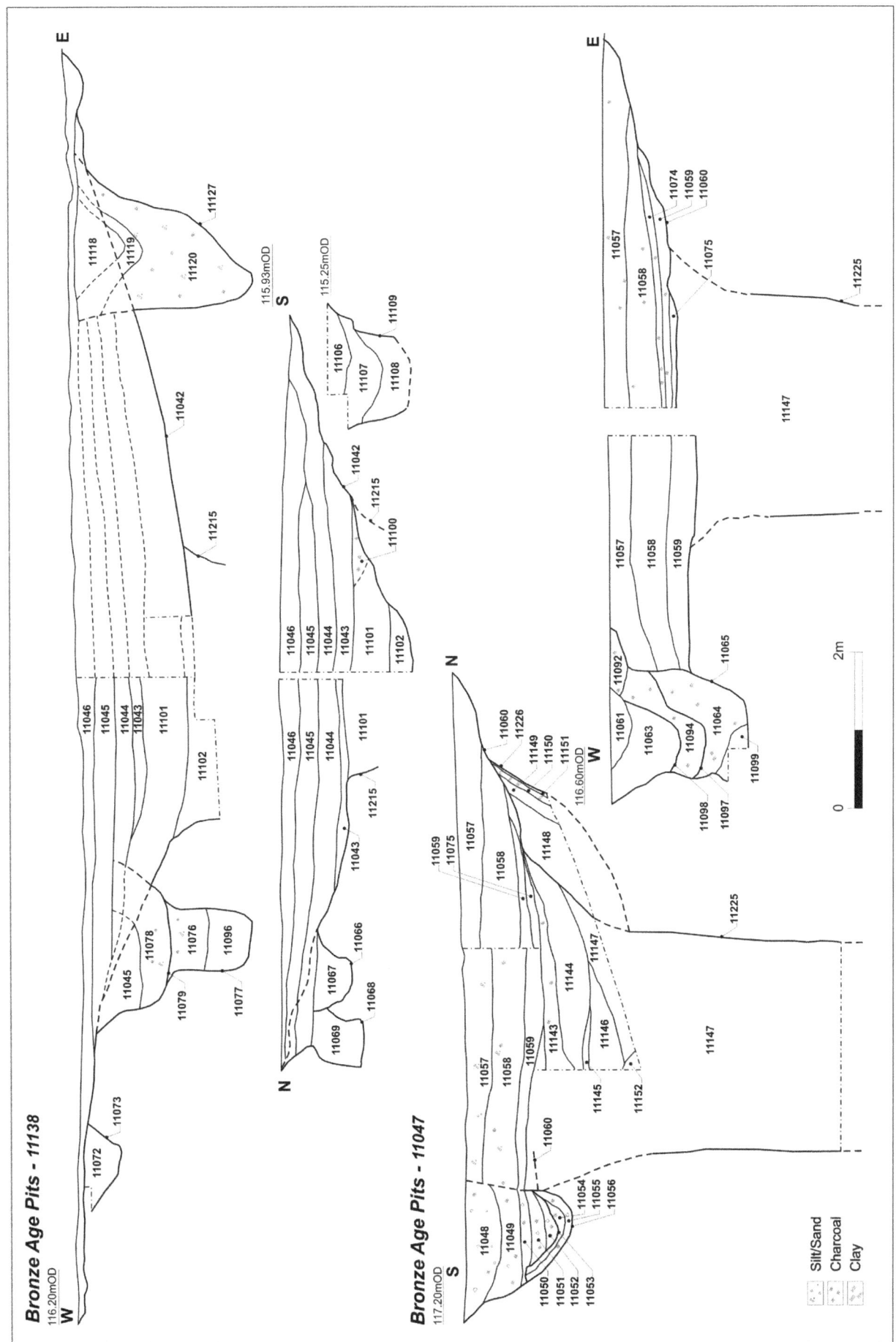

Fig 4.3: Sections of Pit Groups 11047 and 11138 (with projected sections of peripheral pits)

In the light of the later experience of excavating Pit Group 11047 suggests that this was probably a natural depression formed over another solution shaft, although in this case the shortage of any recognisably man-made inclusions, and the harder, siltier subsoil made it impossible to distinguish the slumped natural silt from the undisturbed substrate. The sub-rectangular shape must be seen as fortuitous.

Large Pit 11195 (Figs 4.1 and 4.5)

This was a large circular pit 10m in diameter. It was encountered in the initial evaluation trench (Feature 11009) and was sectioned with a machine bucket to determine whether it was natural or man-made, but the feature remained ill-defined. Later the overburden around it was stripped to clarify the form of the feature.

The sondage was cut to a depth of 1.1m below the top of the pit. The sections were cleaned by hand (Fig. 4.5, S. 133). At this depth the main fills of the feature consisted of horizontally layered silty sands and sands some containing charcoal flecks, but with few other inclusions (Fills 11192, 11191 and 11190). At this level was a layer of iron panning with clayey silt beneath. It was not clear whether the base of the feature had been reached, but the sterile nature of the deposits suggested that little would be gained by continued excavation. The feature was probably a natural solution hollow. Absence of any cultural material may mean that the pit was older (or more recent) than the Bronze Age pits elsewhere.

Linear ditches and related features, Group 11224 (Fig. 4.4)

Two linear ditches, both on an approximate N-S alignment and of similar dimensions were examined to the east of Pit 11110. Ditch 11013 was 1.4m wide and 0.20m deep with steep slopes and flat base. It appeared to cross the width of the trench (>23 m) but was very indistinct toward the south. Its fill was a compact brown silty sand (11012 and 11010) which contained several fragments (68g) of BA pottery and occasional burnt flint. Adjacent to the ditch there was a small circular pit (11015) 0.84m wide and 0.08m deep with gentle slopes and concave base.

The terminal of another linear ditch (11019) was found immediately to the west. It was 0.95m wide and 0.20m deep, with steepish slopes rounding to a flattish base and a similar fill to (11013). There was an adjacent posthole (11017), 0.17m wide and 0.14m deep with vertical sides.

There is no reason to question the pottery evidence, and at face value these features are likely to be of Bronze Age date and probably contemporary with Pit 11024. They would appear to have formed some sort of boundary. They were not traced in the northern trench.

Pit Group 11174 (Figs 4.1 and 4.6)

In the watching brief area a large circular pit, 5.4m wide, was machine excavated to a depth of 1.4m within an 8m by 2m sondage. The section was then cleaned by hand and recorded (Fig. 4.6). Machine excavation subsequently proceeded to a depth of about 2m and the base of the feature observed. No finds were recovered from this feature.

The pit was shown to have a very steep, almost vertical, northern edge plunging to below the base of the initial sondage, and a more gradual southern edge. The pit appeared to have been recut on more than one occasion.

The earliest pit in the sequence, (11184), cut through what appeared to be natural silts, although it is possible that the sediments on the southern side of the cut had been redeposited in a much larger original feature. There was some variation to these sediments. The earliest identifiable 'natural layer' (11185) was a grey clay-silt which contrasted with the orange sandy substrate to the north. Above 11185 was a more orange silty clay (11182) which in turn was overlain by a mottled grey and orange silt loam with some charcoal flecks (11214). While it is possible that these variations were naturally occurring ones, the presence of charcoal in the upper layer suggests that this was not undisturbed. There may therefore have been a large feature here which was not definable in plan.

The earliest pit (11184) was evident only on the northern edge of the sondage where it formed a narrow tapering shaft. Its southern edge had been cut away. Its base appeared to have been reached at about 2m after the second phase of machining. The single fill (11183) was a mid orange clay-silt with frequent ironstone inclusions. The form and fill of this feature suggest that it was a natural solution hole, although it would not have been symmetrical and it was not traceable below about 2m.

The remains of a later pit (11181) was visible in the southern part of the section. This had a gradual slope to about 1.0m deep and a base which was almost flat before being truncated by 11179. Cut 11181 was filled with a mottled grey and brown silty loam (11180). This pit seems to have been deliberately cut into the centre of Pit 11184 after it had largely infilled. Presumably it would have been visible as a hollow.

The third pit (11179) was again cut from the surface and formed a smaller pit about 3.4m in diameter and 1.0m deep. Like the earlier cuts, the northern edge was steeper than the southern one. It had a lower fill of mottled grey and brown silty sand (11178) and a middle fill which was a brown silty loam with frequent charcoal (11177).

The upper part of the pit appeared to have been truncated by a shallow re-cut (11176), to a maximum depth of about 0.7m on the northern side of the feature. This was filled with an orange-brown silty sand (11175).

This interpretation would seem to indicate that the hollow, formed by a natural solution hole, became the subject of repeated pit digging. There were no finds to indicate over what sort of timescale this took place.

Pit Group 11155 (Figs 4.1 and 4.6)

Nearby, 2m to the south-west, was another large circular prehistoric pit about 4.5m in diameter. This was machine excavated to 1.2m within a 2m by 7m sondage and the section cleaned by hand (Fig. 4.6).

The original cut (11173) was truncated in the west but the eastern side showed a gradual slope to a flatish concave base at a depth of 1.0m. It was filled with several layers comprising a primary fill of brown sandy loam with frequent charcoal flecks (11170), a lighter deposit overlying it towards the centre of the cut (11169), a charcoal-rich band (11168) in the middle of the sequence, and upper light (11167) and greyish (11166) silty loams.

Pit 11173 was re-cut on its western side by a 1.4m wide pit (11165) with near-vertical sides. Its base did not appear to have been reached. The earliest visible fill was a mottled grey/brown sandy loam (11164) overlain by a mottled grey/brown silty loam (11161) and further overlain by a mottled grey/brown silty clay (11158). This pit had been re-cut in a virtually identical location, but to a slightly narrower width, by Pit 11157 whose steep slopes broke to a flat base at a depth of 0.8m. This pit contained a single fill of brown sandy loam (11156).

No finds were recovered from these features, although it is clear that they were man-made and entailed the re-digging of pits in the same location after periods of natural infilling. The timescale of this activity remains unknown.

Pit Group 11213

Lying 8m to the SW, another large pit, 5.4m by 6.2m in size, was machine excavated to a depth of 0.8m below the stripped surface within a 7m by 2m sondage. The section was cleaned and recorded (Fig. 4.6).

Three individual cuts were recognised. The earliest cut [11210] had moderately steep sides. It contained several loose fills of a light brown or greyish cast (11209, 11208, 11207, 11206 and 11205), all of which appeared to consist largely of redeposited natural sand.

This pit was re-cut by a smaller pit (11204), 1.6m wide, with steep / near vertical sides and cut to approximately the depth of the sondage (0.8m). The lowest fill of the re-cut was a loose mottled dark brown and whitish blue sandy loam with charcoal traces (11203). It was overlain by a yellowish brown sandy loam (11202). This pit was further re-cut from the surface by Pit 11201, 1.0m wide with regular, near vertical, sides breaking sharply to a flattish convex base at a depth of 0.65m. It had a main fill of loose light brown sandy loam (11200), overlain by a mid-brown sandy loam (11199) which merged with the overlying subsoil.

It seems likely that this group of pits can be interpreted as the re-digging in prehistoric times of a natural solution hollow.

Area E, Trenches 13-29: possible prehistoric features

In the northern part of Area E evidence of prehistoric occupation was identified from the results of the surface collection and trial-pitting surveys (GGP 2000, Oxford Archaeology 2002). In particular, the recovery of large fragments of bucket urn and globular urn from the subsoil in Trial Pit 136 suggests Bronze Age activity here (Timby, Chapter 9). Surface finds of five sherds of probable Bronze Age pottery and three sherds identified as Iron Age reportedly came from this area (GGP 2000, 5), although only two Bronze Age sherds and an early Saxon sherd (originally misattributed as prehistoric) have been positively identified in the present re-assessment (Timby, Chapter 9). The surface distribution of worked flint and of burnt flint may show a slight concentration in the northern part of Area E, with a thinner scatter elsewhere in this field (Figs 8.4 and 8.7).

The excavation of the trial trenches and access road trench resulted in little directly related to these earlier finds. Several small gullies, pits and post-holes were identified, but there were very few finds and the features are all poorly dated or undated. The nature of the earlier prehistoric occupation is made more difficult to determine by the presence of late Iron Age/early Roman and late Roman occupation in this area, while two more early Saxon sherds were also found. The undated features could potentially relate to any of these later occupations. On the whole, the absence of dating evidence is more characteristic of the earlier prehistoric than the late Iron Age/Roman activities, although the extent of early Saxon activity is a problematic factor. Tentatively, however, a small number possible Bronze Age features have been identified (Fig. 4.7) and are described below. Only two contained pottery and their dating is nowhere near secure.

Northern part of Area E (Fig. 4.7)

?Bronze Age Gully 29021
This length of shallow gully (0.50m wide and 0.16m deep) ran east-west for 7m (Plate 5). It was probably originally longer and had been truncated by ploughing. Its mid brown silty fill (29020) contained three relatively large sherds of Bronze Age pottery (Fabric FL3) and some flint shatter. A soil sample (Sample 4) yielded just a few fragments of charcoal.

Undated Ditch 2707
Ditch 2707, running north-south, was a little over 1.0m wide and 0.5m deep. It was a clear feature although it was without finds.

Undated Pit 2704
This pit was about 1.0m in diameter and 0.4m deep, with rather irregular edges. It was without finds, and like the nearby ditch 2707, its date is uncertain.

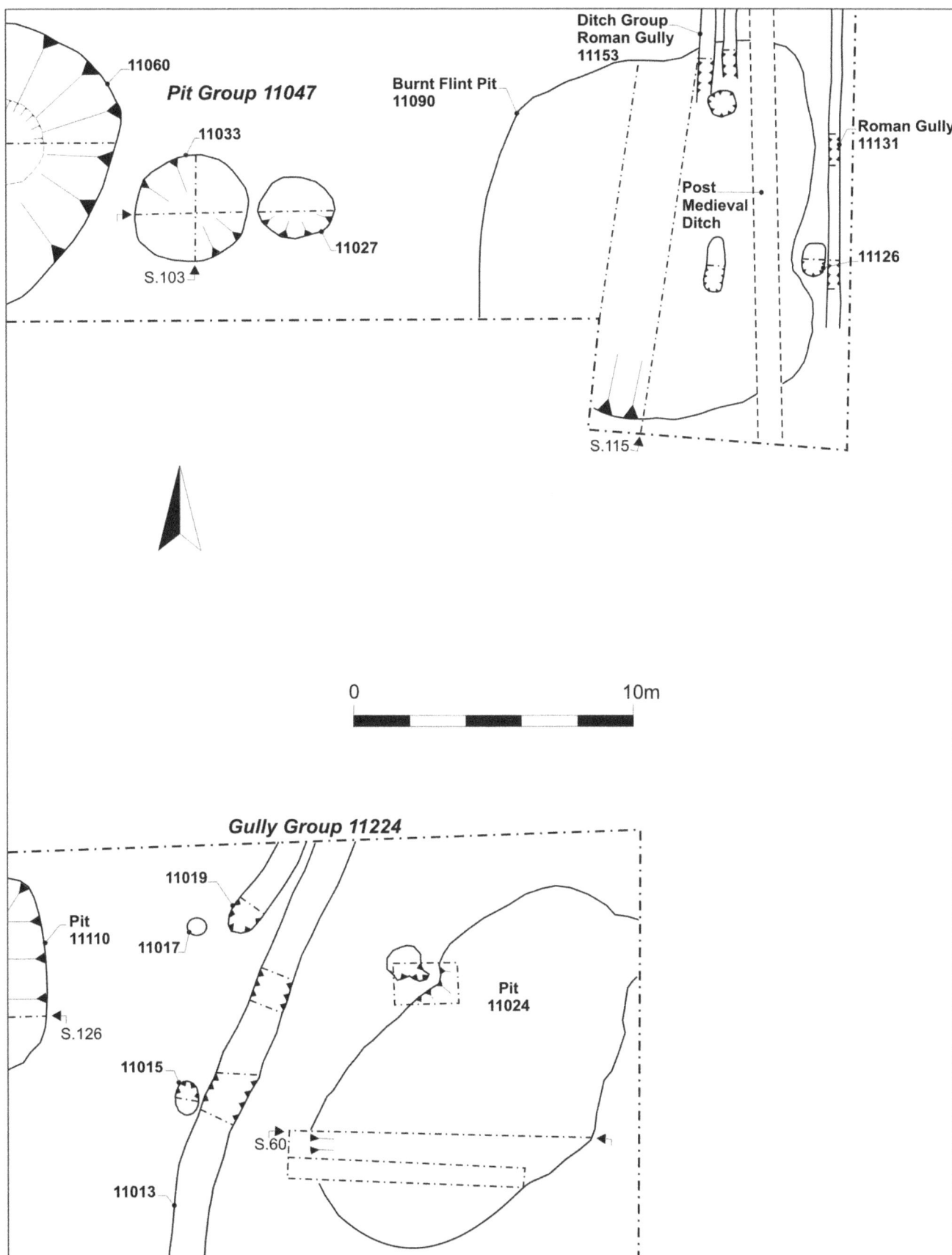

Fig 4.4 Pits 11090 and 11024

Undated Pit 29042
This pit was 0.7m wide and 0.3m deep with regular, moderately steep sides. It was without finds. A soil sample (Sample 24) was assessed and yielded some charcoal and weed seeds.

Undated Pit 29040
This oval pit was 3.0m long and 0.5m wide, with a flat base at a depth of 0.25m. It was filled with dark brown silty loam, which yielded some charcoal and weed seeds (Sample 25), but was without other finds.

Central part of Area E (Fig. 4.7)

Gully 29160 and nearby gullies
Gully 29160 was a very shallow, irregular, linear gully, 0.3m wide and 0.1m deep. It was traced for about 4 m but petered out thereafter. It contained a sherd of pottery in a sandy fabric which has been identified as LBA or IA. It cut a deeper gully, 29076, on a similar but not identical alignment. This was traced for about 5m and must have terminated thereafter. Three re-cuts of 29076 were recognised.

The alignment of 29076 was continued, slightly offset, to the east with another shallow gully 29068, 0.15m deep, which was at least 7m long (extending outside the trench).

Gully 29252
To the north of 29160 was a similar, shallow, sinuous gully, (29252), running east-west, which appeared to cross the width of the trench. Several sections showed it to be of varying profile, between 0.5m and 2.3m wide and 0.14m to 0.24m deep, generally wider but shallower toward the west (Cut 29242). There were no finds from this feature. It was cut by Pit 29062.

Pit 29062
This small ovoid pit was 0.8m x 0.5m in plan and 0.15m deep. It had a lower fill of silty clay, and an upper fill (29063) predominantly of charcoal. Several fragments of fired clay were recovered, and a soil sample (Sample 9) contained mainly oak charcoal and few weeds.

Pit Group 29253
Five small pits lay within an area of 5m by 7m immediately north of Pit 29062. The pits were circular or ovoid in plan, 0.5 - 1.5m dia., with flat bases 0.10 - 0.25m deep.

Plate 5 *?Bronze Age gully 29021. Area E Trench 29*

Ditch 29070
This was a curving, approximately north-south, ditch to the north of Gully 29252. It was traced for about 8m. The ditch was about 1.6m wide and up to 0.4m deep (shallower to the north) with a somewhat irregular profile. The fill (29086) from the northern section yielded a waste flint flake and a notched flake came from the lower fill (29071) of the southern section. The upper fill of this section (29091 - which may have been within a shallow re-cut) contained some burnt flint.

Gully 29256
This was an irregular linear feature on the eastern side of the trench, running approximately at right-angles to 29160. Several sections were excavated and it was shown to be up to about 1.3m wide and 0.3m deep, but narrower and shallower in places, with a flat or rounded base. It was interpreted as being of natural origin, although a 're-cut' was recorded in the central section. A soil sample (19) from cut 29110 yielded traces of charcoal.

Pit 29228
Toward the southern end of this group of features, Pit 29228 was oval in shape 1.6m by 1.4m and 0.33m deep. It was without finds, but an assessed soil sample, (21), yielded occasional charcoal and weeds with indeterminate cereal also present.

Pit 29246
Near Pit 29228, Pit 29246 was similar but slightly deeper at about 0.55m. An assessed soil sample (27) yielded occasional charcoal and weeds.

Post-hole 29204
This oval post-hole had steep sides and a flat base at a depth of 0.17m. A small soil sample (22) yielded some weeds and charcoal in assessment.

Pit 2303
Among the scatter of potential pits revealed in Trench 23, Pit 2303 is thought to be possibly prehistoric. It was a regular circle in shape and about 0.5m across, though only 0.1m deep. Its fill was relatively dark with traces of oak charcoal, but it was without finds.

Area A: Isolated Iron Age pit

A small pit containing Iron Age pottery was discovered in Area A Trench 16, south of the M4 motorway (Fig. 7.1, Pit 1649). This was the only early, datable find of significance in this area. The pit was positioned centrally upon a raised area of natural orange clay which had been scored by ploughing. The pit barely survived, being 0.28m wide and only 30mm deep, but had a substantial pottery base *in situ*. The base was part of an Iron Age vessel (Timby, Chapter 9). Potentially, it could have had some ritual/dedicatory significance (such as an isolated cremation vessel), but there is little upon which to base further speculation.

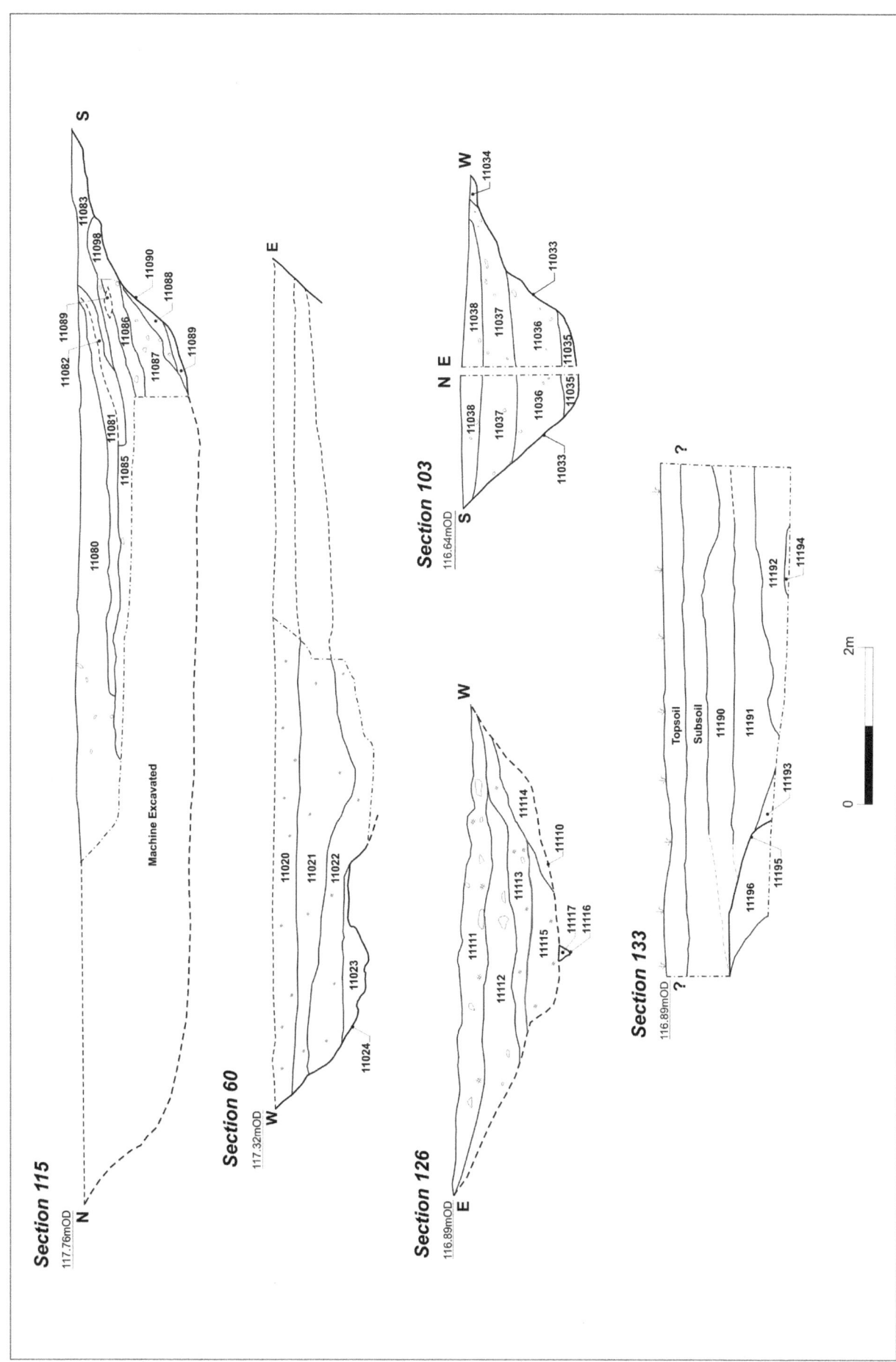

Fig 4.5: Pits 11090, 11024, 11110, 11195 and 11033 (sections)

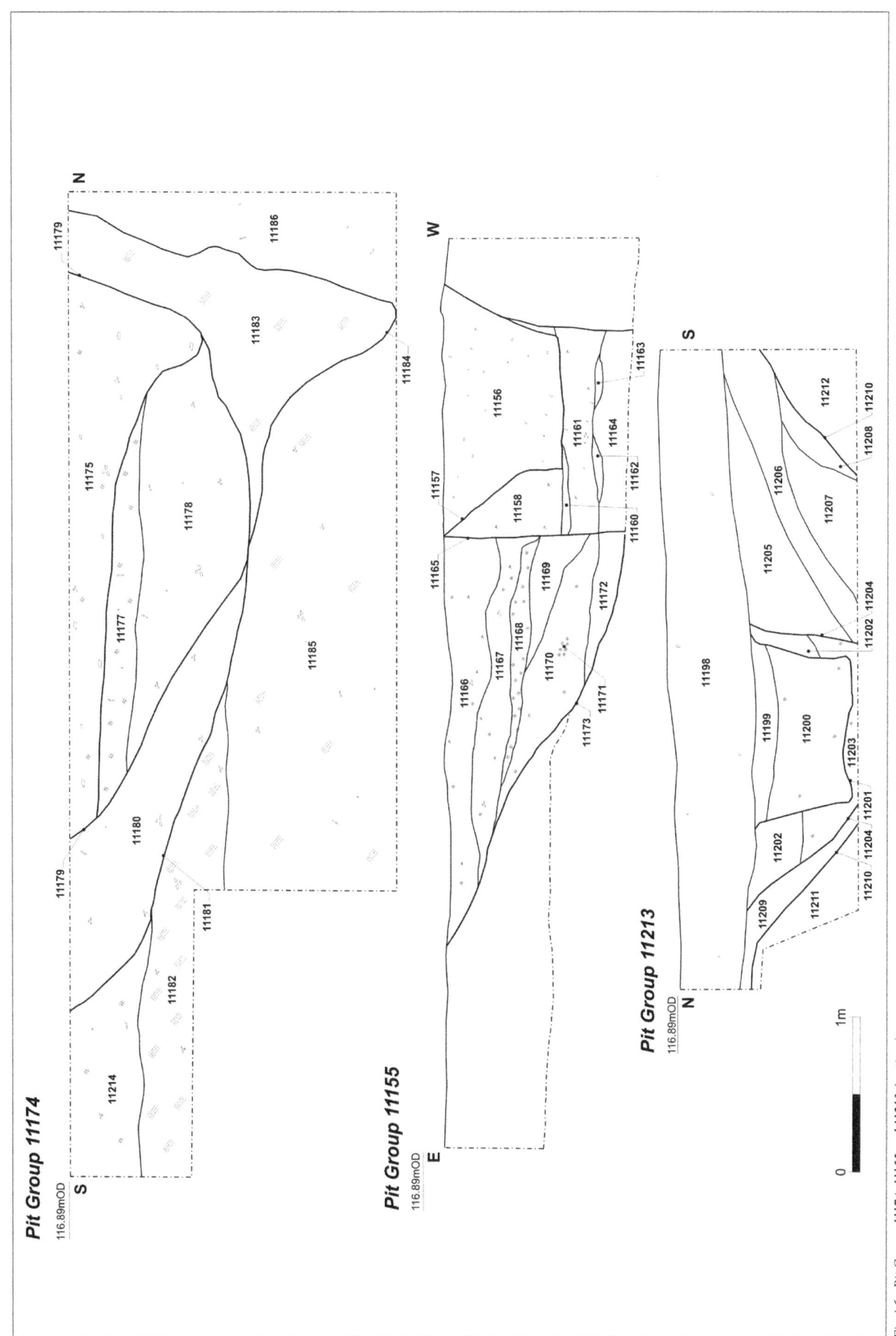

Fig 4.6: Pit Groups 11174, 11155 and 11213 (sections)

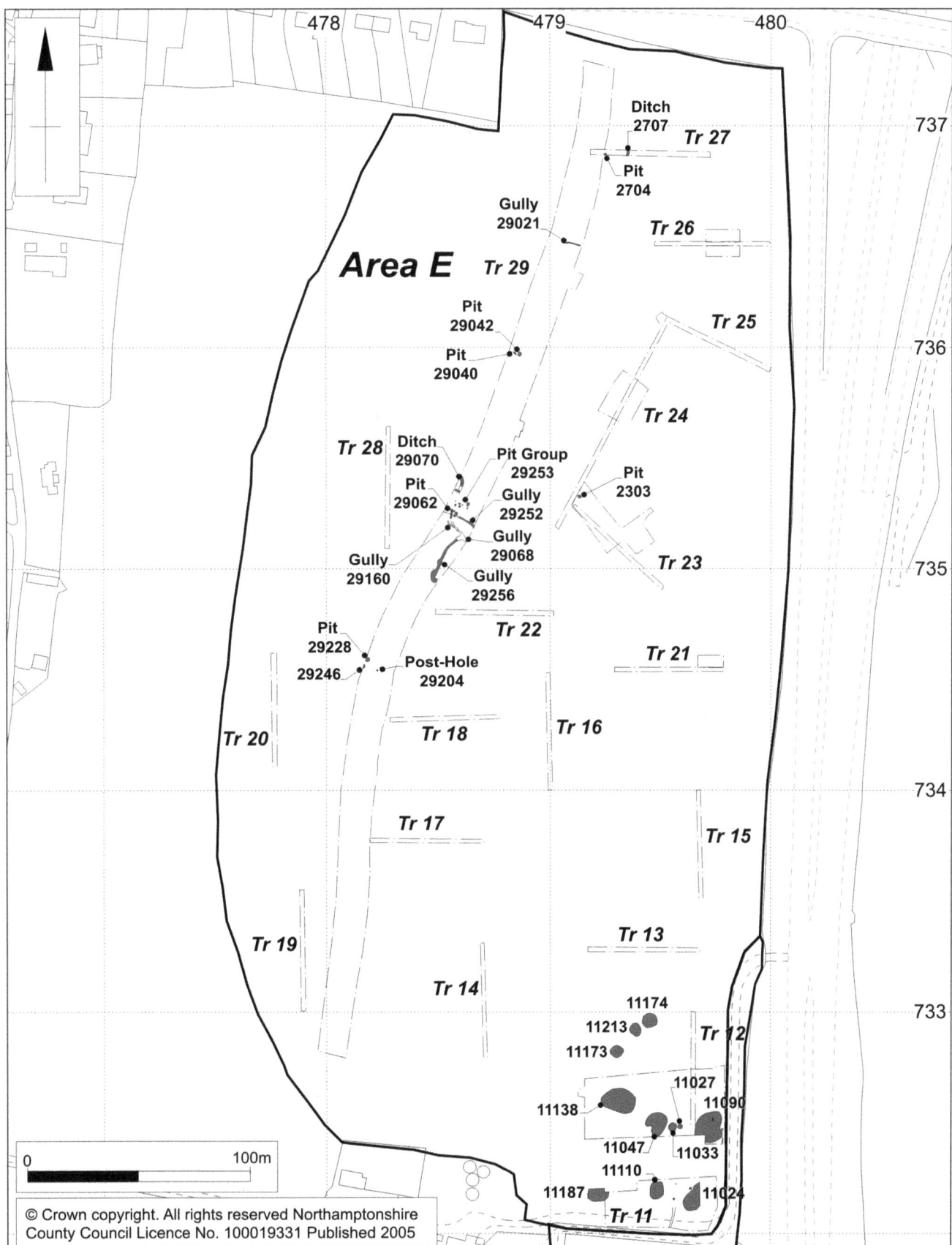

Fig 4.7 Bronze Age features in Area E

Chapter 5: Roman features

Introduction

There were very few Roman finds from the surface collection survey (just four sherds of pottery), leading to the suggestion of an absence of occupation of this period in the survey area (GGP 2000, 7). Two sherds came from the northern part of Area E. The trial-pitting resulted in the recovery of another 21 sherds, 18 of which came from Trial Pit 139 and the features within it (below), and another from Trial Pit 145, also in the northern part of Area E. The possible enclosure and other ditches revealed in the geophysical survey suggested a focus of occupation in the vicinity of Trial Pit 139 (the area demarcated for preservation *in situ*). Trench 28 was targeted in order to define the southern extent of this complex, and the features discovered here were for the most part left unexcavated.

The Roman features found in Trench 29 of the strip and record excavation appeared to be part of an isolated group peripheral to the main occupation further west. They were also significantly later, and add something to the time depth of activity in the area which includes both early and late elements.

Early Roman features in Trial Pit 139

Two ditches were found in this trial pit (Fig. 5.1); one running approximately east-west (13907) was about 0.5 m deep and yielded four sherds of Roman pottery from its single fill (13906). This was cut by a slightly deeper ditch (13905), which was aligned north-west to south-east and which contained two diagnostically early Roman sherds in the lower fill (13904). A further 12 late Iron Age/early Roman sherds came from the topsoil in this pit.

The later ditch would seem to correspond to a curving ditch traced on the geophysical survey, which probably appeared again as one of the three (unexcavated) ditches in Trench 28 (Fig. 5.2). It is possible that the earlier ditch followed this general course and also corresponds to another of the ditches at the northern end of Trench 28, although this is not clear from the survey. The geophysical plot indicates that these ditches terminated a short distance east of Trench 28, and this would seem to be confirmed by their absence in Trench 29.

Possible Roman features in Trench 28

There were a number of small features to the south of the three LIA/ER ditches (2830-2) in this trench (Fig. 5.1). None contained reliable dating, but it is possible that they were part of the Roman occupation to the north.

Pit Group 2829 included a series of possible stake-holes sealed by gravely clay. The stake-holes, numbering seven, of varying depth and irregularly distributed, were within a shallow ovoid cut (2820). This was 0.66m wide, but lay only partly within the trench and the overall form of this feature and what it related to are not known. A fragment of fired clay was recovered from the fill (2822) suggesting that the feature was man-made.

Pit 2827 was a large oval pit which was 0.2m deep and without finds. A little further south, Pit 2826 was a wide pit or possible ditch terminal, 1.6m across and 0.63m deep. It had three shallow post-holes in the base. Two flint flakes were the only finds, but they may well have been residual.

Earlier Roman features at the northern end of Trench 29

Ditch 29250

This shallow ditch ran for over 20 m across the trench on an east-west alignment (Fig. 5.2). It was 0.75m wide and 0.21m deep with steep sides and a flattish, concave base. Although no finds were retrieved, the ditch was cut by the late Roman pit 29018, and is, therefore, early.

Ditch 29029

This ditch lay immediately north of 29250 and parallel to it, crossing the trench (Fig. 5.2). It was of varying width (1.5-2.5m) and about 0.2m deep with a shallow, flat-based profile. It yielded three flint flakes, although this is not considered to be conclusive dating evidence.

Both Ditches 29250 and 29029 correspond quite closely to the clearest geophysical anomaly registered, which is probably part of the early Roman enclosure to the west. It is likely that one or other relates to the geophysical anomaly, while the other is of a similar date, although presumably of a different phase.

Late Roman pits at northern end of Trench 29

An area of Roman activity (Pit Group 29247) comprised a layer overlying two pits, all containing an exceptional amount (273 sherds) of late Roman pottery and other finds (Fig. 5.3). The pits were thought to be possible cremation pits, and this terminology has been retained, although only a few minute fragments of calcined bone were recovered from the soil samples (Fryer, Chapter 11), and it seems that the pits were not themselves intended to receive any human remains.

Plate 6 Late Roman pit 29018 (part of Group 29247). Area E Trench 29

One of the 'cremation' pits, 29229, was sub-rectangular, 1.38m by 0.70m in size and cut on an east-west alignment. It had vertical sides and an irregular, westwards sloping base at a depth of 0.25m. The fill, (29230), which was 100% sampled (Sample 26), was a very dark greyish brown loam with pottery fragments and frequent charcoal. The carbonised remains included seeds of several grassland/ruderal plant species which are quite typical of pyre material (Fryer, Chapter 11). Found at the top of the fill was a small complete jar, its miniature size and completeness suggesting that it may have been a funerary object (Fig. 9.1.4).

Another 'cremation' pit, 29018, 3 m to the north-west, was sub-rectangular, 1.10 m by 0.50 m, cut on a north-south alignment (Plate 6). It had vertical sides and flat base at a depth of 0.28 m. The main fill (29016) was a friable dark brown sandy loam with frequent medium-sized pottery sherds, infrequent very fragmented and larger pieces of animal bones and charcoal flecks. The sharp-edged fragments of an entire dish (Fig. 9.2.11) were found, indicating it may have been either placed or thrown intact into the pit. Also within this deposit were three coins and several iron objects including five cleats, possibly used to re-enforce the soles of boots (Hylton, Chapter 10). The basal fill was a small deposit (29036) of a lighter brown colour than 29016. The presence of sherds from the same vessel as found in 29016 indicated this fill was contemporary with the layer above.

Between the two pits, beneath two quernstone fragments, in an area of 1.0m x 0.8m, was a deposit of brownish red sand (29087), which appeared to have been scorched (Plate 7). This merged with the natural clay which was also scorched red. It is thought possible that this area of burning was the location of a funeral pyre.

The general area was overlain by a hard mid to dark grey brown silty loam (29014) containing frequent large sherds of pottery both sharp-edged and moderately worn and occasional poorly sorted small pieces of burnt clay. This layer was 5.2 by 3.8m in area, filling a depression to a depth of 200-300mm. The carbonised plant remains (sample 16) included charcoal and cereal grains. Also from 29014 were a number of other finds, including four coins, a copper alloy spoon (Fig. 10.1), two fragments of rotary quern, another smooth rubbing stone, eight iron nails and several other fragments of iron sheet and rods.

Trench 11: linear ditches and related features

Cutting, and to the east of, the prehistoric pit (11090) were a group of three shallow ditches or gullies (Group 11153NN). As well as being on a parallel north-south alignment, they were of similar width. A sherd of grog-tempered storage jar from Ditch 11129 indicates that the group are probably Roman.

The easternmost ditch (11123) was 0.6m wide running the full width of the trench (over 30m). The ditch had steep sides to a flattish, concave base at a depth of 0.35m. It had a compact clay fill with occasional burnt flint and charcoal pieces, which yielded a small Bronze Age pottery sherd. Adjacent to the ditch in the south, there was also a small circular pit (11126), 0.85m in diameter, with regular concave profile to a depth of 0.35m and a similar clayey fill.

Four metres west, Gully 11131 was 0.3m wide, but just 0.15m deep, with a fill of compact mottled rusty coloured/grey clay. In the south, the ditch butt ended with a possible posthole (11133) on the same alignment. It was 0.4m wide with a regular concave profile to a depth of 0.2m. It cut the top of Pit 11090.

Alongside, and containing a very similar fill, Ditch 11129 was 0.6m wide and 0.3m deep with an asymmetrical profile. It is assumed to be an earlier or later phase of Gully 11131 and merged with it to the north. On its eastern side it was cut by a post-medieval foundation trench (11221). To the south Gully 11137 lay on the line of 11129 and 11131. It was 0.4m wide and ran a short length of 2.3m. Its depth was just 0.1m and it is unclear whether it had been truncated.

Plate 7 Late Roman quernstone, overlying a patch of burnt clay, base of Layer 29014 (part of Group 29247). Area E Trench 29

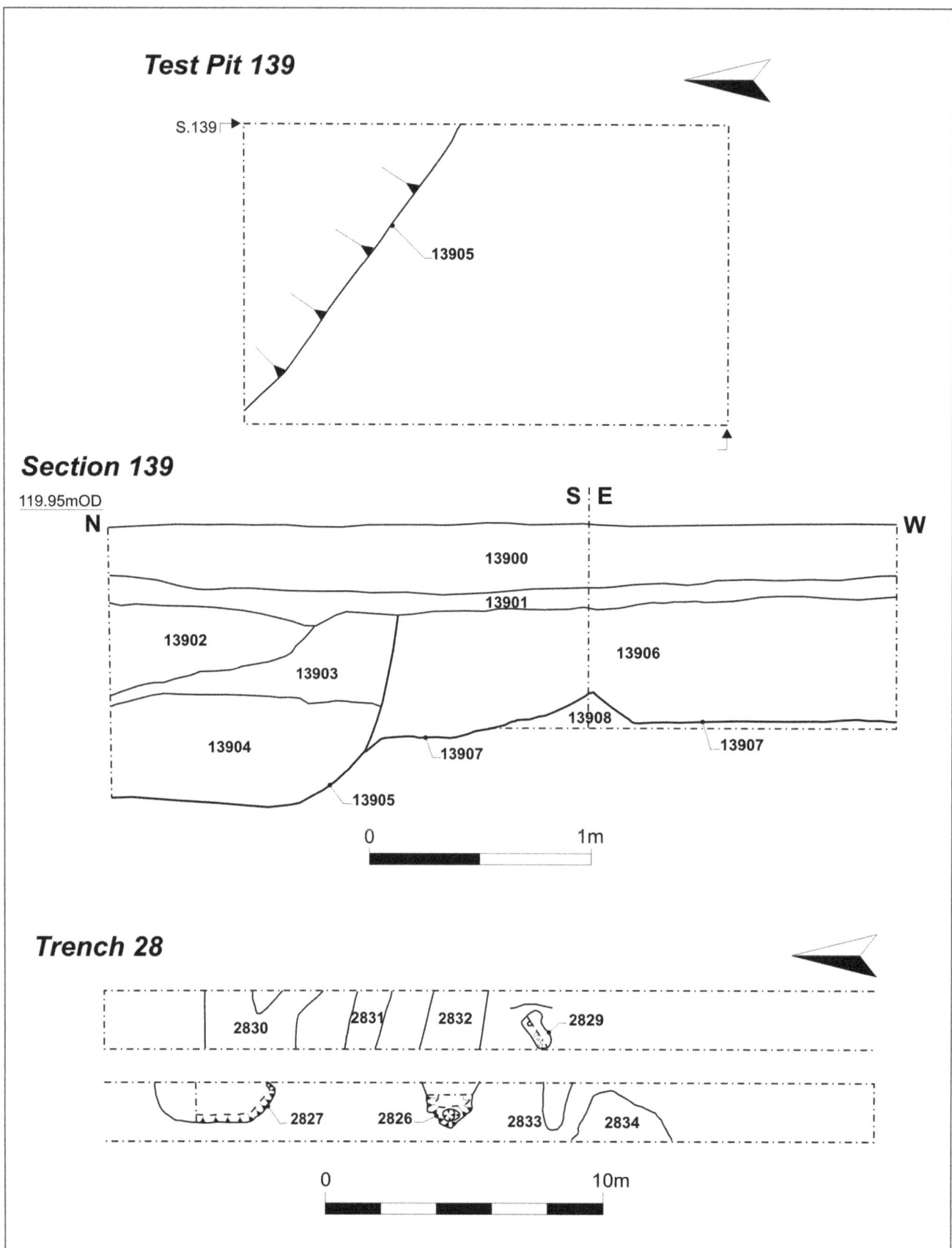

Fig 5.1 Trial Pit 139 (from Oxford Archaeology 2002); Trench 28. Area E

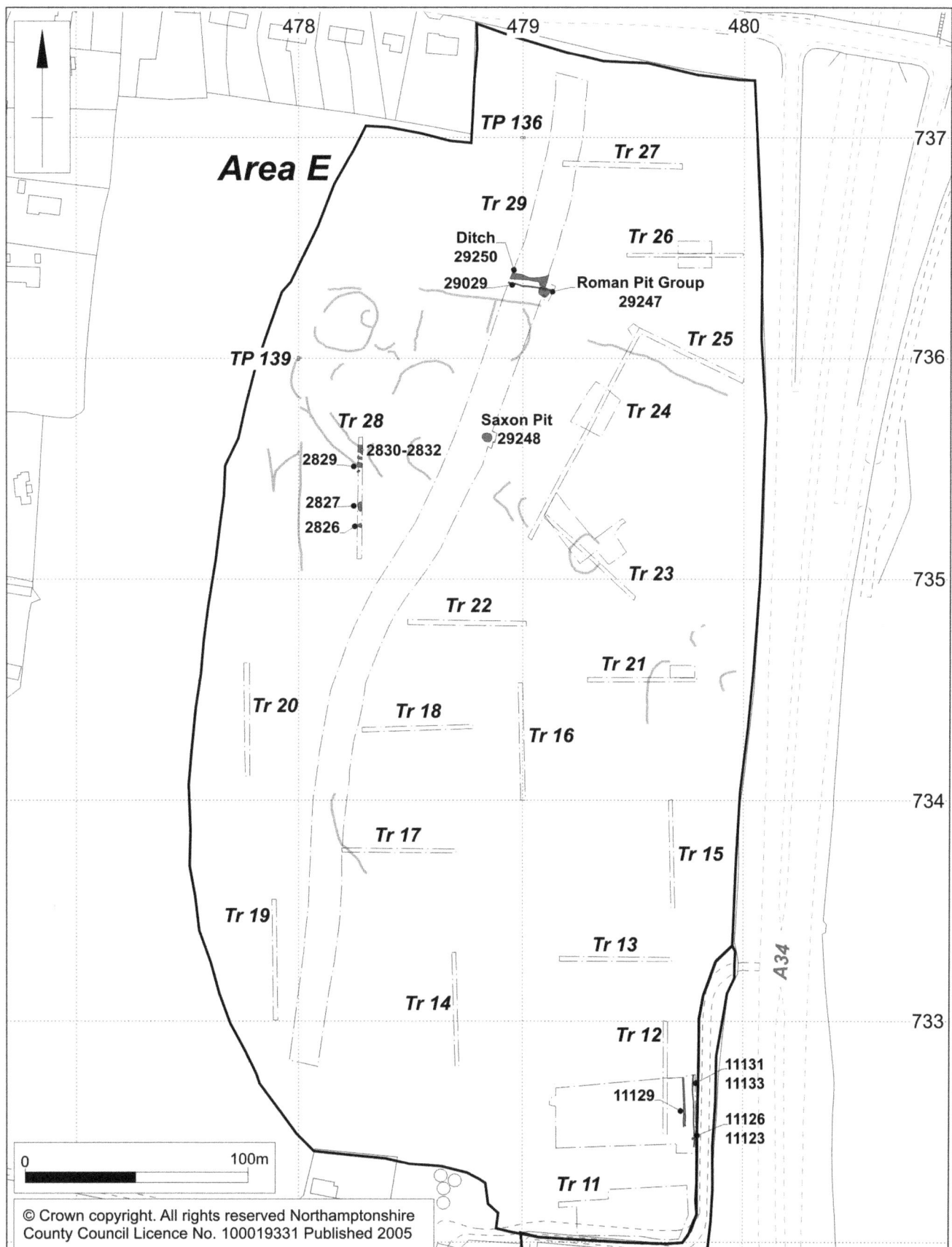

Fig 5.2 Roman and early Saxon features in Area E

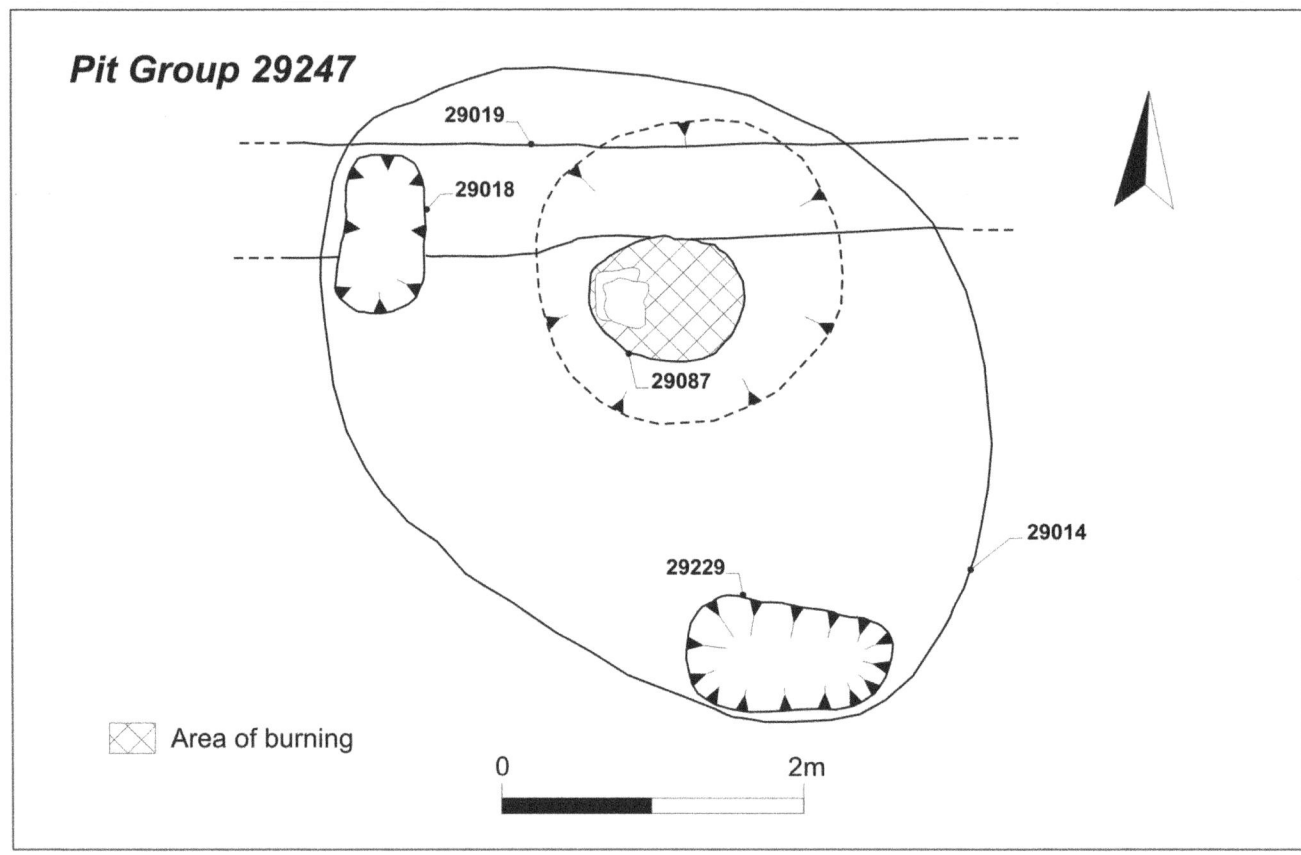

Fig 5.3 Late Roman 'cremation' pits, Group 29247. Area E

Area D Trench 1: miscellaneous Iron Age and Roman pottery

A group of eight small sherds of flint-tempered and sandy Iron Age pottery, together with a larger grog-tempered Roman sherd, were recovered from colluvial layers at the northern end of Trench 1 at the western side of Area D (Timby, Chapter 9; Fig. 3.2). There were no features in this trench, nor in the trenches to the east, and it is assumed that these finds relate to a site lying somewhere to the west of the soil disposal area.

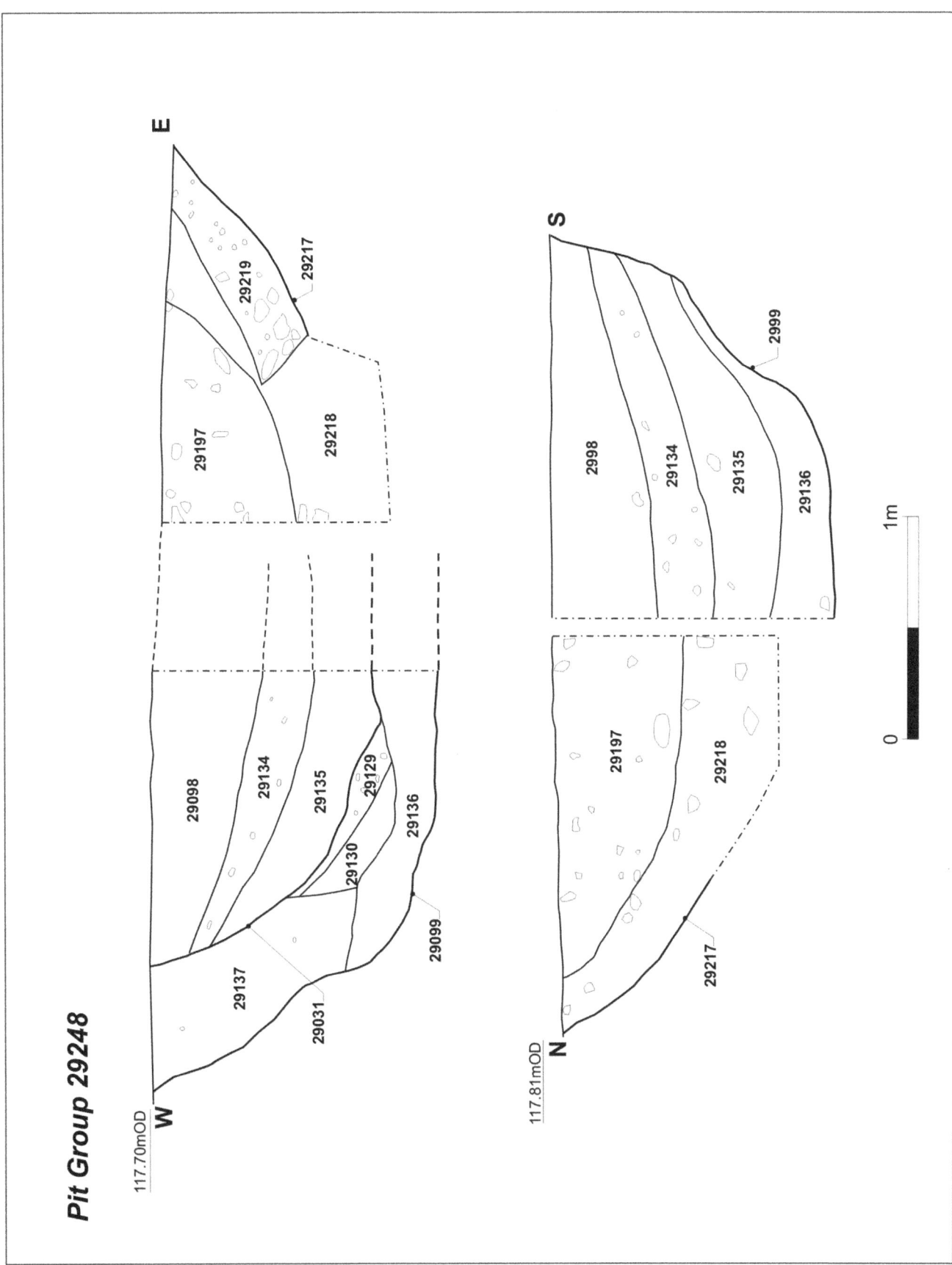

Fig 6.1 Probable early-mid Saxon pit 29248

Bronze Age, Roman and later occupation at Chieveley, West Berkshire

Chapter 6: Saxon features

Introduction

A slight 6th to 8th century presence in the area of Radnall Farm is indicated by five small sherds of Saxon pottery from Area E (Timby, Chapter 9). One was recovered from fieldwalking, two came from the subsoil in Trench 28 and one from the post-medieval ditch 29183. The other came from the upper fill of Pit 29248. This is taken to indicate that the pit is probably of this date. Some of the undated or poorly dated features may also be of Saxon date.

To the south of the M4 motorway, six Saxon sherds were recovered from Pit 1005 in Area C, and a small number of other pits are likely to be of this date.

Area E: Pit 29248

A large, oval pit (Group 29248) was excavated in two sections (Fig. 5.2). It measured 4.6m by 3.9m and was 1.3m deep, with a flattish base. It contained several fills, the lower of which were dark brown silty loams with trace charcoal (Fig. 6.1). Some shell-tempered pottery from the lower fill (29218) may be Iron Age. A soil sample (Sample 20) yielded a few indeterminate cereal grains and some charcoal. Just above this, the south-east quarter of the pit was lined with a layer containing 50% chalk (29219), which is not local to the site.

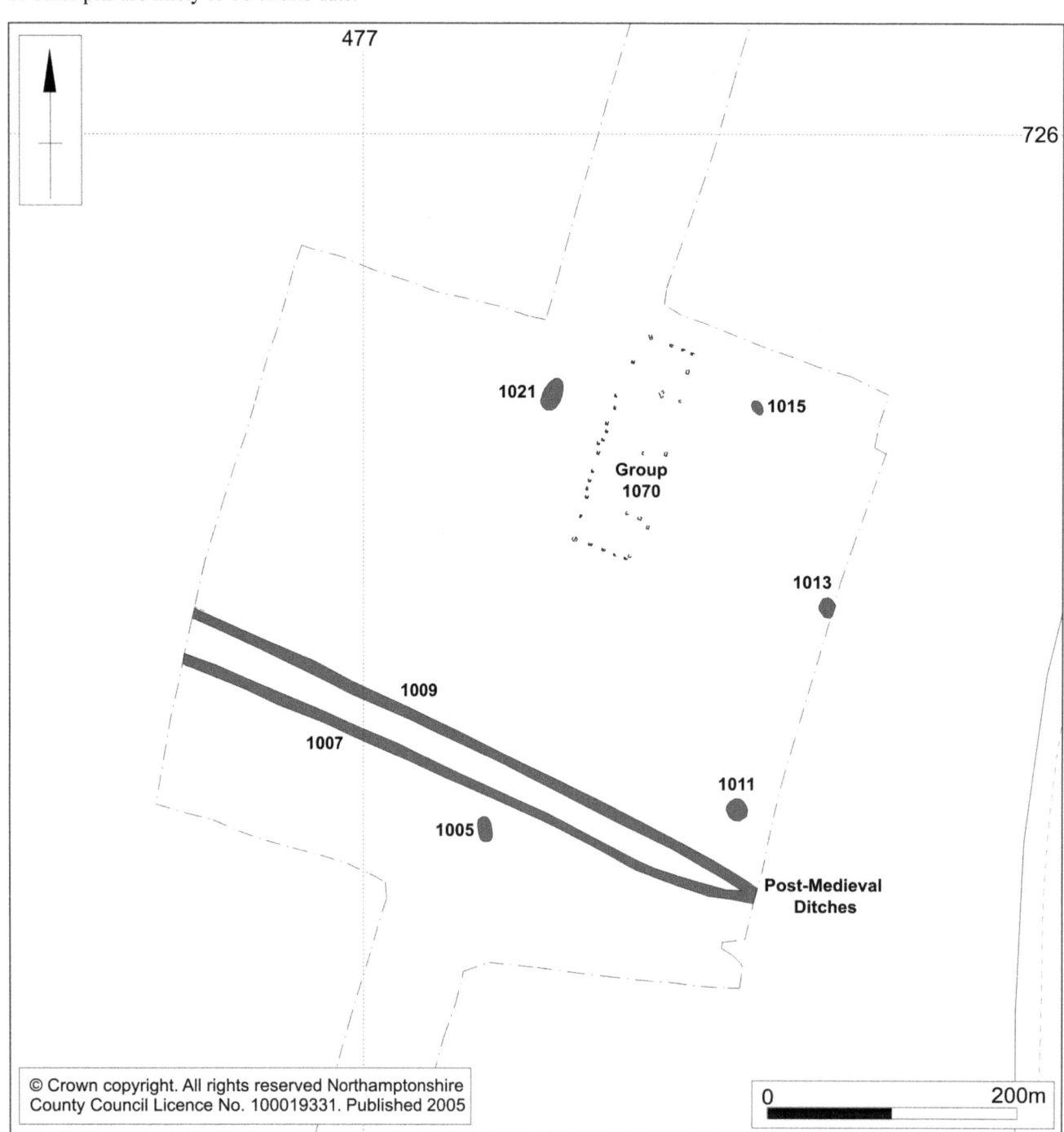

Fig 6.2 Trench 10, Area C, showing early-mid Saxon pits, post-medieval ditches and undated post-built structure

A re-cut was recorded in both sections above this fill, and the pit was subsequently infilled with deposits of brown or grey-brown silt loams with varying amounts of sand and flint gravel. The upper fill (29098) was a light brown loam containing a nail (SF24) and three pottery sherds - two of Roman and one of Saxon date. While the date and purpose of this pit are uncertain the Saxon sherd is considered likely to provide the *terminus post quem*. A post-Saxon date is possible, but the medieval and later activity here seems to have more of an agricultural character, or be related to quarrying, and the pit is anomalous in that respect. Notwithstanding that the pit was probably re-cut, it is most unlikely that it had its origin in the Iron Age and the pottery is probably residual.

Area C Trench 10: group of pits

In the southern part of the trench, an isolated oval pit 1005, approximately 0.51m deep and 1.78m along its main axis, produced pottery of early to middle Saxon date and lava quernstone fragments (Fig 6.2). Fragments of lava quern also came from Pit 1011 in the south-eastern part of the excavation area, which was of a similar size. These were the only features providing material evidence of any antiquity, but it is likely that three other pits were of similar date.

At the northern extremity of the trench extension a large re-cut oval pit (1021) was discovered with burnt material in tip lines visible through the section (Fig. 6.3). The main pit was 0.51m deep below the subsoil and 2.38m across its main axis. There were three cuts in total, (1017, 1019 & 1021), but none produced datable materials.

Soil samples from Pits 1005, 1011 and 1021, contained charred remains of cereals, weeds and wood which are fairly typical of small domestic assemblages (Fryer, Chapter 11). Hazelnut also came from Pit 1021 (Sample 4).

On the eastern extremity of the trench extension, two other circular pits were defined, 1013 and 1015. Pit 1013 was 1.58m across and 0.37m deep, while 1015 was just 0.54m across and 0.15m deep. Both contained friable grey clay-silts with moderate charcoal inclusions. Although pit 1013 contained some animal bone, neither produced any datable evidence. They lay within an area of disturbance possibly caused by roots.

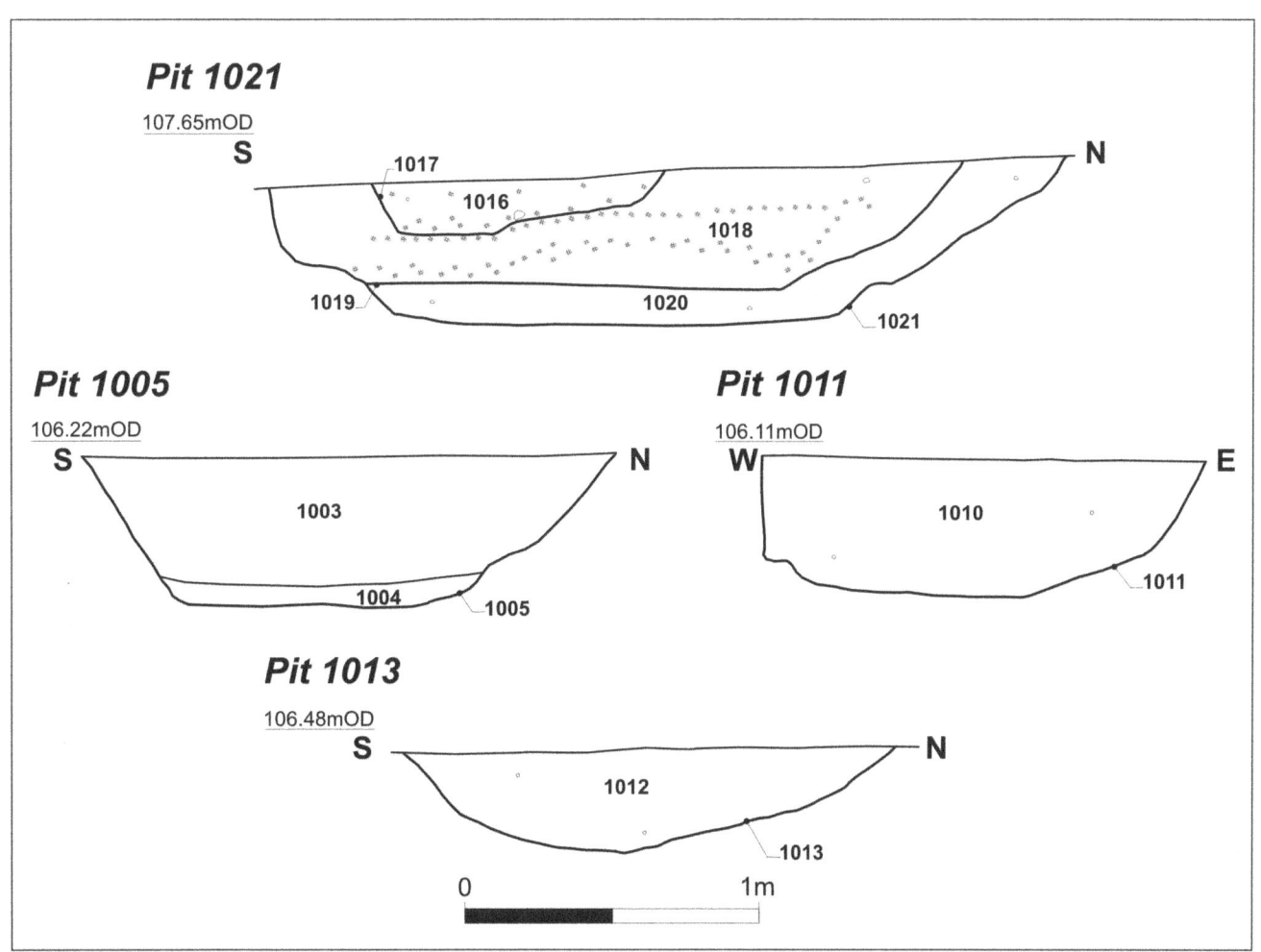

Fig 6.3 Sections of early-mid Saxon pits

Chapter 7: Post-medieval features

Area A Trench 16: Hollow-way and other features

The predominant features on this excavation site consisted of several linear soil marks, which had been identified on aerial photographs, following the same course and inter-cutting at different points. They ran NE-SW from the Green Lane access point by the A34 carriageway for about 100m before turning SE for the remaining extent of the excavated area (Fig. 7.1; Colour Plate 2). Other features included a small number of pits and post-holes, together with boundary ditches aligned perpendicular to the main linear feature and which were probably post-medieval in date.

There were also two large circular pits of 19th or 20th century origin. One of the pits (1647) was 14.8m in diameter. It was investigated to a depth of 0.99m below the subsoil. It was found to comprise a long sequence of deposits containing relatively recent debris. The other pit was larger and was left unexcavated. It is unclear what these pits were for.

Hollow-way

The main linear soil mark was sectioned in four places. At the southern end of the trench it was more heavily truncated than elsewhere on the site. The far southern portion revealed a very shallow cut (1604), only 0.21m deep, although its breadth extended 3.1m. Its fill (1603) was a grey/brown clayey silt which was heavily compacted. The base of 1604 was very gently concave, but flattened towards the centre. The base was cut by a narrow gully (1608) at the eastern end which measured 0.21m wide by 0.14m deep with almost sheer sides and a flat base. The fill of this (1607) was a much lighter, soft and crumbly orange/brown sandy silt and could be seen extending through the base of 1604 on a slightly different alignment. Gully 1608 ran parallel to a second gully (1619), which was more heavily truncated, offset from 1608 by 1.8m and had a comparable fill. It is thought that these represented wheel ruts sunk into the base of 1604. This interpretation suggests that the main linear feature was a road or track which had developed into a hollow way.

To the north, on the central western side of the trench, these linear features were less truncated. Here a section measuring 6.8m long and 0.6m deep was excavated through them and revealed a much more complicated stratigraphic sequence than that in the southern section (Fig. 7.2). On the inside arc of the main linear feature (here 1623) was a ditch (1625) measuring 0.87m wide and 0.35m deep, running across the site roughly parallel to the main linear soil mark. This feature was cut by the main linear at this point and was therefore the earliest feature in this sequence. It was equivalent to 1699, 1671 and 1667 (re-cut by 1665) on the plan. A fragment of clay tobacco pipe bowl came from Cut 1697. This is not closely dateable, but may be as late as the 18th or 19th century.

At the base of the section two narrow gullies were visible, 1617 and 1619, set apart by 1.8m and following the same alignment as the potential wheel-ruts seen further south. These features cut the base of the main linear feature 1623, where substantial amounts of stone were revealed as an irregular and uneven surface.

Cut 1623 of the hollow-way was only visible for 1.24m of the section, to a depth of 0.44m, where it had a gradual sloping side and flat base. Like 1604, the cut was filled with a thick deposit of soil (1614), showing a clear period of disuse and a gradual process of deposition, probably at least partly resulting from ploughing, which filled the hollow-way. The date of the upper fill (1613) derives from artefacts recovered which included 19th-century pottery, tile, clay pipe, and an iron horse shoe from the equivalent fill 1662 in Cut 1663.

On the western side, these deposits were cut by a ditch (1612) following the outer edge of the hollow-way and equivalent to 1673, 1659 and 16993. This would seem to be part of a later post-medieval boundary rather than a ditch beside the hollow-way as it did not follow the hollow-way precisely. Another horseshoe came from 1672 (Cut 1673). The complete sequence of features here suggests a long-lived boundary which became used as a routeway for some part of its existence.

Two further sections to the north and east confirmed the nature and extent of the ditches and the hollow-way, and identified evidence for another ditch (1675) on the outer arc of the main linear soil mark. This was 0.8m wide and 0.2m deep below the subsoil. This ditch is equivalent to 16995, 1687 and 1661, and yielded post-medieval tile from fill 1686 and 19th-century pottery from fill 16994.

Pits and post-holes

Within the perimeter of the main linear features a number of smaller post-holes and pits were investigated. Two clear post-holes were identified (1639 and 1629), set close to Ditch 1625. They were 0.31 m and 0.28 m deep respectively, with near vertical sides and flat bases. Although other potential post-holes were investigated in this area the cuts proved to be shallow, ill defined and no deeper than 0.1 m and so may have been of natural rather than archaeological origin. No datable materials were retrieved from any of these features and the evidence is insufficient to indicate the form of any structures.

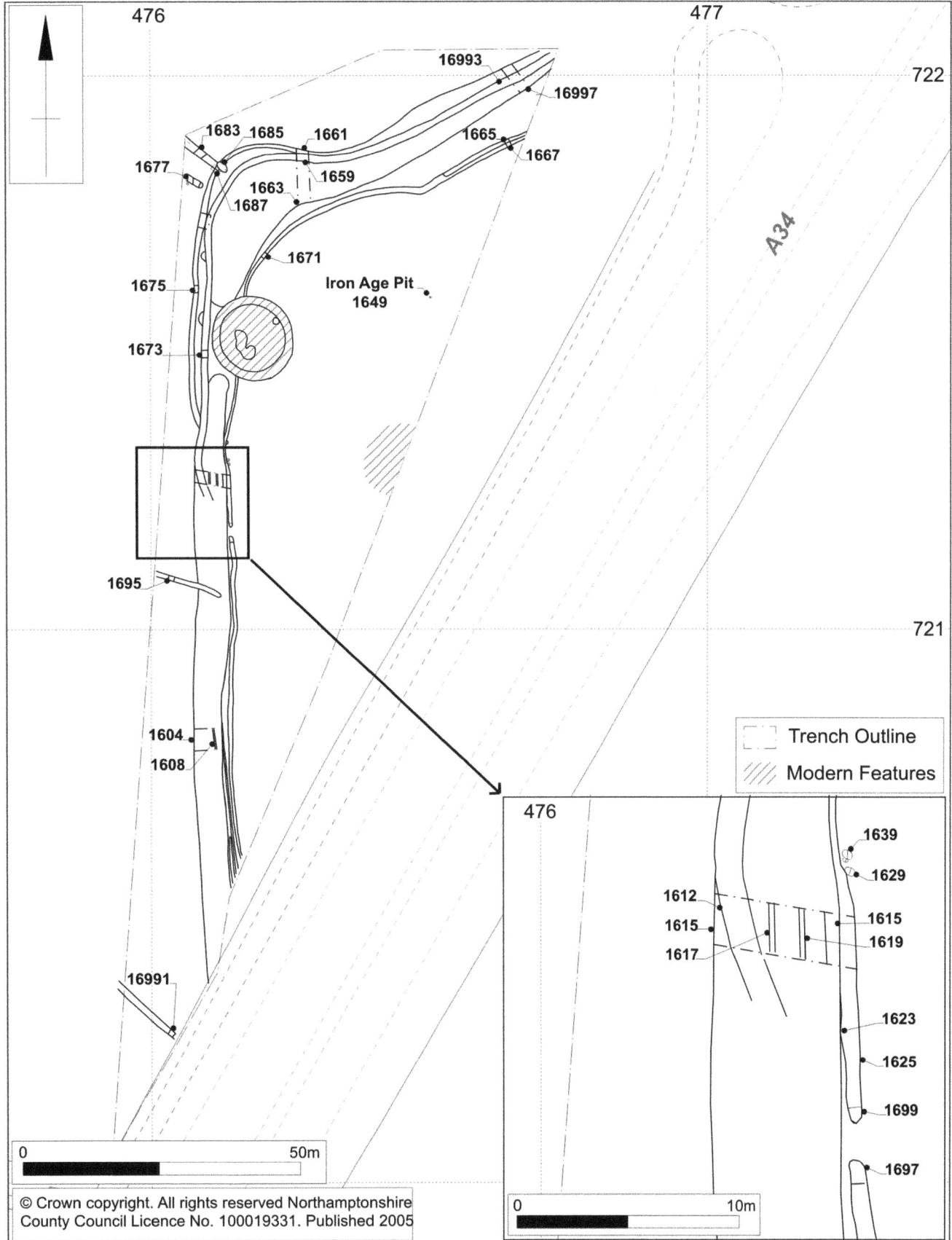

Fig 7.1 Plan of post-medieval hollow-way and other features, Trench 16, Area A

Field boundaries

Outside the perimeter of the main linear features, four ditches running out of the trench on a roughly east-west or NE-SW alignment were recorded and investigated. All were roughly perpendicular to the main linear soil mark. Ditch 16991, towards the very southern end of the trench, was 1.52m wide and 0.44m deep. A strip of ironwork, probably a bucket binding, came from its fill (16990). The second ditch (1695), located halfway along the trench on the western side, was 1.1m wide and 0.39m deep. This ditch produced no datable material but could clearly be seen cutting the post-medieval fills of the hollow-way, which suggests that it was relatively recent.

The northernmost ditches, 1677 and 1683, ran on a NE-SW alignment, roughly parallel to one another and 3.4m apart. Ditch 1677 was 1.21m wide and 0.16m deep with an uneven base and gently sloped sides. Ditch 1683 was 1.56m wide and 0.25m deep with an irregular convex sloping side running sharply down into a narrow round based gully. Their fills were both of friable sandy loams. Pit 1685 cut Ditch 1687 but produced no datable finds. Ditches 1677 and 1683 are likely to be post-medieval like the majority of features in this area.

Area B: Field boundaries

Trial trenching in this field revealed a ditch running approximately north-south through trenches 18, 20 and 22 (Fig. 7.3). The ditch was 0.3-0.4m deep and a little over 1m wide. It was buried beneath 0.33-0.46m of subsoil which may explain why it did not show up clearly on the geophysical survey. The ditch corresponds to a field boundary shown on the 1840 Tithe map of Snelsmore (Fig. 13.1).

Area C Trench 10: Timber structure and field boundary ditches

There was very little dating evidence from this area, but a group of post-holes, forming an apparently open-sided timber structure, and three ditches are all considered likely to be post-medieval in date (Fig. 6.2).

Timber structure

In the northern part of the trench, a group of post-holes were discovered, Group 1070, comprising 20 clearly definable features. These post-holes each had vertical or near vertical sides and were rectangular in plan, varying between 0.13m and 0.16m in diameter and 0.12m and 0.18m in depth. The fills were all of similar nature, being for the most part grey silty clay with a slight gritty texture and with few inclusions. The post-holes formed a rectangle, aligned north-south, and open on the eastern side. It was thought that the group represented either a small fenced enclosure or the heavily truncated remains of an insubstantial timber structure, about 17m long and 5m wide. Attempts to identify possible internal features were made, plotting the light grey/blue soil marks, but none of these produced substantial evidence for cut features in section. In any event, no dating evidence was recovered.

Although early/middle Saxon pits were found nearby, it is most unlikely that this structure was of a similar date, the form and fills of the post-holes and the plan of the structure itself being untypical of structures of that period. It is far more likely to have been some form of shelter shed or agricultural outbuilding of more recent origin. The structure does not appear on any historical maps.

Ditches

Two parallel ditches, 1007 and 1009, of approximately equal size and 0.36m deep, crossed the trench on an east-west alignment. Post-medieval clay pipe was recovered from one of these.

Area E Trench 11: Ditch and related features

Early maps show that there has been a building on the side of the A34 Oxford Road (to the east of Trench 11) since at least 1761, as shown on Rocque's map of Berkshire (Fig. 13.2) and later maps, until the road was widened in 1971 with the construction of the M4 and the junction roundabout. The building appears always to have been a roadside dwelling and was associated with a well, indicated on maps from 1900 (although it may have existed earlier) and a rear boundary. A concentration of roof-tile from this part of the field in the fieldwalking survey (Fig. 2.2 from GGP 2000, fig. 6) undoubtedly came from this building.

On the eastern margin of Trench 11 layers of modern debris associated with this building were cleared by machine to expose the underlying Bronze Age pit (11090). The remaining post-medieval features comprised a north-south ditch, 11221, which cut the prehistoric and Roman features in this area, and another smaller linear feature (Fig. 7.4). These features were not excavated, but Ditch 11221 is likely to have been the rear property boundary shown on the maps.

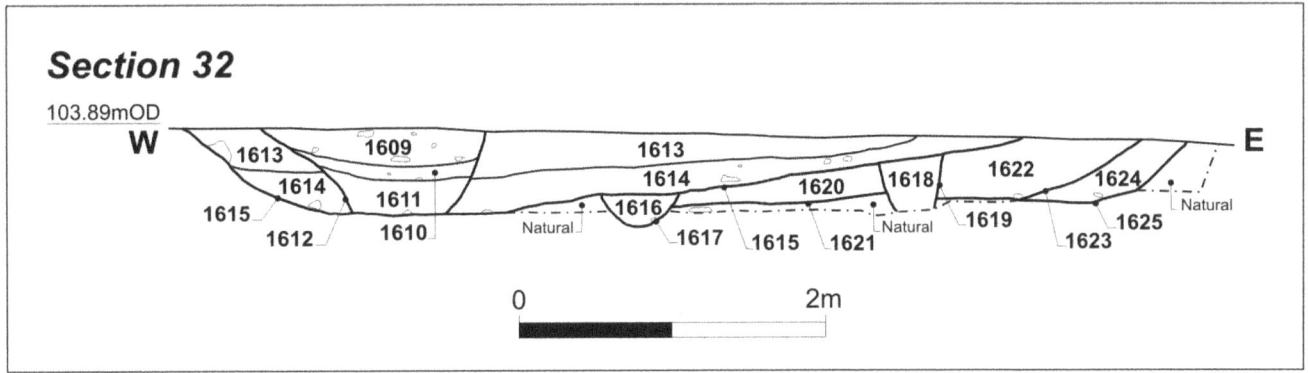

Fig 7.2 Section through post-medieval hollow-way, Trench 16, Area A

Area E: Other linear features

In Trench 15 was a gully (1504) running approximately east-west (Fig. 7.4). It was without finds but cut the subsoil and it considered to be relatively recent. It does not correspond to any mapped features.

In Trench 29 were three linear ditches, possibly forming part of a field division. Ditch 29183 was over 15m in length on an east-west alignment. It was 0.4m wide by 0.5m deep and filled with a mid greyish brown sandy loam (29184).

Ditch 29114 abutted 29183, and was 0.15m wide by 0.3m deep, curving to the south-east. It contained a light brown and orange sandy silt (29115).

Continuing the alignment of 29114 to the north, was a linear gully (29255), over 15m long, 0.75m wide and 0.2 m deep, becoming shallower at its southern terminal. It had a fill of mid greyish brown silty sand which was numbered individually in the several sections excavated. The fill contained a small, possibly Iron Age, sherd (from 29102) and a post-medieval sherd (from 29132).

Area D: Field boundaries

A gully was found running WNW-ESE in Trench 3, stratified between two deep layers of colluvium (Fig. 7.4). This is undoubtedly a post-enclosure field boundary which is shown on the 1882 and 1900 editions of the OS 1:10,560 map, but which had disappeared by 1913.

Trenches 7 and 9 also contained shallow gullies, running east-west, which are likely to be of post-medieval date although there was no dating evidence and they do not correspond to known field boundaries.

Bronze Age, Roman and later occupation at Chieveley, West Berkshire

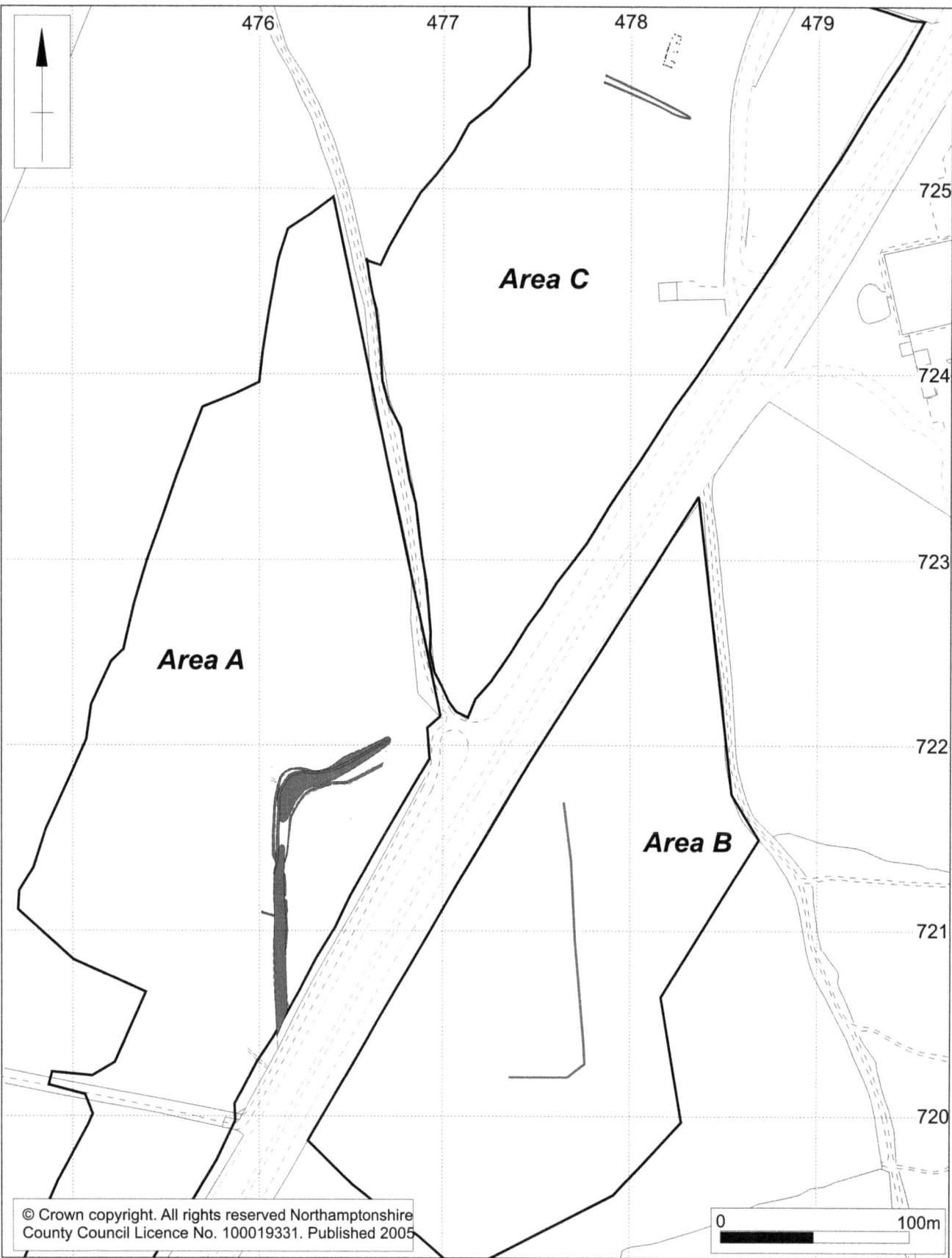

Fig 7.3 Post-medieval features in Areas A, B and C

Chapter 7: Post-medieval features

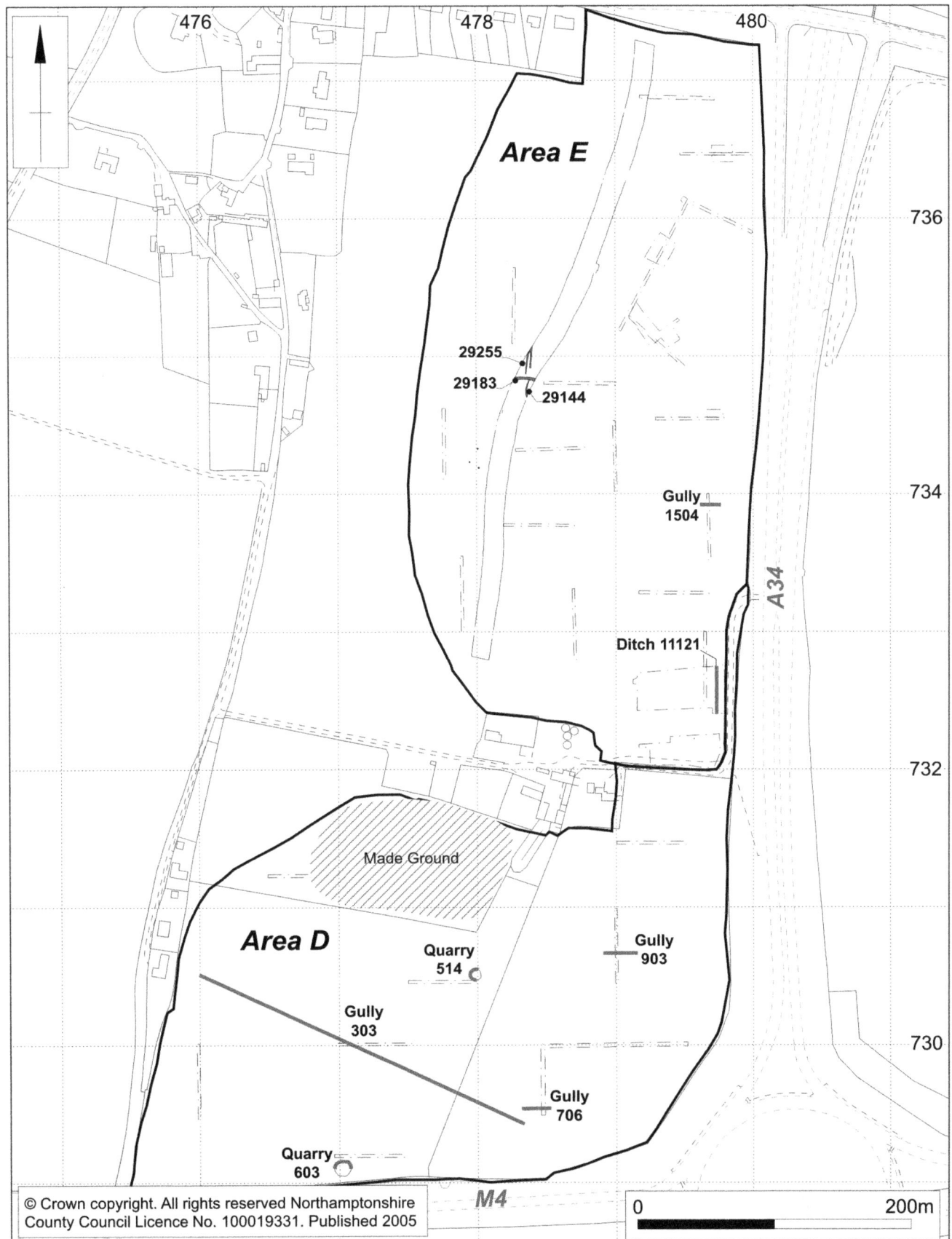

Fig 7.4 Post-medieval features in Areas D and E

Chapter 8: Worked and Burnt Flint

by Alex Thorne

Worked Flint: Introduction

A total of three hundred and eighty-nine pieces of worked flint were recovered from the three phases of fieldwork at Chieveley. Of these, two hundred and twenty-five flints (58%) were collected during the fieldwalking evaluation of most of the study area in 2000 (GGP 2000). In this phase, a general scatter was recovered from most of the area covered, but there was a marked concentration of material in Area E, possibly indicating one or more sites of domestic occupation. The assemblages were suggested to be mainly Bronze Age due to their association with burnt flint and a few sherds of Bronze Age pottery although there was also some probable late Neolithic/early Bronze Age material (ibid, 6-9).

Subsequent test-pitting by the Oxford Archaeology in 2002 recovered sixty-three flints (16%) from a total of forty-one contexts (mainly topsoil) from thirty-five of the one hundred and eighty-three test pits excavated (Oxford Archaeology 2002). There was a low scatter of flint across the site, with a single concentration of flint from TP 130 (Area E) in association with middle/late Bronze Age pottery, and generally higher amounts of flint from immediately adjacent test pits. The assemblage was characterised as being broadly later Neolithic or Bronze Age, but the character of the irregular, thick flakes, and the lack of blades, suggested a date in the latter end of the range. A small component of earlier material was also identified within the assemblage (Cramp 2002, 9-10).

Excavations by Northamptonshire Archaeology in 2003 recovered one hundred worked flints (26%) from 48 contexts in Trenches 1, 2, 5, 11, 20, 23, 28, and 29, mainly from the northern, Radnall Farm site (CHRF), with only five flints recovered from Trench 16 at the southern Snelsmore Farm site (SNEL).

The flint collection from all stages of the work is quantified in Table 8.1. It forms a significant group of stratified and unstratified prehistoric artefacts whose re-examination for this report provides an opportunity for a critical assessment and overview of this aspect of the archaeological fieldwork. The account presented here starts with a description of the flintwork from the sealed contexts excavated in Trench 11 which were associated with mid-late Bronze Age pottery. This provides a point of comparison with the remaining unstratified material.

Category of flint	Gifford 2000	Oxford Archaeology 2002	Northamptonshire Archaeology 2003	Total
Palaeolithic flake	2 (0.5%)	-	2 (0.5%)	4 (1%)
Adze	-	-	1 (0.4%)	1 (0.4%)
Arrowhead	1 (0.4%)	-	-	1 (0.4%)
Fabricator	1 (0.4%)	-	-	1 (0.4%)
Scraper	31 (8%)	4 (1%)	6 (1.5%)	41 (10.5%)
Scraper/knife	18 (4.6%)	2 (0.5%)	-	20 (5.1%)
Core	16 (4.1%)	2 (0.5%)	6 (1.5%)	24 (6.1%)
Core rejuvenation flake	6 (1.5%)	2 (0.5%)	3 (0.7%)	11 (2.7%)
Hammer stone	7 (1.8%)	-	1 (0.4%)	8 (2.2%)
Notched flake	13 (3.3%)	3 (0.7%)	1 (0.4%)	17 (4.4%)
Miscellaneous retouched	33 (8.5%)	7 (1.8%)	7 (1.7%)	47 (12%)
Utilised flake	13 (3.3%)	6 (1.5%)	7 (1.7%)	26 (6.5%)
Utilised blade	-	1 (0.4%)	3 (0.7%)	4 (1.1%)
Waste flake	70 (18.0%)	25 (6.4%)	54 (14.1%)	149 (38.3%)
Waste blade	3 (0.8%)	2 (0.5%)	3 (0.7%)	8 (2.2%)
Burnt flake	-	6 (1.5%)	1 (0.4%)	7 (1.9%)
Shattered piece	11 (2.8%)	3 (0.7%)	6 (1.5%)	20 (5.0%)
Total	225 / 58%	63 / 16%	101 / 26%	389

Table 8.1: General composition of the Chieveley flint assemblages. Percentages are given as a proportion of the entire collection.

Excavated assemblage from Trench 11

Of the material recovered in the excavations, a group of 54 flints was found in Trench 11, most of it stratified and some in association with middle/late Bronze Age pottery. This assemblage is quantified in Table 8.2.

Key to Tables:
N/K: Not Known
U/S: Unstratified
OA: Oxford Archaeology
NA: Northamptonshire Archaeology

Category of flint	U/S	Roman Ditch 11123	Pit 11024	Pit 11033	Pit Group 11138	Pit Group 11047	Pit 11110	Strat. Total
Palaeolithic flake	1	-	-	-	1	-	-	1 (3%)
Adze	1	-	-	-	-	-	-	-
Core	-	-	-	-	3	1 (re-used)	-	4 (11%)
Scraper	1	-	-	-	-	-	-	-
Core rejuvenation flake	1	-	-	1	-	-	1	2 (5%)
Retouched flake	-	-	1	-	-	-	-	1 (3%)
Notched flake	-	-	-	1	-	-	-	1 (3%)
Utilised flake	-	-	-	-	1	-	-	1 (3%)
Utilised blade	-	-	-	-	-	1	1	2 (5%)
Waste flake	11	-	5	3	6	4	-	18 (49%)
Waste blade		1				3		3 (8%)
Shattered piece	1	-	-	-	2	2	-	4 (11%)
Total	(16)	(1)	6	5	13	11	2	37

Table 8.2: Composition of the flint group excavated from CHRF Trench 11 middle/late Bronze Age and other contexts. Percentages relate to the stratified assemblage from the pits.

This group of material contains some pre-Bronze Age flintwork. Two rolled flakes, one of them from Pit Group 11138 and the other superficial, are certainly Palaeolithic, while two of the 15 unstratified flints - the adze (Fig. 8.10.1) and the scraper (Fig. 8.10.10) - are likely to be Neolithic. The Bronze Age pit groups may well contain a proportion of residual earlier material, but other than the Palaeolithic flake, there are no diagnostic pieces to help determine whether or not this is the case.

The sealed assemblage of 37 pieces is characterised by a low overall incidence of tools (five, or 13%) comprising retouched/utilised flakes/blades and one notch. There were no scrapers, despite these forming a relatively high proportion of the project assemblage as a whole (Table 8.1). The assemblage was dominated by apparently unutilised debitage including waste flakes (49%) and cores (11%). This observation should be qualified by the note that no use-wear analysis has been carried out, and where this is undertaken it tends to show that utilised pieces are more common than is apparent to the naked eye. Of the four cores, one (Pit 11098, Group 11047) showed a rejuvenated platform, indicating a certain degree of care in core maintenance (Fig. 8.10.11), although the others were irregular lumps of flint with few flake removals. This group of material is similar to other late Bronze Age assemblages, including that from Green Park, Reading Business Park (Bradley 2004, 50-2), where the typically limited range of tools comprised piercing and cutting implements and a single scraper. The Chieveley assemblage contains a relatively high occurrence of blades (13%), which are commonly considered to be typical of more careful knapping traditions, although it is possible that they formed part of a specific range of cutting implements at this site. The quantity (five) is too low to be sure that this is significant, but as a point of comparison the much larger Green Park (Reading) assemblages included only 1.7% blades from both the late Neolithic and late Bronze Age groups.

Figures 8.1 - 8.3 illustrate the breadth: length ratios of the flints from each of the stages of fieldwork. In shape, flakes from the excavations range from being equal in length to breadth to rather more squat, and wider than they are long (Fig. 8.1). There are equal proportions of secondary and tertiary flakes (13 of each) but only five primary flakes, so perhaps there was some initial core preparation carried out elsewhere. There are several instances of miss-hits, hinged fractured flakes, and the large quantity of shattered pieces suggests poor quality of workmanship, a characteristic of late Bronze Age assemblages generally. There is only one example of a soft-hammer struck flake. The range of raw material appeared similar to that from the excavated site as a whole. The worked flint was associated with moderately large quantities of burnt flint (below). Again this association is often characteristic of late Bronze Age 'burnt mounds' and other sites of this period.

Worked flint from other trenches (Northamptonshire Archaeology 2003)

The composition of the Northamptonshire Archaeology flint collection is summarised on Table 8.3.

Category of flint	U/S	CHRF Tr.1	CHRF Tr.2	CHRF Tr.5	CHRF Tr.11	CHRF Tr.20	CHRF Tr.23	CHRF Tr.28	CHRF Tr.29	SNEL Tr.16	Total
Palaeolithic flake	-	-	-	-	2	-	-	-	-	-	2
Adze	-	-	-	-	1	-	-	-	-	-	1
Scraper	-	-	1	-	1	-	-	1	2	3	8
Core	1	-	-	-	4	-	-	1	-	-	6
Core rejuvenation flake	-	-	-	-	3	-	-	-	-	-	3
Retouched flake	-	-	-	-	1	-	-	-	1	1	3
Notched flake	-	-	-	-	1	-	-	-	3	-	4
Utilised flake	-	1	-P	-	1	-	-	-	5	-	7
Utilised blade	-	-	-	1	2	-	-	-	1	-	4
Waste flake	-	-	-	1	29	1	1	3	13	1	49
Waste blade	-	-	-	-	4	-	-	-	1	1	6
Burnt flake	-	-	-	-	-	-	-	-	1	-	1
Shattered piece	-	-	-	-	5	-	-	-	1	-	6
Total	1	1	1	2	54	1	1	5	28	6	100

Table 8.3: Composition of the Northamptonshire Archaeology flint assemblage

There are no major differences between the stratified flints from Trench 11 and the flints from the remainder of the trenches. Other than the unstratified adze and the scraper already noted from Trench 11, there are no diagnostically earlier prehistoric pieces, although the overall number of scrapers is noteworthy and may suggest that there was a significant prehistoric presence predating the activity associated with the pits.

Eight of the flints were recovered from Roman contexts, and a further four from a post-medieval ditch. This represents a redeposited component of at least 12%. It would perhaps not be unreasonable to expect a similar percentage of earlier material in middle/late Bronze Age pits.

Flint from surface collection (Gifford 2000)

The composition of the Gifford flint collection has been divided into the different areas of the site as defined in the subsequent stages of fieldwork, although the precise extents of surface collection areas differed to some degree from those used later (Table 8.4). In particular, Area B was much smaller, investigated with a block of transects measuring only 100m by 40m. Area A included what became defined as Area F. Area D was not suitable for this survey. The flint was collected from transects spaced at 20m.

The overwhelming majority of the flint was recovered from Area E, with concentrations apparent on the western side of the area. There was relatively little from Areas C and A, despite the similar acreage covered. The relatively high number of tools is also noteworthy. It should be noted that due to the heavy edge abrasion of a high percentage of this assemblage, it was often difficult to ascertain whether edge damage was caused by ploughing or other post-depositional disturbance, or whether it resulted from utilisation or deliberate retouch. The pieces identified as having original edge wear or retouch are included in the totals in Table 8.4, but it is possible that items in these categories are slightly over-represented. There are twice as many retouched items as compared with those excavated by Northamptonshire Archaeology (Table 8.3). The wider range of tools, including a large number of scrapers, does however suggest that the surface material derived from a range of activities different from that recovered in the excavations. The greater range of size and shape of the flintwork perhaps also suggests this (Fig. 8.2).

Category of flint	N/K	Area A	Area C	Area B	Area E	Total
Palaeolithic flake	-	-	1	-	1	2 (0.9%)
Leaf-shaped arrowhead	-	-	-	-	1	1 (0.4%)
Fabricator	-	-	-	-	1	1 (0.4%)
Scraper	-	3	3	-	24	30 (13.4%)
Scraper on blade	-	-	-	-	1	1 (0.4%)
Scraper and knife tool	-	-	-	-	4	4 (1.8%)
Scraper/ scraper knife with notch	-	1	2	-	11	14 (6.2%)
Cores	-	1	1	3	11	16 (7.1%)
Core rejuvenation flake	-	-	1	-	5	6 (2.7%)
Hammer stone (all re-used cores)	1	-	1	-	5	7 (3.1%)
Retouched	-	-	-	1	10	11 (4.9%)
Retouched and notched	-	-	-	-	10	10 (4.4%)
Retouched and utilised	-	-	1	-	7	8 (3.5%)
Retouched, notched and utilised	-	1	1	-	2	4 (1.8%)
Notched	-	-	5	1	7	13 (5.8%)
Utilised flakes	-	1	4	-	8	13 (5.8%)
Utilised blades	-	-	-	-	-	0
Waste flakes	-	3	7	3	57	70 (31.1%)
Waste blades	-	-	-	-	3	3 (1.3%)
Burnt flakes	-	-	-	-	-	0
Shattered pieces	-	1	-	-	10	11 (4.9%)
Total	1 (0.4%)	11 (4.9%)	27 (12%)	8 (3.6%)	178 (79.1%)	225

Table 8.4: Gifford flint categories per field.

Category of flint	N/K	Area A	Area B	Area C	Area D	Area E	Area F	Total
Scrapers	1	1	-	-	-	1	-	3 (4.8%)
Scraper/knife	-	1	-	-	-	-	-	1 (1.6%)
Scraper/ scraper knife with notch	-	1	-	-	-	1	-	2 (3.2%)
Core	-	1	-	-	-	1	-	2 (3.2%)
Core rejuvenation flake (modified)	-	1	-	-	-	1	-	2 (3.2%)
Knife on a flake	-	-	-	-	-	1	-	1 (1.6%)
Retouched flake	-	2	-	-	-	1	3	6 (9.7%)
Retouched and notched flake	-	1	-	-	-	-	-	1 (1.6%)
Retouched and utilised flake	-	-	-	-	-	1	-	1 (1.6%)
Notched flake	-	2	-	-	-	1	-	3 (4.8%)
Serrated blade	-	-	-	-	-	1	-	1 (1.6%)
Utilised flake	-	3	-	-	-	2	2	7 (11.3%)
Utilised blade	-	1	-	-	-	-	-	1 (1.6%)
Waste flake	-	14	1	-	-	9	1	25 (40.3%)
Waste blade	-	2	-	-	-	1	-	3 (4.8%)
Shattered piece	-	1	-	-	-	2	-	3 (4.8%)
Total	1 (1.6%)	31 (50%)	1 (1.6%)	0	0	23 (37.1%)	6 (9.7%)	62

Table 8.5 Oxford Archaeology flint categories

Flint type	Description	Flint source	Percentage of assemblage			
			Gifford	OA	NA	TOTAL
A	Generally very dark grey glossy flint with pale grey cherty patches. Up to 2mm thick rough brown weathered cortex. White or mottled blue patina where absent. Uneven nodules with generally rounded projections	Surface flint from nearby chalk land	21.5%	18.5%	17.5%	19%
A2	As A but has a thin, up to 1mm, paler yellow brown cortex, generally fresher, less weathered-looking. Some of this flint is similar and hard to distinguish from non-percussed river gravel G	Chalk land flint possibly mined	5.5%	2%	16%	8%
B	Generally a medium-dark grey glossy flint with rough white cherty patches. Up to 1mm rough creamy or brown weathered cortex. Uneven nodules. Some of exposed surfaces have a tabular fracture and are patinated white	Surface chalk land flint	24%	17%	2%	14%
C	A very fine-grained flint which is patinated a milky-grey. Inclusions of large cherty areas Nature of cortex is not known	Unknown Unusual, may be locally occurring or imported	0.5%	3%	0%	2%
D	Mid or dark-grey flint with a matt, pale grey patina Usually lacks cortex, but when present varies from being identical to A and percussed like K, with a grey or brown surface patina. Includes large cherty areas	Chalk land flint.	9%	29%	20%	19.5%
E	Medium dark grey glossy flint with darker grey bands and small speckles of white chert Large nodules with a thin and vesicular slightly weathered yellowish brown cortex surface. Some which are very abraded are similar to type A	?Chalk land flint	13%	7%	10%	10%
F	Dark grey glossy flint, sometimes paler & matt Paler grey cherty patches and or lines, sometimes diffuse. Ochreous brown iron staining occurs below cortex. Occasional fossiliferous patches. Mottled patina where absent. Cortex is rough, ridged and varies from brown to pale yellowish brown over a brown patina of 1-2mm thickness. Cortex can be quite thick	Locally occurring 'Bullhead' flint	15.5%	18.5%	17.5%	17%
G	Flint identical to A2. Only differs from it in that it occurs in rounded nodules with a smoothed or slightly grainy, non-percussed cortex in pale yellowish brown to grey brown.	River gravel	4%	5%	10%	6%
	Rounded nodules with a heavily percussed grey or brown surface patina. Some old exposed surfaces have a blue/grey patina		2%	0%	2%	1%
H	Medium-dark grey cherty flint with some iron staining. Has a thin cortex with a dark line below it, or where the cortex is absent, thick white patina as B.	Locally occurring Chalk land flint?	2%	0%	0%	1%
I	Dark grey glossy patina with matt freshly exposed surfaces. Has distinctive and frequent small sandy speckles as well as grey cherty patches. A single piece is from a small rounded nodule with rough grainy, greeny-grey to brown cortex.	?Chalk land flint	1.5%	0%	5%	2%
J	Matt to slightly glossy mid grey flint with ochreous patina and other staining. Traces of cortex occur within surviving deep vesicular hollows within the flint, which is otherwise identical to type A.	Surface chalk land flint?	1.5%	0%	0%	0.5%

Table 8.6: Categories of raw material

Flint from trial pits (Oxford Archaeology 2002)

The composition of the individual Oxford flint assemblage plotted by field is shown on Table 8.5.

Almost all the worked flint came from Area A and Area E, with little found elsewhere. As with the Gifford collection there are a relatively large number of retouched pieces. Among these is a serrated bladelet of probable earlier Neolithic date from Area E, TP 162 (Fig. 8.10.4). The debitage includes some smaller flakes, as might be expected with recovery using meshes (Fig. 8.3).

Raw material

There were twelve distinct types of raw material used and present as unworked natural nodules (see Table 8.6). The predominant types A and D were chalkland nodular flint of small to medium size. Most is likely to have derived from surface exposed deposits of flint on chalkland locally occurring within 0.5km of the site. Some other variants of chalkland flint A2, B, E, H and I were used in lesser proportions. Seventeen percent of the raw material used was the locally occurring 'Bullhead' flint (Cramp 2002). These nodules of either grey or brown cherty flint have a distinctive brown cortex and ochreous brown staining below. This appears to be the same material noted within the burnt flint assemblage with a distinctive fire-reddened/blackened sub-cortical layer, probably as the iron-rich layer had oxidised in the heat of the fire. The smallest proportion of flint was of small to large rounded gravel nodules, some of which have heavily battered surfaces, probably from water rather than glacial action. A few pieces exhibit frost damage or were pot-lidded flakes. This type of material also occurs within the burnt flint assemblage.

Discussion

Comparisons between the stratified assemblage of flintwork from the middle-late Bronze Age pits in Trench 11, and the material recovered from elsewhere on the site show some significant differences, suggesting that the land here was utilised for a long time before the Bronze Age occupation. While the flintwork is normally not particularly diagnostic of date, artefact forms not represented in the stratified assemblage include probable Neolithic pieces such as a serrated bladelet (Fig. 8.10.4.), a leaf-shaped arrowhead (Fig. 8.10.2), and a possible early Bronze Age fabricator (Fig. 8.10.6). There are also a large number of scrapers from unstratified deposits, particularly from the surface collection, of which some are neatly formed and are probably late Neolithic/early Bronze Age (Fig. 8.10.5 and 10). The majority, however, are crudely made and are likely to be middle/late Bronze Age (Fig. 8.10.7), although none were found in the pits. The pieces include a scraper/knife combination tool which occurs quite widely in the fieldwalking collection, often with an additional notch. This is not a diagnostic tool of either Neolithic or earlier Bronze Age periods, and may represent a local middle/later Bronze Age variant. Notched flakes (Fig. 8.10.3) and a variety of utilised forms also occur dating from the Neolithic period onwards.

There is a high proportion of apparent 'waste' material from all phases of work, although the proportion from the Bronze Age pits is higher than that from the unstratified deposits. The possibility that a certain proportion of the edge-wear on 'tools' may be post-depositional has already been mentioned and may account for some of this difference. It is also unclear how many of these 'waste' pieces may in fact have been used as tools without leaving any trace of the evidence. In general, it has not been possible to separate middle/late Bronze Age debitage from later Neolithic/early Bronze Age material, and so the collection has been looked at as a single entity.

Characteristics of the flint collection
Four examples of Palaeolithic material were recovered comprising extensively rolled flakes, one of which may have been worked (Gifford Transects B2.F and F4.J [Areas C & E respectively]; NA Trench 11 contexts 11002 and 11045). These flints are unlikely to have derived from the natural gravel and may have been brought in as raw material perhaps from a nearby river.

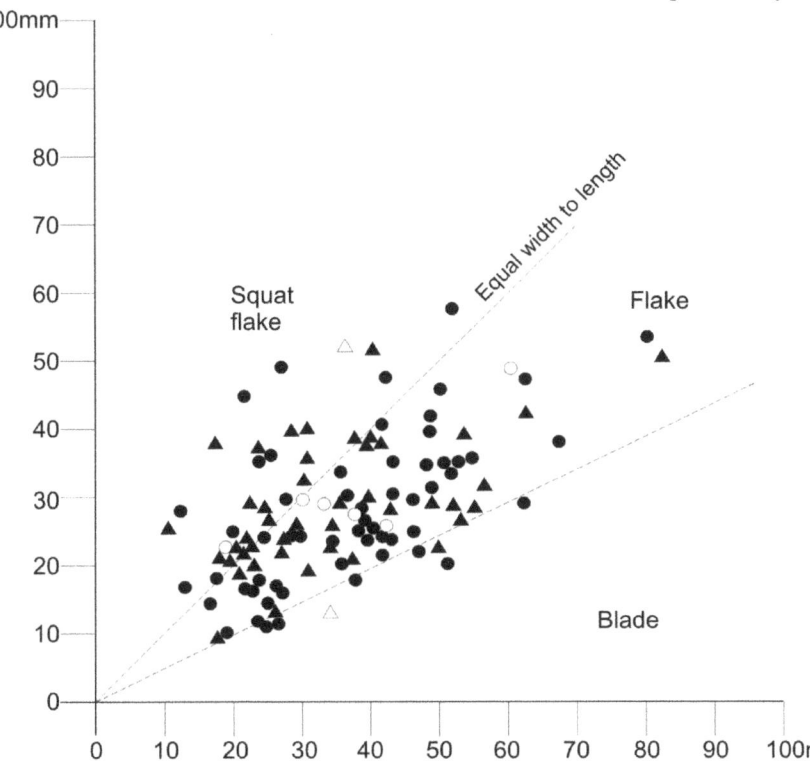

Fig 8.1 Length and breadth dimensions of flint artefacts, Northamptonshire Archaeology collection

Northampton Archaeology Hard Hammer Struck Flint in solid black and Soft Hammer Struck Flint in white. Triangle represents material from Trench 11.

A single possible later Mesolithic/early Neolithic end scraper on a small microlith-like blade was recovered (Gifford transect F1.L [Area E]; not illustrated). A diagnostic earlier Neolithic leaf-shaped arrowhead was recovered from the fieldwalking (Fig. 8.10.2). A small pear-shaped adze, probably for woodworking, came from Trench 11 (Fig. 8.10.1). Its rounded cutting edge would ensure that the tool did not dig into the flat surfaces of worked wood. Such items can date from the earlier Neolithic period through into the early Bronze Age. There are several examples of other possible early Neolithic material: a soft-hammer struck, serrated bladelet (Fig. 8.10.4), and a blade struck from a prepared blade-core (Gifford transect F4.M [Area E]). Other pieces which comprise unusually neatly formed scrapers (eg. Fig. 8.10.5) and retouched flakes may also be earlier pieces rather than the work of later periods by persons with greater aptitude.

The majority of the flint comprised debitage (over 170 pieces, and about 50% of the material). All waste flakes and blades had been detached from cores with a prepared striking platform, and there were many instances of tertiary flakes. Where the bulbar end of the flake had survived it showed that the majority of flakes had been detached by means of a hard hammer of flint or stone. Several pieces also exhibited distinctive percussion marks from miss-hits.

Forty-six pieces of flint were detached using a soft hammer. There seems to be little correlation between soft-hammer work and blades, blade-like material or the stratified Northamptonshire assemblage (Figs 8.1 - 8.3). Of the twenty-five recovered from fieldwalking, a single example is a blade, the rest being a mixture of flakes and squat flakes, with a cluster of smaller flakes. Four soft-hammer struck flakes were from Field E, (Transect F1.E). Six of the eleven soft hammer struck flakes from the test pitting were recovered from Area E, three were from Area A and two pieces from Area F.

Of the soft hammer struck group, the serrated blade is characteristic of the earlier Neolithic. Four other utilised or retouched flakes, together with a bladelet and a spall may also be early. Most of these pieces fall within the flake category and, although they range in size, tend to be small. Of the eight examples from the excavations, two were from pits in Trench 11 - one a blade and one a flake. Three of the rest are scrapers (one from CHRF Trench 29 and two from SNEL Trench 16). All these examples occur across the spectrum of widths, with one blade-type and few smaller pieces.

The plots of length/breadth ratios of the complete flakes and blades show that the collection does not fall into distinct categories of size or shape. While some of the OA flint, in particular, is of a generally smaller size, this is likely to be a result of finds being retrieved by sieving rather than indicating a difference in lithic technology. There are few examples of blades (length: breadth ratio at least 2:1), with the majority of all flint being flakes (ratio 2:1 - 1:1) or squat flakes (breadth greater than length). There is no apparent correlation between size or tool use and primary, secondary or tertiary flakes (plots remain in archive).

Of the twenty-four cores present, only three were expertly worked (e.g. a keeled core from Gifford transect C1.E [Area B]). The majority of cores were nodules, or naturally, frost-shattered fragments of nodules, unsystematically worked or with only several exploratory flakes removed. Most cores still had potential for further working, which suggests that raw material was readily available. Eight former cores had then been used as hammer stones. Some of these exhibit extensive percussion damage (e.g. Fig.8.10.11). There were generally smaller proportions of cores and hammerstones compared to other tools.

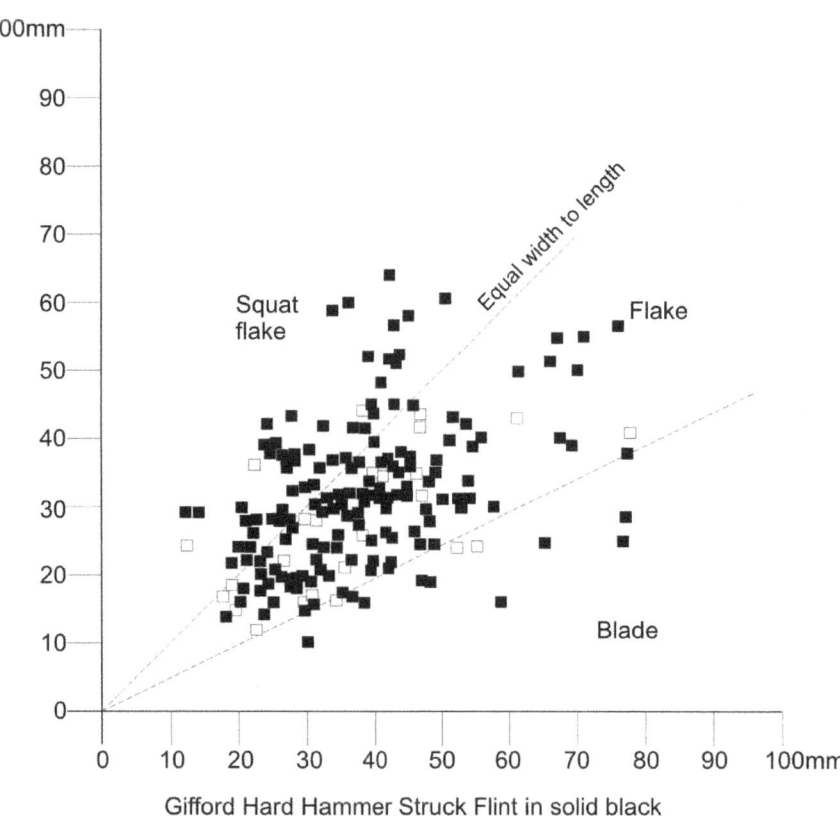

Gifford Hard Hammer Struck Flint in solid black and Gifford Soft Hammer Struck Flint in white.

Fig 8.2 Length and breadth dimensions of flint artefacts, Gifford collection

Overall there were fewer than half the number of core rejuvenation flakes compared with cores, but there were three from Trench 11 (Table 8.2; Fig. 8.10.9). This shows that the cores were being worked on site, and in particular near Trench 11, where the largest number of waste flakes were also present (contexts 11036-8, 11104 and 11112). Core rejuvenation is not generally characteristic of the middle to late Bronze Age and it is possible that these flakes are earlier pieces. Pit 11110 (which contained only a core rejuvenation flake and a utilised blade) may be earlier than the main group of pits.

The general nature of the debitage, with largely irregular flakes suggests that most probably dates from the later Neolithic/early Bronze Age into the middle and later Bronze Age. Earlier Neolithic assemblages tend to contain more regularly-shaped flakes and blades, which were detached from carefully prepared cores. Diagnostic later Neolithic/early Bronze Age pieces such as small thumbnail scrapers are, however, all but absent from the assemblage, which could suggest that the area was not intensively occupied until after the early Bronze Age (the single thumbnail-type scraper is about 50% larger than a normal example). The few scrapers present are mostly both large and clumsy, or small with barely any retouch present, which again is suggestive of later prehistoric manufacture.

Apart from a single and very crude fabricator (Fig. 8.10.6) there are few diagnostically Bronze Age tool types. Instead, tools mainly comprise miscellaneous retouched pieces, while tools such as scrapers, knives and notched pieces occur in combination on single pieces. These include twenty examples of a scraper/knife with one or more scraping edges combined with a single cutting edge. Only one of these is roughly discoidal in shape and profile, which is a characteristic of the earlier Bronze Age. None exhibit any trace of polish.

There are a number of utilised flakes, the sharp edges of which had been used, without modification, for cutting and then discarded (some after apparently heavy usage). Many flakes showed a degree of retouch, use-damage and/or possible notching which shows that there was not a specific 'tool-kit', but that unspecialised flakes may have served a variety of purposes. There are few examples of simply notched flakes (e.g. Fig. 8.10.3), but many of the core rejuvenation flakes are either notched or retouched in some manner. The general lack of specific tools, for example knives and axes, could suggest that either bronze was being used for most everyday tools, or that such items were not needed for the activities carried out. Only a single, very crude awl-like point was noted in the assemblage (Gifford transect E6.B [Area E]).

Distributions

The combined surface and excavated collections show a concentration of flint on the sandy ridge occupied by Area E (Figs 8.4 - 8.6). There is a marked fall off in flint density to the south of this (Areas D and C), although it seems likely that the shortage of flint in Area D is to a large degree due to its unsuitability for surface collection and the extent of modern disturbances. There were also few surface flints at the southern end of the site (Areas A and F), but a relatively high proportion (*c.* 60%) of the test-pit collection came from this area, a figure which is difficult to explain. This cannot be a result of surface conditions since a large amount of burnt flint was recovered from these areas (below).

The superficial flint from both the fieldwalking and test-pitting gave no indication of the focus of occupation characterised by the mid-later Bronze Age pit groups revealed by excavation in Trench 11. This is where the vast majority of the excavated flint came from. The second largest group of excavated flints came from various features in Trench 29, some of which are likely to be Bronze Age or earlier, and others Roman and later. This is also the location of the majority of superficial flints but again the distributions do not coincide with any great precision, the group of superficial flints in the south-western corner of this area, for instance, having no counterpart in the excavated assemblage.

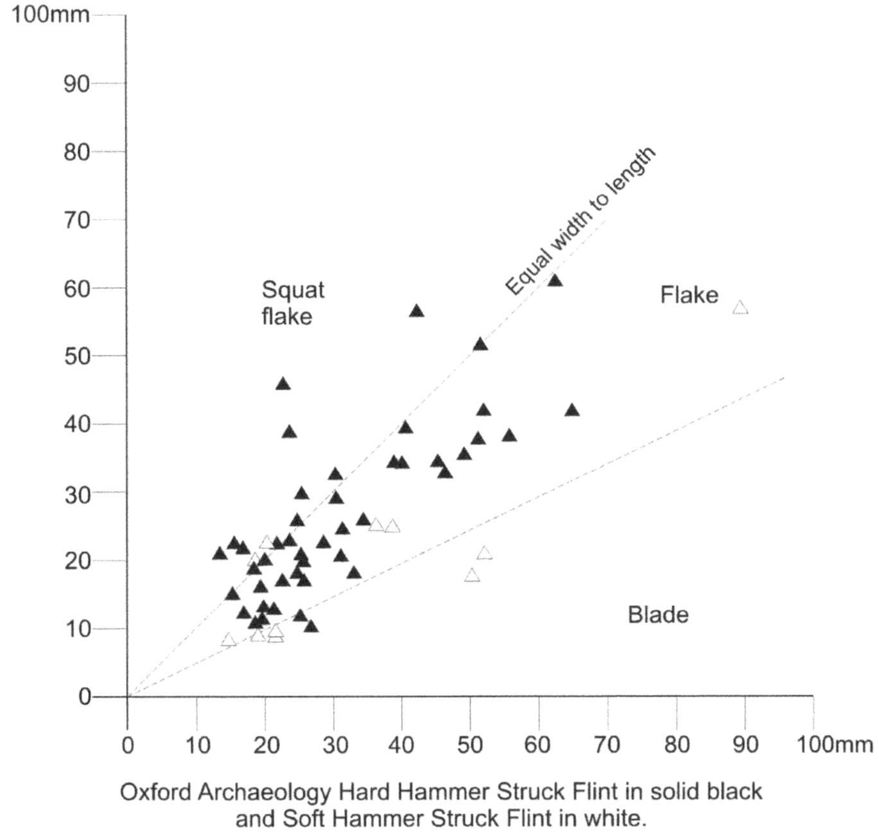

Fig 8.3
Length and breadth dimensions of flint artefacts, Oxford Archaeology collection

Oxford Archaeology Hard Hammer Struck Flint in solid black and Soft Hammer Struck Flint in white.

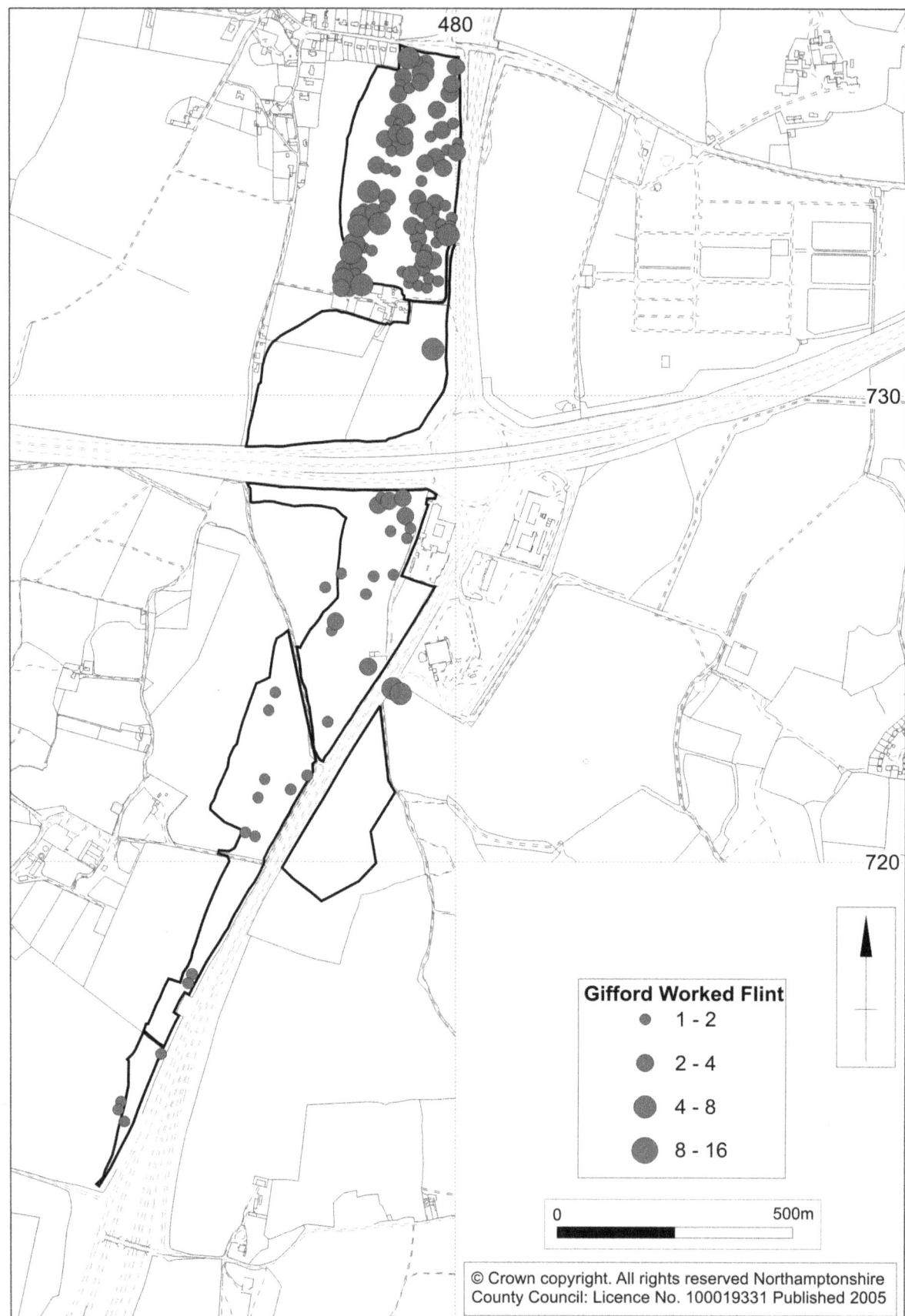

Fig 8.4 Worked flint distribution from surface collection (from GGP 2000 archive)

There seems little doubt that the superficial flint from Area E derives from a series of occupations commencing in the earlier Neolithic which left little sub-surface traces. It is suggested that occupation intensified in this area in the later Neolithic and early Bronze Age, although the character of much of the flintwork and the absence of diagnostic tools of this period perhaps indicates that most of the occupation material relates to the middle and late Bronze Age. The presence of middle Bronze Age pottery in the northern part of Area E, both from the test-pitting and surface collection (Chapter 9), perhaps supports this interpretation.

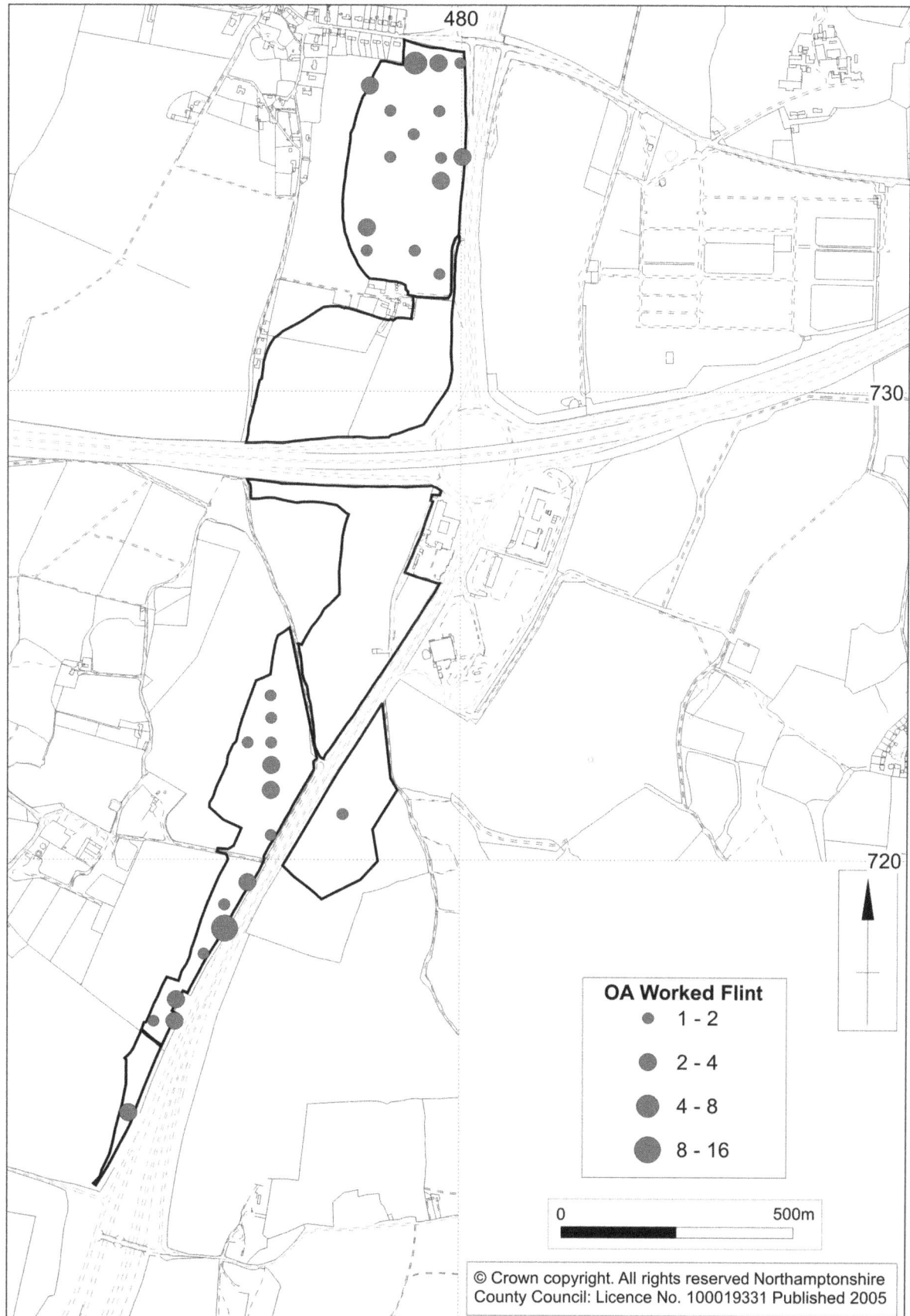

Fig 8.5 Worked flint distribution from trial pits (from OA 2002 archive)

It is worth noting that a greater proportion of tools were recovered from surface contexts, while relatively few were deposited in the pits or other sealed contexts. The implication is that such material was either generally discarded on the ground surface at distance from the activities associated with the pits, or that there was a significant group of flint with a high proportion of tools which pre-dated the pits.

There is no suggestion that the flint within Roman and Saxon contexts was deliberately buried and all is undoubtedly simply residual.

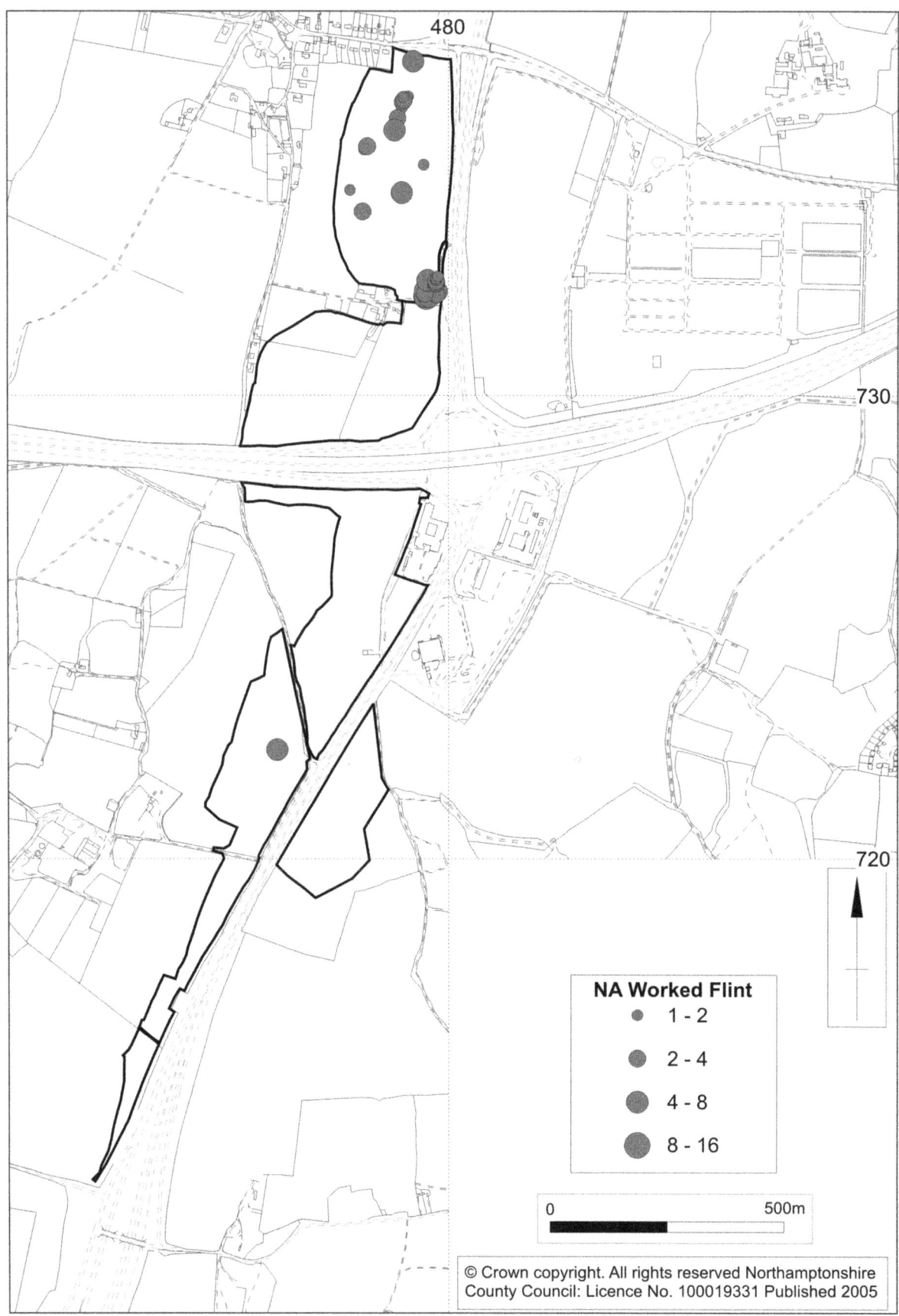

Fig 8.6 Worked flint distribution from excavations (NA 2003)

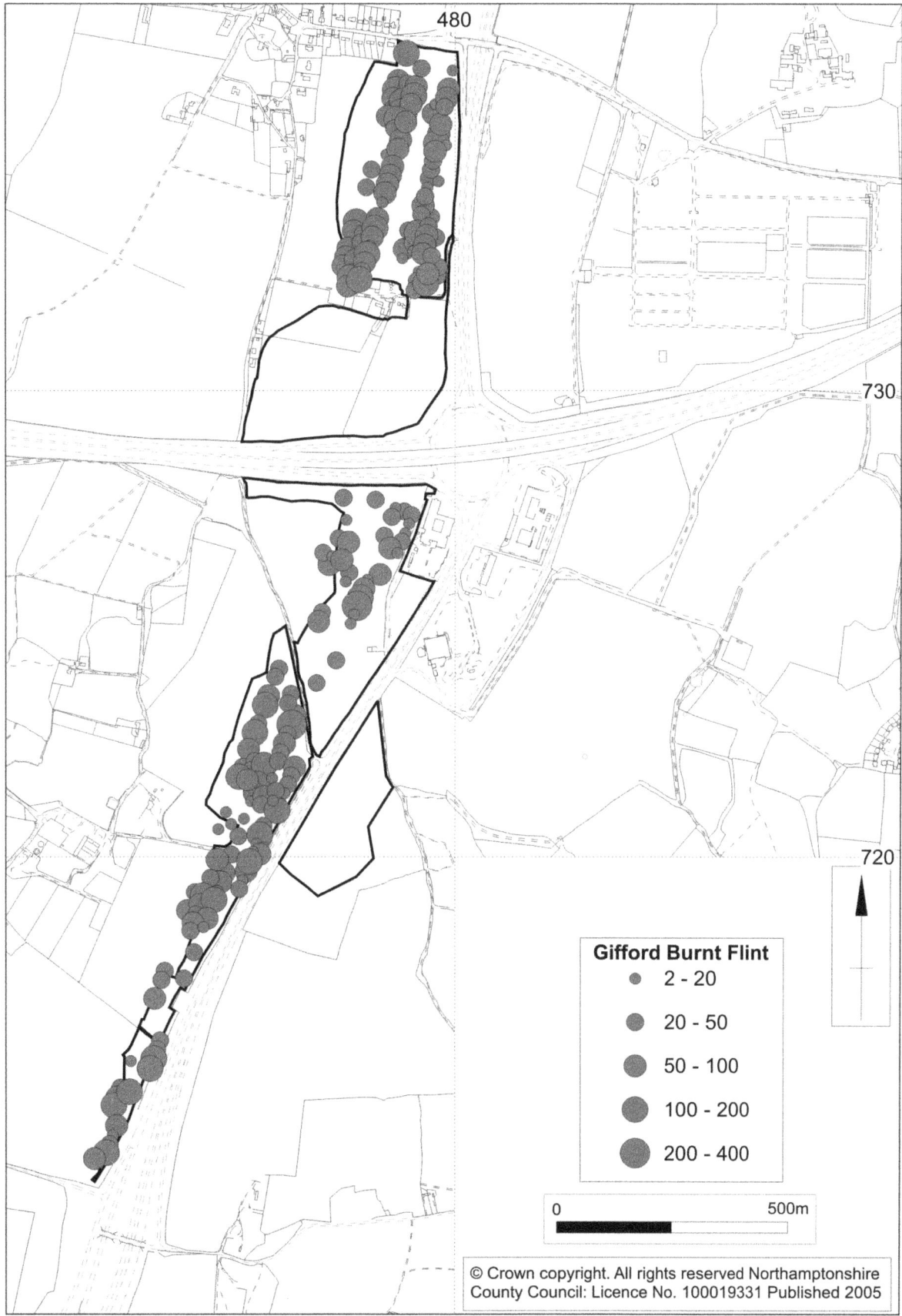

Fig 8.7 Burnt flint distribution by weight from surface collection

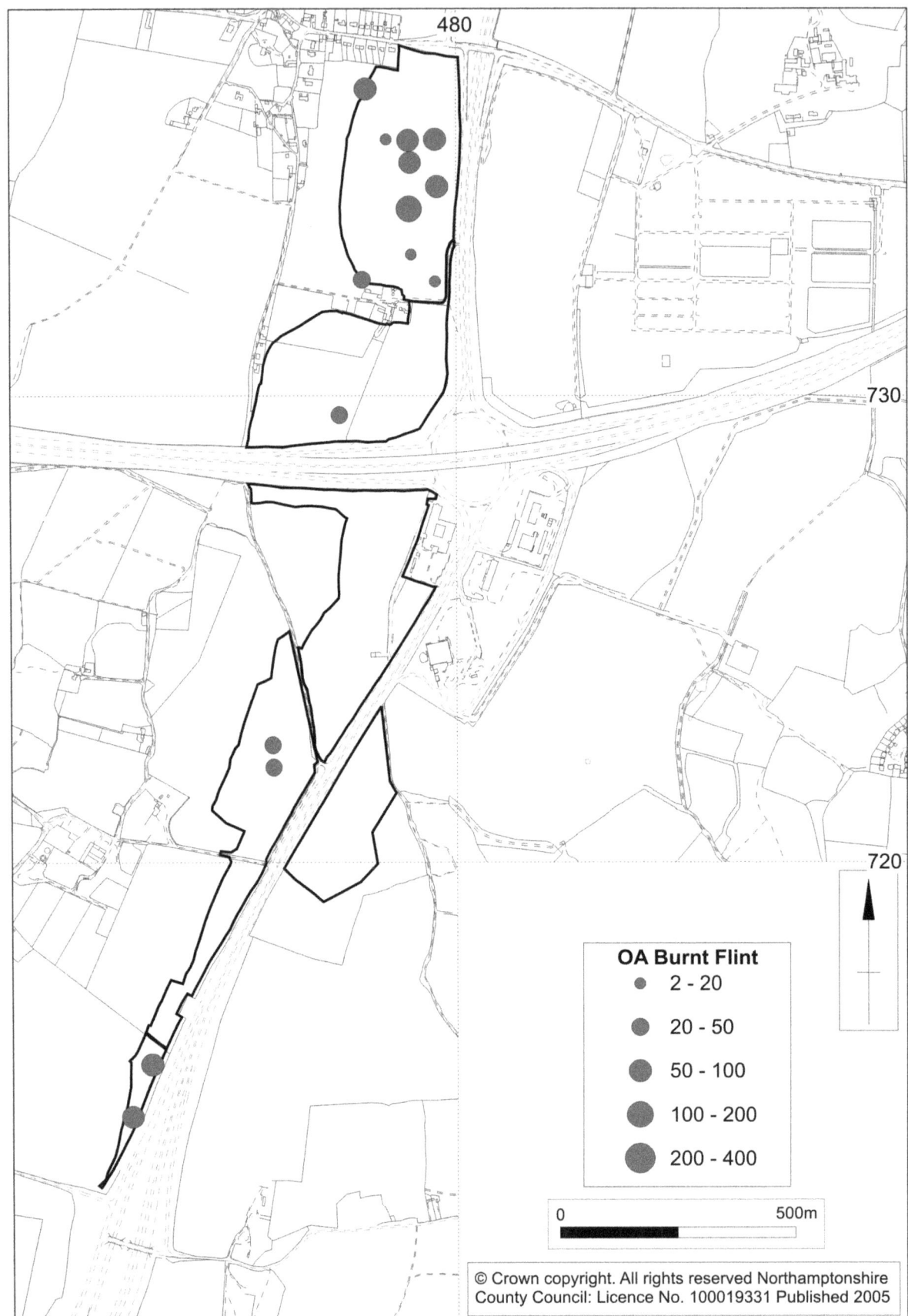

Fig 8.8 Burnt flint distribution by weight from trial pits

Burnt flint

Burnt flint was recovered from all the phases of fieldwork. The hand-retrieved quantity, by weight for each Area, is shown on Table 8.7. In addition, the burnt flint from the sieved soil samples was quantified (Table 8.9).

Area	Gifford (2000) (g)	OA (2002) (g)	NA (2003) hand-retrieved only (g)
A/F	3200	180	0
C	2506	0	0
B	0	0	0
D	(not walked)	46	0
E	4786	487	14 954
Total	8236	713	14 954

Table 8.7: Total weight of burnt flint recovered by Area

The surface flint recovered in the Gifford survey was plotted and quantified in the original report but not retained. The distribution is shown on Fig.8.7. The burnt flint shows a wide distribution with apparent concentrations in the northern and southern parts of Area E and another in Area A. The concentrations in Area E were associated with worked flint (Fig. 8.1) and prehistoric pottery, but these artefacts were not present in Area A, where it was suggested that the flint might have derived from a ploughed out 'burnt mound' (GGP 2000, 7). The subsequent test-pitting by Oxford Archaeology recovered much smaller quantities of burnt flint from fifteen of the one hundred and eighty three test pits excavated (Oxford Archaeology 2002), without noticeable concentrations (Fig 8.8).

The excavations by Northamptonshire Archaeology yielded the largest quantity of burnt flint. The hand-retrieved component weighed 14.954kg - all from Area E Trenches 11, 28 and 29. All but 755g came from the prehistoric features in Trench 11 (Table 8.8). In addition, nineteen bulk soil samples yielded 9.04kg of burnt flint, again mostly from Trench 11, and this material has been quantified in Table 8.9.

The distribution of excavated burnt flint (Fig 8.9) by weight emphasises the disproportionate amount of material deposited in the Bronze Age pits in Trench 11, compared with the background scatter in other features and that recovered from fieldwalking. There is a general residual scatter of burnt flint in later, Roman and other contexts. It can be noted that the surface distribution of burnt flint is not an obvious indicator of the features present below (Fig. 8.7).

Nature of the material

In common with the worked flint, the burnt flint was predominantly nodular, of small to medium size, with variations of thin to thick creamy coloured or brown cortex, some of which had been weathered. It was likely to have derived from chalk land, the nearest surface outcrop of which lies in the field to the north of the site. Other pieces may have been exposed and eroded in the local gravel.

Feature	Feature Group	Context	Date	Weight (g)	No.
topsoil		11001	-	479	26
subsoil		11002	-	937	28
Pit 11006	11024	11005	BA	55	4
Ditch 11011	11224	11010	BA	29	1
Ditch 11013	11224	11012	BA	43	1
Pit 11024	11024	11021	BA	94	3
Pit 11027		11028/11029	BA	1887	65
Pit 11033		11036-11038	BA	1571	82
Pit 11042	11138	11045	BA	444	11
Pit 11042	11138	11046	BA	297	8
Pit 11053	11047	11048/11049/ 11050	BA	1533	58
Pit 11060	11047	11026	BA	649	33
Pit 11060	11047	11047	BA	731	17
Pits 11053/ 11056	11047	11051/11052/ 11054/11055	BA	94	12
Pit 11060	11047	11057	BA	26	3
Pit 11060	11047	11057/11058	BA	3553	155
Pit 11060	11047	11059	BA	436	17
Pit 11060	11047	11061	BA	154	10
Pit 11098	11047	11063	BA	171	17
Pit 11065	11047	11064	BA	336	18
Pit 11066	11138	11067	BA	147	6
Pit 11068	11138	11069	BA	405	18
Pit 11060	11047	11074	BA	39	3
Pit 11077	11138	11076	BA	136	2
Pit 2826		2825	Roman?	197	5
Pit 29042		29041	prehistoric?	42	1
Ditch 29070		29091	prehistoric?	62	1
Pit 29131		29098	Saxon	244	8
Gully 29183	29249	29184	post-med.	210	3
		TOTAL		14954	616

Table 8.8: Quantities of hand-retrieved flint from excavated features. (Northamptonshire Archaeology 2003)

Sample	Feature	Feature Group	Context	Date	Weight (g)	Sample vol. (l)	Weight (g) per litre
9	Pit 29062		29063/4	unknown	26	40	0.6
16	Layer		29014	Roman	20	20	1.0
26	Pit 29229		29230	Roman	245	70	3.5
33	Pit 11027		11028	BA	118	20	5.9
36	Pit 11042	11138	11044	BA	21	20	1.0
38	Pit 11042	11138	11046	BA	36	20	1.8
39	Pit 11065	11047	11064	BA	81	15	5.4
42	Pit 11053	11047	11048	BA	187	20	9.3
43	Pit 11053	11047	11049	BA	809	20	40.4
45	Pit 11053	11047	11051	BA	620	20	31.0
46	Pit 11053	11047	11052	BA	128	10	12.8
55	Pit 11090		11080	BA	327	20	16.3
56	Pit 11090		11081	BA	2324	20	116.2
57	Pit 11090		11082	BA	725	10	72.5
58	Pit 11090		11083	BA	2242	20	112.1
63	Pit 11090		11087	BA	487	20	24.3
70	Pit 11060	11047	11074	BA	485	20	24.2
73	Pit 11065	11047	11099	BA	114	10	11.4
83	Pit 11127		11120	BA	48	10	4.8
TOTAL					9043		

Table 8.9: Quantity of burnt flint recovered from bulk soil samples (Northamptonshire Archaeology 2003)

Two contexts (11069, 11076) contained fragments of a distinctive flint with frequent vesicular irregularities.

A smaller proportion of flint was of small rounded gravel nodules, some of which had heavily battered surfaces, probably from water rather than glacial action, in common with the gravel present in the worked flint assemblage. A few pieces exhibited frost damage or were pot-lidded flakes. A single piece of tabular flint was present.

A few nodules were only heat reddened, most were heavily heat crazed and showed much spalling and were shattered into small fragments, from repeated and prolonged heating. Only 11 fragments conjoined. Many of the less-heavily spalled flints were roughly squared as though they had been pre-prepared prior to burning, and two examples, from contexts (11002 and 11026), retained large bulbs of percussion from hard hammer blows, possibly as part of this process. Many nodules had instead been heated without any signs of prior modification.

A single example of a burnt flint flake has been included in the worked flint report. Five other examples of burnt flints showed evidence of prior working, but this was limited to a single flake detached from the piece in four cases (Contexts 11012, 11026, 11048/11049/11050 and 29184). The fifth, an angular piece from 11002 may have been a core rejuvenation flake, but as there were no surviving waves of percussion, the possibility that the several negative flake scars had been formed by natural means could not be ruled out.

The vast majority of the burnt flint in the soil samples comprised small shattered fragments under 10mm, with only a small proportion of small pieces from 10 to 40mm present. There was no burnt flint in the remaining samples. The material will not be retained.

Figure 8.10

1. Small adze formed by retouching sides and end of a tertiary flake. Butt missing (recent break?) and there is a small area of damage to the cutting edge. Neolithic?. Area E, NA Tr. 11 (unstratified).
2. Leaf-shaped arrowhead basal fragment. From a thin flake wholly retouched on the ventral side and partly on the dorsal side. Area E, Gifford Transect F2.K.
3. Notched flake, with deep retouch and bulb removed. Area A, OA Test-pit 88 (8801).
4. Serrated bladelet. Fine serrations along one edge show edge damage. Area E, OA Test-Pit 162 (16200).
5. Side scraper with light retouch. Area E, Gifford Transect F1.L.
6. Fabricator on a flake with retouch all round. Area E, Gifford Transect F6.L.
7. Double end scraper on a primary flake. Soft hammer struck. Area A, NA Tr. 16 (unstratified).
8. Side and end scraper. Hard hammer struck. Area A, NA Tr. 16 (unstratified).
9. Core rejuvenation flake. Hard hammer struck. Area E, NA Tr. 11, Pit 11110 (11112).
10. End scraper on a blade. Utilised on one side. Detached from a prepared core using a hard hammer. Neolithic? Area E, NA Tr. 11 (unstratified).
11. Core. Flakes were initially detached from one face. A rejuvenation flake created a second working platform on the opposing face from which flakes were detached using a hard hammer. It was later used as a hammer stone. Area E, NA Tr. 11, Pit 11098 (11063).

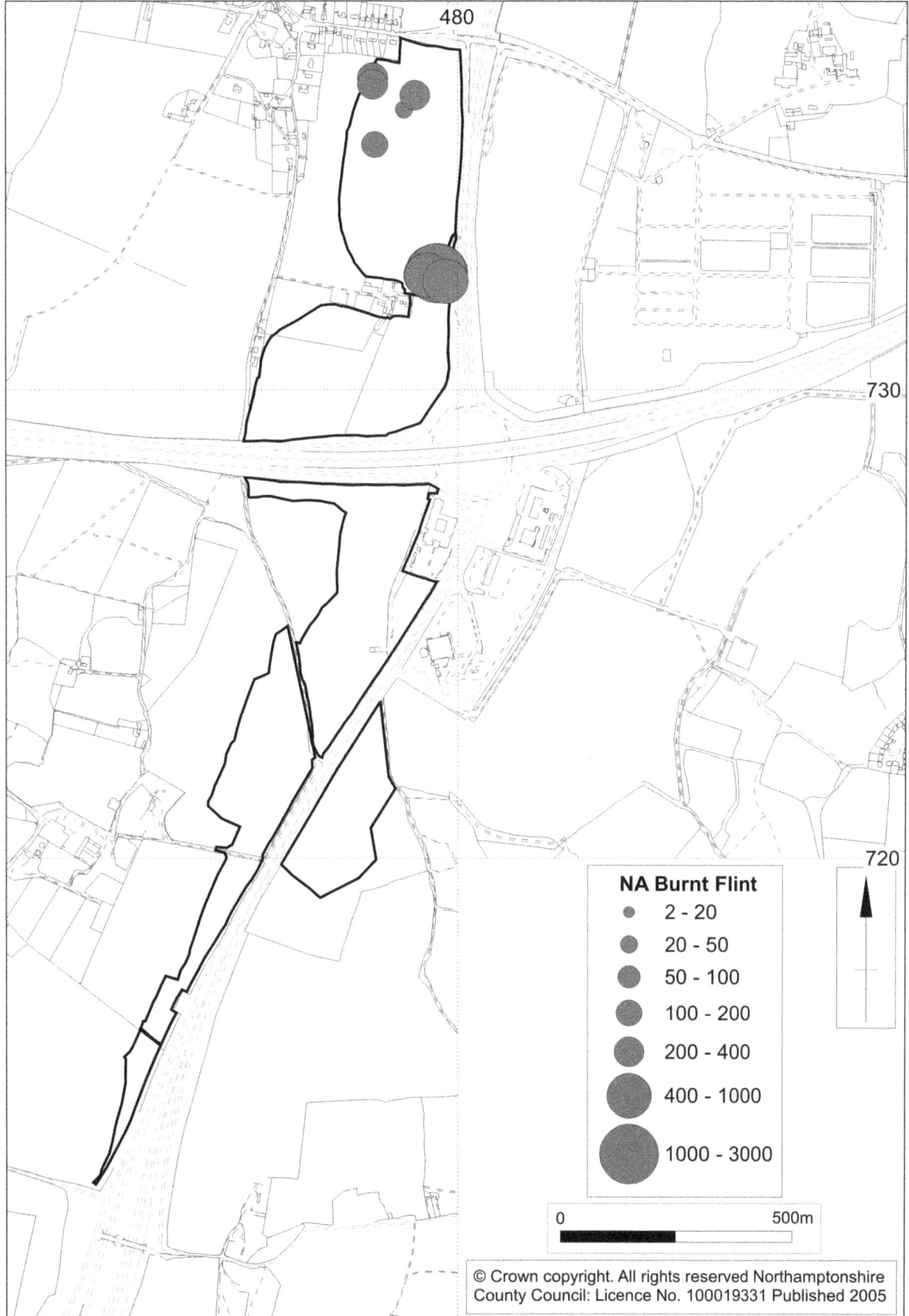

Fig 8.9 Burnt flint distribution by weight from excavations

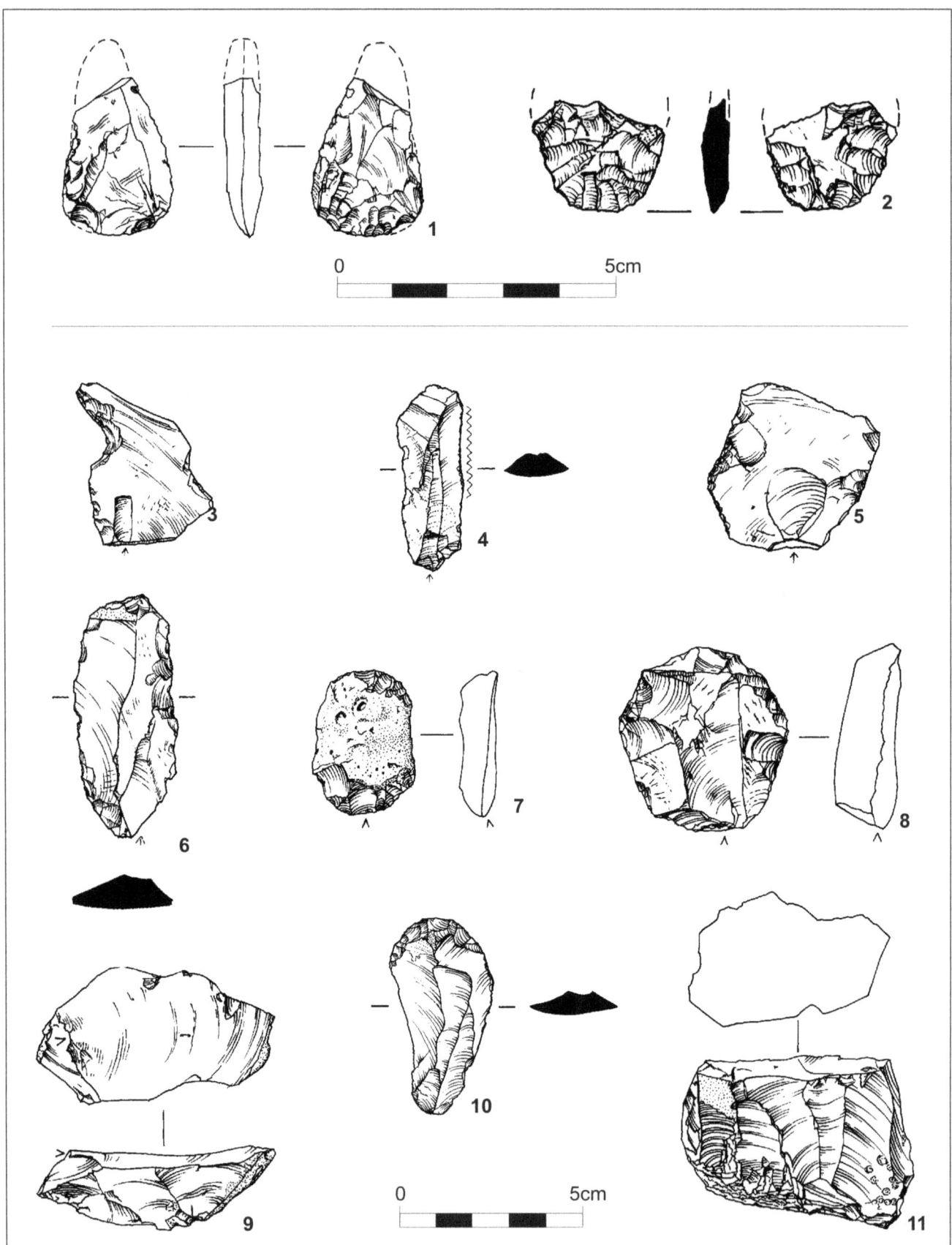

Fig 8.10 Flint artefacts from all stages of fieldwork. See catalogue for details.

Chapter 9: The Pottery

By Jane Timby

Introduction

The archaeological excavations resulted in the recovery of some 580 sherds weighing 6.2kg from the main (northern) site (CHRF) with a further small assemblage of 38 sherds, 382g, from the southern Snelsmore Farm site (SNEL). Most of the pottery was recovered from Trenches 11 and 29 in Area E. In addition seven fragments of fired clay and seven small pieces of ceramic building material (CBM) were noted. Earlier work on the site produced some 13 sherds (112g) from fieldwalking and 114 sherds (892g) from trial-pitting.

The pottery shows a particularly extensive date range from at least the Middle Bronze Age through to modern times. The assemblage is of variable condition. The prehistoric sherds are, with a few exceptions, particularly poorly preserved, many just represented by rounded crumbs. By contrast the Roman material is generally well preserved, particularly that from Trench 29 where several semi-complete vessels were recovered. Four sherds of Saxon date were recovered from the excavation areas with a further sherd amongst the fieldwalking finds. A single medieval cooking pot rim (Newbury fabric B) (Vince 1997) was recovered from the topsoil along with 29 (502g) post-medieval sherds from various features and layers. A further five medieval sherds came from the fieldwalking (Newbury fabrics B and C) along with one post-medieval sherd and CBM. The trial-pitting yielded four medieval and 17 post-medieval sherds.

The medieval and later pottery is of little interest and is not described further. A catalogue has been presented in the Assessment Report (NA 2004, Appendix 12) which is retained in archive.

The extensive date range for the assemblage, combined with the fragmentary nature of many of the deposits, the relatively small groups from most contexts and a marked lack of diagnostic sherds, has some impact on the degree of confidence that can be placed on the dating of some contexts. The prehistoric material is particularly problematic from this perspective.

Methodology

The assemblage was sorted into fabrics based on the dominant macroscopically visible inclusions present, combined with surface finish. For the prehistoric material the sherds were coded following the recommendations outlined in PCRG (1992). The known named or traded Roman wares are referred to using the national Roman reference collection codes (Tomber and Dore 1998) and these are not described further. The assemblage was quantified by sherd count, weight and estimated vessel equivalence (rim) (EVE) for each recorded context and the data put onto an Excel spreadsheet, a copy of which is deposited with the site archive. A summary of the fabrics identified is given in Table 9.1. The pottery is discussed by chronological period below.

Bronze Age

The earliest recognisable material appears to date to the Bronze Age period, amounting to some 96 sherds, weighing 609g, (18 EVEs) from the excavation, two sherds (8g) from fieldwalking, and 71 sherds, 618g, from the trial-pitting. The most diagnostic material is that from the trial pits representing two vessels: a bucket urn and a globular urn dating to the Middle Bronze Age period (1500-1100 cal BC) (Barclay 2002), and two plain walled bucket urns of comparable date from Pit 11024 (Area E Trench 11).

Many of the sherds from the excavation are single one-off bodysherds with no diagnostic features, and in one or two cases the material would not be out of place in a Neolithic context. However, in the absence of any corroborative evidence it is treated here as probably Bronze Age.

Two main ware groups have been identified, grog-tempered and flint-tempered. The latter has been sub-divided into three sub-groups (FL1-3) with a general FLINT group for fragments too small to categorise.

Fabrics and forms

Grog-tempered
EPGROG: A smooth, fairly soft ware oxidized throughout and with a soapy feel. The paste contains a common frequency of sub-angular, dark orange and grey grog up to 3mm in size. Restricted to a single bodysherd from Pit 11062 (Group 11047), with a wall thickness of 10mm. Not associated with any other material, the sherd is probably urn material and has Bronze Age currency.

Flint-tempered
FL1: A finely micaceous clay matrix, oxidized on the exterior and grey-brown on the interior. The paste contains a sparse scatter of angular white, calcined, flint up to 2mm in size, in some cases protruding from the vessel surface. The paste also contains sparse organic inclusions or linear voids from such. A similar fabric was noted at Reading Business Park (Hall 1992, fabric T). Restricted to a single rim sherd (Fig. 9.1.3) from a thin-walled, concave sided vessel from Pit 11053 (Group 11047). This is the only sherd from this feature and is provisionally dated to the later Bronze Age. Broadly similar vessels are recorded from Reading Business Park (ibid 64, fig 41, type 7).

FL2: A moderately fine fabric with an oxidized orange exterior and light brown interior. The paste contains a

Date	Fabric	Description	No	Wt (g)	EVE
BRONZE AGE	EPGROG	soapy, oxidised grog-tempered	1	7	0
	FL1	sparse flint and organic	1	7	3
	FL2	sparse coarse flint	2	39	0
	FL3	coarse, hackley flint-tempered	75	539	15
	FLINT	other flint-tempered	16	17	0
	MISC	grey sandy with grog	1	8	0
sub-total			**96**	**617**	**18**
IRON AGE	FL4	sparse flint	18	72	5
	SF1	sand and flint-tempered	3	18	0
	SA1	dark brown sandy	3	4	0
	SA2	sandy with calcareous	2	4	0
	SA3	glauconitic sandy	3	9	0
	SA4	red-brown sandy	5	22	0
	GROG	grog tempered	2	22	0
	SAND	other sandy	2	2	0
sub-total			**38**	**153**	**5**
ROMAN					
Imports	CGSAM	Central Gaulish samian	5	152	25
Regional	ALH RE	Alice Holt grey ware	11	67	9
	DOR BB1	Dorset black burnished ware	4	66	0
	LNVCC	Lower Nene Valley colour-coat	2	3	0
	HAM GT	Hampshire grog-tempered	7	48	5
	OVY WH	Tilford ware	3	49	7
	OXF RS	Oxfordshire colour-coated ware	47	584	92
	OXF WHM	Oxfordshire whiteware mortaria	5	129	23
	OXF WS	Oxon white slipped ware	1	1	0
	ROB SH	late Roman shelly ware	41	168	0
local/unknown	GREY1	grey/black sandy/ red core	246	3336	592
	GREY	misc grey /black wares	4	37	10
	OXID	misc oxidised sandy	13	53	26
	GRSA	grog and sand tempered	4	167	0
sub-total			**393**	**4860**	**789**
SAXON	SXORG1	fine micaceous organic-temper	3	18	0
	SXORG2	sandy organic-tempered	1	1	0
sub-total			**4**	**19**	**0**

Table 9.1 Pottery fabrics and quantification

sparse frequency of angular, calcined flint up to 2mm. The fabric has a harsh feel. Finds are limited to just one bodysherd and one base sherd in the fabric from pits 11077 and 11090. The base sherd is flat with a slightly protruding foot typical of late Bronze Age vessels (cf. Hall 1992, fig. 51.218). The former is the only sherd present, the latter appears to be in an Iron Age pit and thus probably residual. Again a later Bronze Age date is suggested for this fabric.

FL3: A very poorly consolidated fabric with a hackley fracture. The paste contains a common frequency of coarse angular, calcined flint up to 3-4mm in size. The resultant fabric is very friable. Vessels include both oxidized and grey reduced examples. This is the commonest of the flint fabrics recorded with some 75 sherds from the excavation and a further 55 sherds from Trial Pit 136 (13600 and 13602). Many of the excavation phase sherds come from two plain-walled urns of Middle Bronze Age date (Fig 9.1. 1-2) from Pit 11024. Context 11021 in this feature also produced a bodysherd with a shallow finger depression. A very small rim fragment in Pit 11060 (11058) and a group of c. 8 very friable bodysherds from

Pit 11090 (11087) are also likely to come from urns.

FL5: A moderately hard, well-compacted black fabric. The paste contains a moderate to common frequency of very fine crushed angular white calcined flint, up to 1 mm but mainly finer. Six thin-walled (8mm) bodysherds from a globular urn were recovered from Trial Pit 136 (topsoil 13600) associated with the bucket urn.

Iron Age

A total of 39 sherds have been designated later prehistoric, encapsulating the later Bronze Age-early Iron Age period. This may include the middle-late Iron Age, although featured sherds were too sparse to confirm this. The fabrics include one flint-tempered ware, one sand and flint-tempered ware, four sandy wares and two general categories of grog and sand.

Fabrics

Flint-tempered
FL4: A black, moderately hard, fairly thin-walled ware (5mm) containing a sparse frequency of white calcined flint, 1-2mm in size. The only featured sherd is a beaded rim jar with a burnished finish, from Pit 11042 (Group 11138), which could be later Iron Age.

Sand and flint-tempered
SF1: A brown, fine sandy textured ware with a sparse scatter of fine, calcined flint (up to 1 mm), rounded dark brown iron and occasionally larger rounded inclusions, possibly quartz/quartzite, up to 7mm in size. At x20 magnification the matrix contains a sparse scatter of fine, ill-sorted quartz sand. No featured sherds.

Sandy wares
SA1: A dark brown-black, moderately hard, sandy ware. At x20 magnification the paste contains a sparse frequency of fine, ill-sorted rounded quartz sand. Three bodysherds from pits 11098 (Group 11047) and 11068 (11138), and one rimsherd from Trial Pit 139 (topsoil 13900).

SA2: A pale brown ware with a black core contained a sparse to common frequency of ill-sorted rounded quartz sand, a mixture of clear and iron-stained grains and rare, rounded, white calcareous inclusions. Two bodysherds, both from Pit 11042 (Group 11138).

SA3: A red-brown ware with a black core. The paste contains a moderate frequency of moderately fine, well-sorted glauconitic sand and rare flint (up to 3mm). Three bodysherds, all recovered from the subsoil.

SA4: A red-brown ware with a black core, moderately soft. The paste contains a common to dense frequency of very fine, well-sorted quartz only visible at x20 magnification. Four bodysherds and one basesherd from pits 11053, 11060 (Group 11047) and Gully 29160.

Roman

Roman sherds form the bulk of the recovered assemblage, some 394 sherds weighing 4.87kg and with 789 EVEs. Most of the assemblage, 95.7% by count, came from group 29247. Of these, some 253 sherds came from Layer 29014 and a further 92 sherds from Pit 29018 (29016), with 32 sherds from Pit 29229 (29230). The remaining sherds came from one pit (29196 – part of Saxon pit 29248) and topsoil/ residual contexts. In addition, four Roman sherds were recovered in fieldwalking and 20 sherds from the trial pits.

Fabrics and forms

Continental imports
Samian: five sherds represented samian ware from one Central Gaulish dish (Curle 23) from pit 29018. Approximately 25% of the vessel is present, 25% by rim EVE (Fig. 9.1.7).

Regional imports
Alice Holt ware (ALH RE) (Tomber and Dore 1998, 138). A total of 11 sherds of this ware is present, again all from group 29247. Vessels include expanded rim necked jars and a flagon decorated with radiating burnished lines on the neck (cf Lyne and Jefferies 1979, class 8). A further two rimsherds came from fieldwalking (F5L) one of which is from a late Roman jar (ibid, class 1A).

Dorset black burnished ware (DOR BB1) (Tomber and Dore 1998, 127). Limited to four sherds all from group 29247, including both jar and bowl base sherds.

Lower Nene Valley colour-coated ware (LNV CC) (ibid, 118). Two very small sherds from group 29247.

Hampshire grog-tempered ware (HAM GT) (ibid, 139). Seven sherds, including one necked jar, five of which are from group 29247.

Overwey (Tilford) ware (OVW WH) (ibid, 146). Three sherds including one jar rim from group 29247. The ware is generally regarded as current from *c.* AD 325.

Oxfordshire colour-coated ware (OXF RS) (ibid, 174). OXF RS is particularly well represented with 47 sherds, 12% of the total Roman assemblage by count and weight. Forms present include Young (1977) types C45, C51, C77 (Fig. 9.1.8, 9.2.9, 9.3.18), beaker and mortaria C99. Most of the sherds, 44 in total, came from group 29247, the remaining three sherds came from Pit 29196, subsoil and topsoil. The latest type is the white-painted necked bowl C77 probably not made before AD 340. A single abraded sherd of probable OXF RS came from fieldwalking (F4D).

Oxfordshire white ware (OXF WH) (Tomber and Dore 1998, 174). All the sherds in this fabric are present as mortaria with Young (1977) types M17 (two examples) and M22 present again from group 29247. These types were current from the later 3rd to 4th centuries.

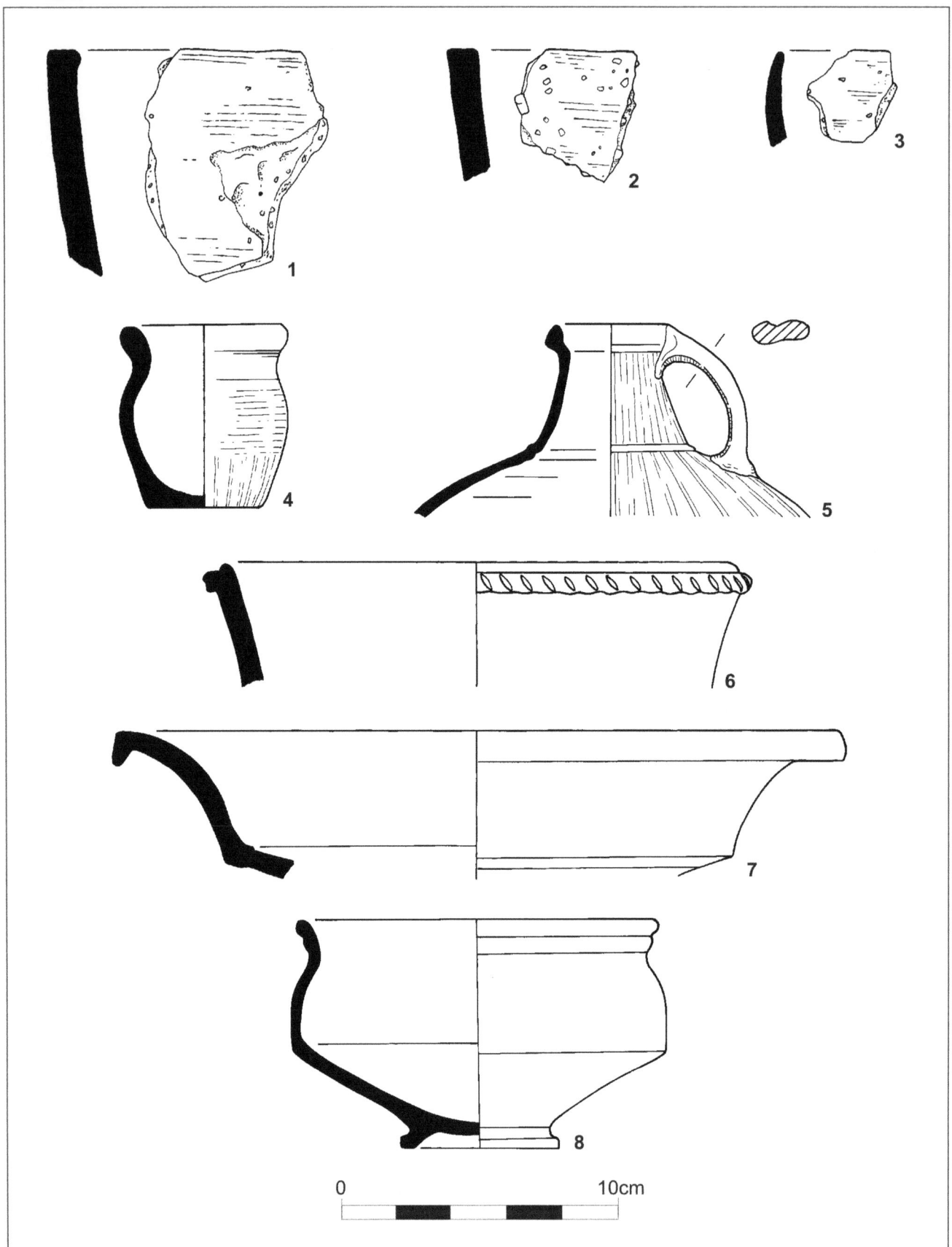

Fig 9.1 Bronze Age pottery (1-3) and Roman pottery (4-8) from excavations

Oxfordshire white-slipped ware (OXF WS) (Tomber and Dore 1998, 176). A single very small sherd was present in Pit 29131.

Late Roman shelly ware (ROB SH) (ibid, 212). This ware, regarded as particularly late in the Roman repertoire dating to the last quarter of the 4th century and beyond, was represented by 41 bodysherds, probably from jar, and all from group 29247.

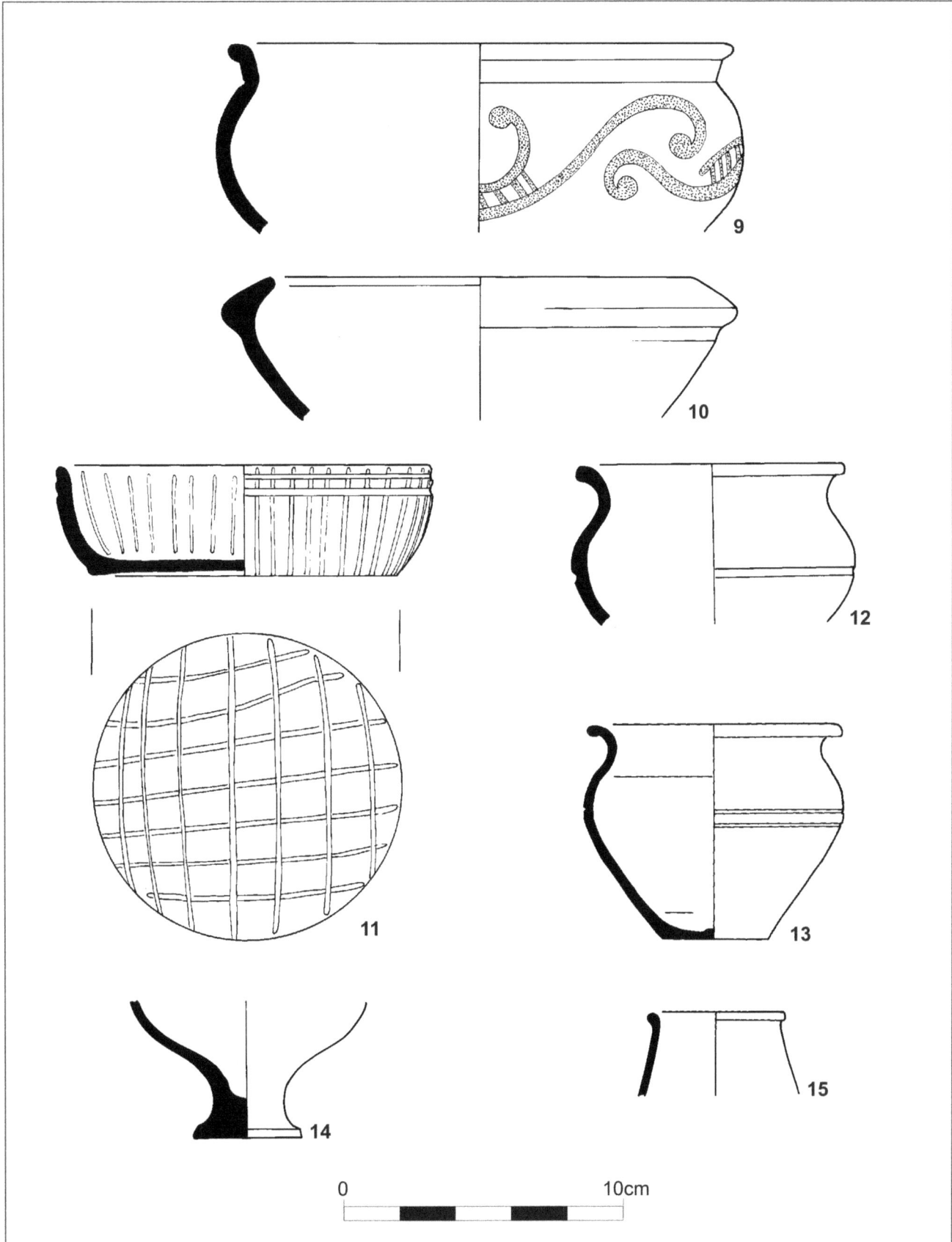

Fig 9.2 Roman pottery (9-15) from excavations

Local/ unknown wares

GREY1: a light blue-grey, occasionally dark grey-black, sandy ware with a red-brown to orange core. Generally very well fired. At x20 magnification a sparse to moderate frequency of moderately well sorted, sub-angular quartz sand are black iron grains (less then 0.5mm) are visible.

On the slightly lower fired vessels, fine mica is visible. This ware is particularly common, accounting for 62.5% of the Roman assemblage, arguing for a relatively local source. Many of the semi-complete vessels occur in this fabric. Forms include a complete small shallow dish (Fig. 9.2.11), necked jars (Fig. 9.2.12-13), necked beakers (Fig.

9.2.15), flasks (Fig, 9.1.5), flanged bowls, including one with a pie-crust rim (Fig. 9.1.6) and necked jars (Fig. 9.3. 16-17). One angled basesherd has several perforations in the base made before firing. The complete miniature jar (Fig. 9.1.4) is also probably this ware. Of the 246 sherds recorded in this fabric, 245 came from group 29247, the other sherd coming from Pit 11042.

GRSA: grog-tempered sandy ware. Handmade ware containing sub-angular to rounded, ill-sorted quartz sand (less than 1 mm) and rare sub-angular grog. Probably from a storage jar.

Discussion

Where datable, most of the Roman material appears to date to the second half of the 4th century with the presence of the late Roman shelly ware pushing it to the last quarter of the 4th century or beyond. The bulk of the Roman assemblage, 387 sherds, came from the various components of group 29147, provisionally interpreted as a cremation site. Layer 29014 produced some 253 sherds weighing 2164g (232 EVEs). The assemblage is quite well fragmented with an overall average sherd size of just 8.5g. It includes a number of Oxfordshire products including colour-coated wares (Young 1977 forms C45 and C99) and three whiteware mortaria (ibid forms M17 and M22) and 38 sherds of later Roman shelly ware. The bulk of the other wares comprise grey sandy wares.

Underlying this deposit were two possible cremation pits, 29229 and 29018. Pit 29229 produced 32 sherds in slightly better condition to 29014 with an average sherd size of 11g. In addition a complete miniature jar in a black sandy ware (Fig. 9.1.4) was recovered from gully 29023 cutting the top of the context. The main assemblage was quite mixed with just three rimsherds and mainly greyware bodysherds. Four Oxfordshire red colour-coated wares were present including a bowl (Young 1977, form C77) (Fig. 9.3.18). The assemblage was not particularly noteworthy and did not appear to represent smashed single vessels.

Possible cremation pit 29018 did, however, present quite an unusual assemblage with several joining sherds from single vessels but also a range of broken sherds from other vessels. The overall average sherd size was 20g, more than twice that from layer 29014. Amongst the complete vessels is a small greyware dish with burnished line decoration (Fig. 9.2.11) and most of a small necked greyware jar (Fig. 9.2.13). The semi-complete vessels include two OXF RS (ibid, form C77), a Central Gaulish samian dish (Curle 23) and the base of a greyware flask. Two large sherds from two further small, necked jars and two sherds from a greyware bowl were noted. Amongst the more fragmentary material associated with these vessels were two sherds of Lower Nene Valley colour-coated ware, further OXF RS, one sherd of Dorset black burnished ware, three sherds of later Roman shelly ware and various miscellaneous grey sandy wares. A further six sherds were recovered from the base of the pit (29036) amongst which are three further OXF RS sherds, one from a flanged bowl (ibid, C51) and two from beakers.

The semi-complete vessels do appear to form a quite neat complement of coarse and fine wares with serving, eating and drinking forms present as often found in burials furnished with grave goods. Only one large jar was present and then only as a rimsherd. The mixture of semi-complete and broken sherds along with the other various small finds is a curious one with no immediately apparent parallels. If seen in a domestic context the complement of wares indicates a fairly high status assemblage with fine and specialist wares well represented. If all the finewares and mortaria are totalled up they account for 18.5% of the whole assemblage by weight, 15% by count. This alone would argue for a non-domestic group as normally a late Roman domestic assemblage would be dominated by coarseware jars. The absence of any obviously residual material is also noteworthy and the fact that none of the material appears to have been burnt. One would not expect to find any continental imports at this time, especially inland, and the samian dish is presumably either a salvaged or curated vessel. Late Roman cremations with inhumation-sized pits whose pyre had been in the immediate neighbourhood were identified at Lankhill cemetery, Winchester (Clarke 1979, 350). In this case however, the cremated remains were interred in single vessels and the grave fills did not incorporate a large range of material as the pits at Chieveley did. Cremations in the topsoil were also identified at Lankhills (ibid, 128) but overall the practice of cremation in the later 4th century appears to be a relatively rare feature. The presence of Saxon occupation in the vicinity and the presence of the shelly ware might argue that the cremation group could date to the 5th century.

Saxon

Five Saxon sherds are present, two from the subsoil (2802), one from Pit 29131 (29098) – part of Group 29248 - one from Gully 29183 (29184), and a superficial find from fieldwalking (F5J). Two fabrics are present, both organic tempered. This is a fairly long-lived tradition and these sherds could date anywhere from the 6th to 8th centuries. The sherd from gully 29184 (Group 29249) is very worn, suggesting redeposition.

SXORG1: a dark grey or oxidized with a black interior, very finely micaceous, smooth, silky fabric. The paste contains a moderate to common frequency of coarse organic material, grass or straw-like in character. Three handmade bodysherds.

SXORG2: a sandy textured paste containing fine rounded quartz sand and sparse to moderate organic matter. Brown in colour with a black core. One bodysherd.

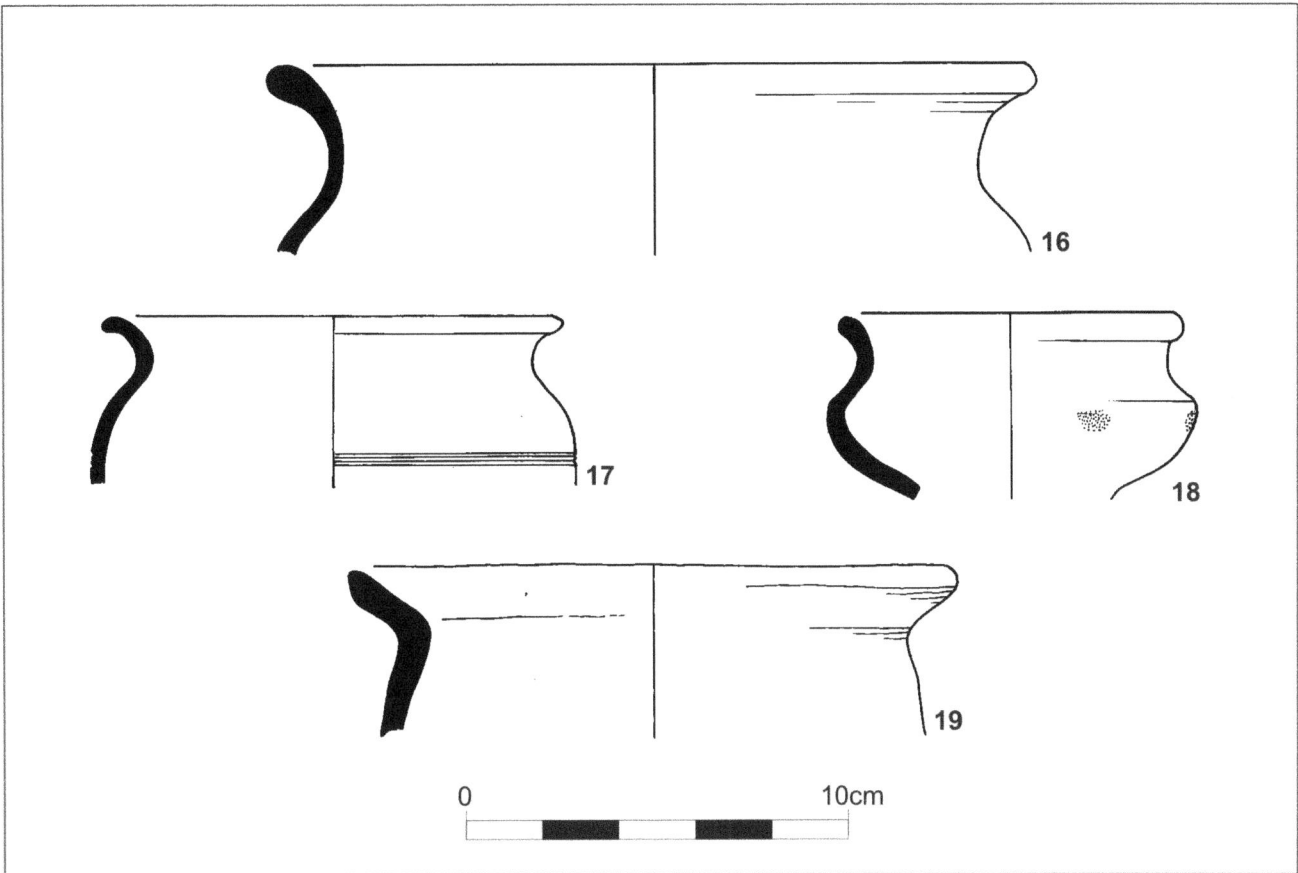

Fig 9.3 Roman pottery (16-18) and late Saxon / medieval pottery (19) from excavations

Pottery from Snelsmore Farm site

Work in Areas A and C (Trenches 10 and 16) resulted in the recovery of 38 sherds of pottery including sherds of prehistoric, Saxon, medieval and post-medieval date.

Iron Age

The prehistoric sherds (*c.* 25 in total) all come from a single flat, sandy ware base from Pit 1649. The base has a diameter of around 90 mm and is 20 mm thick. The paste contains a few grog and flint inclusions and rare visible rounded quartz. The ware could be regarded as typical of the Iron Age.

Saxon

Six Saxon sherds were also recovered all from Pit 1005. One large organic tempered sherd from the base of round-based jar (fabric SXORG1) and five greyware bodysherds, probably from one vessel, are present. The latter sherds are pale grey in colour with a sparse scatter of macroscopically visible clear and white, rounded quartz up to 1.5mm. In addition the paste contains sparse clay pellets, fine mica and rare large quartz up to 5mm. Two of the sherds join and probably come from a spout; the remaining three are bodysherds.

Medieval

The rim of a sharply everted rim jar (Fig. 9.3.19) with a fabric containing flint, quartz and calcareous inclusions came from 1600 (topsoil in Trench 16). Typologically this could be later Saxon or early medieval.

Catalogue of illustrated sherds

1. Plain walled urn with a slightly internally expanded rim. Fabric FL3. Pit 11024 (11022). Middle Bronze Age.
2. Plain walled urn with an undifferentiated rim. Fabric FL3. Pit 11024 (11021). Middle Bronze Age
3. Thin walled concave-rimmed vessel with a tapering rim. Fabric FL1. Group 11047, Pit 11053 (11052). Late Bronze Age.
4. Complete miniature jar. Black sandy ware with a red core. Pit 29229. Late Roman.
5. Handled flask decorated with burnished lines. Fabric GREY1. Group 29247, layer 29014.
6. Flanged bowl with pie-crust rim. Black, slightly micaceous ware. Fabric GREY1. Group 292N47. Layer 29014.
7. Central Gaulish samian dish, Curle type 23. Approximately 25% complete. Group 29247. Pit 29018 (29016).
8. Oxfordshire colour-coated bowl, probably originally with white-painted decoration, now lost. Approximately 50% complete. Young 1977, form C77. Group 29247. Pit 29018 (29016).
9. Oxfordshire colour-coated bowl with white-painted scroll decoration. Approximately 33% complete. Young 1977, form C77. Group 29247. Pit 29018 (29016).
10. Bowl. Fabric GREY1. Group 29247. Pit 29018 (29016).
11. Complete small dish decorated with burnished line decoration on the interior extending into the bases and on the exterior with lattice work on the exterior. Fabric GREY1. Group 29247. Pit 29018 (29016).
12. Small necked bowl. Fabric GREY1. Group 29247. Pit 29018 (29016).
13. Small necked jar. Fabric GREY1. Approximately 75% complete. Group 29247. Pit 29018 (29016).
14. Pedestalled base, probably from a beaker. Fabric GREY1. Group 29247. Pit 29018 (29016).
15. Beaker. Fabric GREY1. Group 29247. Pit 29018 (29016).
16. Everted rim wide-mouthed jar. Fabric GREY1. Group 29247. Pit 29018 (29016).
17. Everted rim jNar. Fabric GREY1. Group 29247. Pit 29018 (29016).
18. Small Oxfordshire colour-coated bowl with faint traces of white-painted decoration. Young 1977, type C77. Group 29247. Pit 29229 (29230).
19. Handmade, everted rim jar. Dark grey ware, with a red-brown interior and blackened interior rim. SNEL, context 1600, u/s.

Acknowledgement

I am grateful to Alistair Barclay for discussing some of the prehistoric material with me.

Chapter 10: Metal and other finds

by Tora Hylton, with Ian Meadows

Introduction

The excavations produced a collection of metal, stone and miscellaneous finds dating from Roman through to post-medieval times. The assemblage is dominated by Roman finds recovered from an area of activity in CHRF Trench 29.

In total there are 49 individual or group recorded small finds in four material types. Each object has been described and measured, and a descriptive catalogue is retained in archive. Bulk finds include ceramic tile, brick, fired clay and clay tobacco-pipe fragments, all of which have been recorded under the bulk-finds system. All the artefacts were recovered by hand.

A total of 25 iron objects (excluding identifiable nails and small fragments) were submitted for X-ray. This was undertaken by David Parish, Dip.Cons. of the Buckinghamshire County Museum Conservation Service. This not only provided a permanent record, but it enabled identification and revealed details not previously visible. All sensitive finds are packaged in air tight plastic containers with silica gel and an indicator card, to maintain a low humidity and reduce deterioration.

Roman Finds

In total 37 non-pottery objects were recovered from late Roman deposits in CHRF Trench 29. All were from a series of features in the northern end of the trench relating to possible cremations (Group 29247). Small numbers of finds were recovered from two possible cremation pits (29018, 29229), while the majority of finds were located in a deposit (29014) sealing the pits. The assemblage is represented by domestic related artefacts, miscellaneous fittings, nails and seven coins, all but one dating to the 4th century (Meadows, this report).

Pit 29018

The finds from 'cremation' pit 29018 include three coins (SFs 4, 7, 10) one hob nail, five cleats, one nail, four unidentifiable iron fragments and three large undiagnostic fragments of ceramic tile (2,372kg), most probably for structural use.

Of particular interest is the presence of five iron cleats. They are roughly oval with a tang at each end protruding at right angles, and measure 25-48mm in length. Cleats are generally assumed to have been used on the soles or heels of boots to prevent wear, or, for fastening strips of wood together (Manning 1985, 131). Manning recalls that Pitt-Rivers uncovered seven cleats at the feet of a skeleton at Rotherley (Pitt-Rivers 1887, 86, plate XXVIII, 16) and there are other examples, including some of the burials at Lankhills (Borrill 1981, fig 38). Therefore it is possible that these five cleats were originally used as "boot plates" on shoes. Like the illustrated examples from Lankhills, where there are cleats of different sizes present within a single burial, these examples graduate in size, measuring 25mm, 30mm, 36mm, 43mm and 48mm in length, with tangs, where present, measuring $c.$15-16mm in length. This may suggest that more than one or two were used on each shoe, the graduation in size reflecting changes in the width of the sole of the shoe.

Pit 29229

There are only two finds from Pit 29229, a complete ceramic vessel (SF 25, reported above) and an iron nail.

Layer 29014

Layer 29014 produced four coins (SFs 3, 12, 15, 26), a fragment of a copper alloy spoon, three querns, an iron fitting, eight nails, four unidentifiable iron fragments and seven fragments of ceramic tile.

The spoon is incomplete, part of the bowl missing; it is therefore it is difficult to determine if the bowl of the spoon would originally have been oval or round. The cranked handle is slender with a circular cross-section and tapers to a point; the handle is ornamented with a small motif, comprising transverse grooves and notched cut outs (Fig. 10.1).

The quern fragments include two rotary querns manufactured from Millstone Grit, which were found together. Both are upper stones with well worn grinding surfaces; originally, when complete, they would have measured in excess of 500mm in diameter. In addition there is a part of a saddle quern.

There is a perforated strip, although incomplete. It is possible that it is part of a reinforcing strip/bracket. It has parallel sides and a rounded terminal with a centrally-placed square perforation. It displays similarities to a bracket/tie-strip from Colchester (Crummy 1983, fig 130, 4079). It is possible that it is part of an iron corner bracket/binding from a wooden box, rather like the iron bindings from a wooden box recovered from a burial at Skeleton Green, Hertfordshire (Borrill 1981, fig116, a, b).

All the identifiable nails recovered are Mannings Type 1b (1985, fig 32). They have flat sub-circular heads, square-sectioned shanks and range in length from 65-80mm; they were presumably used for light structural fixings.

There are seven pieces of ceramic tile weighing 0.959kg. Diagnostic fragments represent parts of a tegula (1), imbrex (3), pilae/subfloor tile (1) and two pieces of undiagnostic tile.

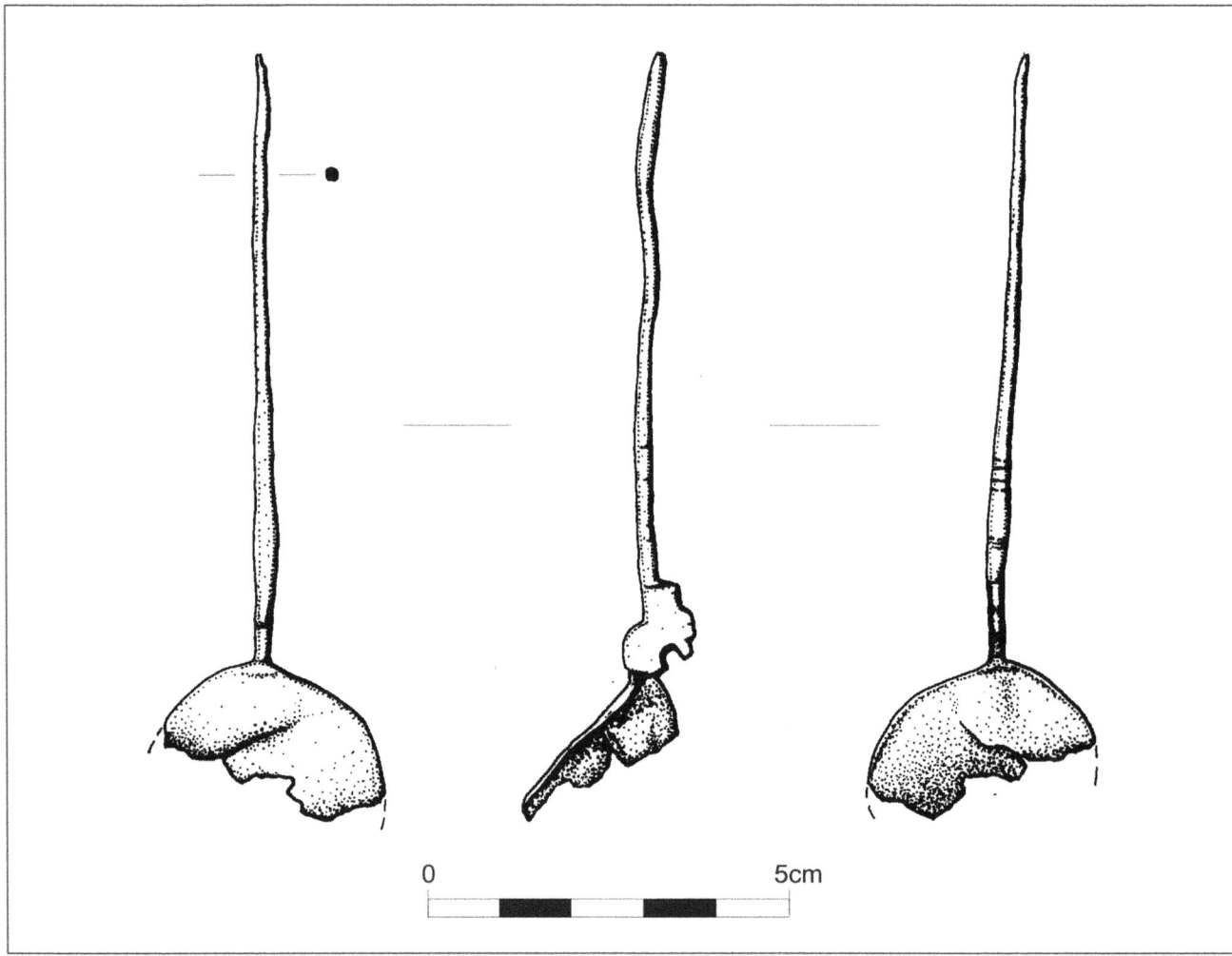

Fig 10.1 Roman spoon from layer 29014

Saxon lava quern

The only Saxon small finds recovered are 27 fragments of lava quern weighing 2.8kg from SNEL Trench 10. Although these quern fragments were recovered with Saxon pottery, it is possible that they are residual Roman items. Lava querns are grey and vesicular, and probably come from the Mayen-Niedermendig area of Eiffel, Germany. A useful discussion of possible alternative sources is contained in the Tamworth report (Wright 1992, 72-73). The majority (16) were recovered from Pit 1005, most are amorphous fragments, and there is only one diagnostic piece, part of an upper stone with a worn grinding surface. Surviving features indicate that it would originally have measured in excess of 400-500mm in diameter. A vestige of the central hole survives measuring 28-30mm in diameter. In addition, 11 amorphous and abraded fragments, some with vestiges of the grinding surface, were recovered from Pit 1011.

Post-medieval finds

Finds from post-medieval features were recovered from SNEL Trenches 10 and 16. They include two horseshoes, one from the hollow-way Cut 1663, which dates to the 18th/19th century and was probably for use on a draught horse, and an incomplete shoe from the later ditch cut 1673. Fragments of undatable clay tobacco-pipe bowl were recovered from ditches, five from field boundary ditch 1009 and one from inner Ditch cut 1697. There are two pieces of ceramic roof tile, one each from hollow-way cut 1615 and the outer ditch 1687. Other finds include miscellaneous fragments of brick, bottle/vessel glass and undiagnostic pieces of iron (catalogue in archive).

Catalogue of Illustrations

10.1   Spoon, copper alloy. Length of handle: 85mm. SF 13, Trench 29, Layer 2914

Coins

by Ian Meadows

A total of nine coins were recovered from the excavations (all from CHRF). Of these, two are 18th century copper halfpennies recovered from the subsoil and therefore indicative of casual loss possibly during cultivation. The remaining coins are all in a poor state, presumably as a result of the ground conditions, resulting in the loss of surface detail such as the mintmarks or legends. A catalogue is presented in Table 10.1.

The seven remaining coins are all Roman in date. Five are House of Constantine issues, both at AE3 and AE4, dating from the second and third quarter of the 4th century. The coins came from two contexts, Layer 29014, where the dateable issues (SF3, 15 and 26) are from the second quarter of the 4th century and 29016 (Pit 29018) where the dateable issues (SF4 and 7) are from the third quarter of the 4th century. The remaining two coins comprise the illegible 4th-century flan from 29014 and a presumably residual 3rd-century radiate from 29016.

Small find no.	Feature	Description
3	Layer 29014	A very corroded AE4 flan with very little original surface. Possibly a CONSTANTINOPOLIS issue (330-35)
4	Pit 29018	An AE3 GLORIA ROMANORUM issue Kneeling captive reverse. The obverse bust is clear but the legend is too fragmentary to discern. The reverse type shows the emperor with no cloak (LRBC Type 8). The mintmark is missing but there are two officina that would suggest either Lugdumum or Arles as the source (364-78)
7	Pit 29018	An AE3 SECURITAS REIPUBLICAE issue. The mintmark is missing and the obverse legend is fragmentary and illegible (364-78)
10	Pit 29016	An AE3 radiate. No obverse or reverse legend is legible. The reverse portrays an unrecognised standing figure. Second half of 3rd century
12	Layer 29014	An AE4 flan otherwise illegible but probably 4th century
15	Layer 29014	An AE3 URBS ROMA issue probably either Trier or Arles (330-335). The mintmark is missing
16	subsoil	A George III Half penny dated 1771
17	subsoil	A George II Half penny old bust type obverse legend GEORGIVS 1746-54
26	Layer 29014	An AE4 flan of 4th century date. Possibly a CONSTANTINOPOLIS issue (330-35)

Table 10.1 Catalogue of coins

Chapter 11: Environmental evidence

Charred plant remains

by Val Fryer

Introduction

A total of 95 soil samples were taken for the recovery of charred plant remains from a range of features of Bronze Age through to Saxon date, as well as from a number of undated features. The majority (89) came from site CHRF (the northern side of the M4 motorway), and the remaining four from site SNEL (the southern side). Sample sizes varied, but most were 20 litres. Of these, 57 samples from CHRF and the four from SNEL were selected for assessment. The assessment indicated that the range of material was limited and the potential for further analysis not high (NA 2004, Appendix 17).

Nonetheless, in order to maximise the amount of information from a generally 'unproductive' site, 29 samples were selected for full analysis. It was hoped that study of this material would:

- indicate the function of the features from which the material was taken
- highlight any differences in the composition of the assemblages from different periods of site use
- provide supplementary data on agricultural practises and the local economy

An additional six samples from features of unknown date in trenches 11 and 29 were processed and assessed, making the total number of assessed samples 67. A note on these samples is presented below (Deighton, this report). They generally confirm the poor quality of the data, but the occasional presence of weeds and seeds suggest some anthropogenic input.

Wood charcoal from 14 samples was sent to Rowena Gale for reporting. Again the quality of the remains was poor and no further work was recommended (NA 2004, Appendix 18). The edited report is included below.

Coarse residues were sorted for burnt flint which was weighed (Chapter 8).

Methods

All samples were bulk floated by Northamptonshire Archaeology, collecting the floats in a 0.5 mm mesh sieve. For detailed analysis the dried floats were sorted under a binocular microscope at magnifications up to x 16, and the plant macrofossils and other remains noted are listed on Tables 11.1 - 5. Identifications were made by comparison with modern reference specimens and nomenclature with the tables follows Stace (1997). All plant remains were charred. Modern contaminants, including fibrous roots, seeds and fungal sclerotia, were present throughout.

As none of the samples contained sufficient plant remains (i.e. 100+ specimens) for full quantification, the density of material within the assemblages has been expressed in the tables as follows: x = 1 - 10 specimens, xx = 10 - 100 specimens and xxx = 100+ specimens. Other abbreviations used in the tables are explained at the end of the text section.

Sample composition

Plant macrofossils

Cereal grains, chaff and seeds of common weeds were present at a low density in only twelve samples. Preservation was generally poor, with many grains and seeds being either puffed and distorted as a result of high temperatures during combustion, or fragmented.

Oat (*Avena* sp.), barley (*Hordeum* sp.), rye (*Secale cereale*) and wheat (*Triticum* sp.) grains were recorded from the assemblages, although frequently as single specimens. With the exception of the examples from site SNEL Trench 10, all wheat grains were of an elongated 'drop-form' type typical of spelt (*T. spelta*), and although chaff was very scarce, double-keeled spelt glume bases were recovered from samples 16 and 29.

Weed seeds were extremely rare, occurring in only six samples. Grassland taxa were predominant and included goosegrass (*Galium aparine*), mallow (*Malva* sp.), medick/clover/trefoil (*Medicago/ Trifolium/Lotus* sp.), indeterminate grasses (Poaceae), dock (*Rumex* sp.) and vetch/vetchling (*Vicia/Lathyrus* sp.). A single sedge (*Carex* sp.) fruit in sample 26 is possibly indicative of nearby damp grassland habitats.

Charcoal fragments were abundant in most samples along with pieces of charred root or stem. Other plant macrofossils were rare, although occasional indeterminate seeds were recorded. A single thorn or prickle, possibly of *Rosa* type, was noted in sample 16.

Other materials

Fragments of black porous 'cokey' material and black tarry material were noted in most assemblages. Most are probable residues of the combustion of organic materials at extremely high temperatures, although some may be derived from waste products from small-scale 'industrial' activities.

For the purposes of this discussion the samples will be dealt with by site, period and context type.

Sample No.	55	56	57	59	60	62	63	64
Context No.	11080	11081	11082	11084	11085	11086	11087	11089
Feature No.	11090	11090	11090	11090	11090	11090	11090	11090
Other plant macrofossils								
Charcoal <2mm	xx	xx	xx	xx	xx	xxx	xxx	x
Charcoal >2mm		x	x	x		x	xxx	x
Charred root/rhizome/stem	xx							
Other materials								
Black porous 'cokey' material	xxx	xx	x	x	x	x		
Black tarry material	xx	xx	x		x	x		
Burnt stone				x	x			
Small coal frags.	xx	x	x		x			
Sample volume (litres)	20	20	10	5	15	15	20	10
Volume of float (litres)	<0.1	<0.1	<0.1	<0.1	<0.1	<0.1	0.1	<0.1
% float sorted	100%	100%	100%	100%	100%	100%	100%	100%

Table 11.1: Charred plant macrofossils and other remains from Bronze Age pit 11090 (Area E)

Sample No.		28	29	30	31	32
Context No.		11034	11035	11036	11037	11038
Feature No.		11033	11033	11033	11033	11033
Cereals	**Common name**					
Cereal indet. (grains)					xfg	
T. spelta L. (glume bases)	Spelt wheat			xcf		
Other plant macrofossils						
Charcoal <2mm		xx	xx	xx	xx	x
Charcoal >2mm						x
Charred root/rhizome/stem			x			
Other materials						
Black porous 'cokey' material			x	x		
Black tarry material					x	x
Sample volume (litres)		10	20	20	20	20
Volume of float (litres)		<0.1	<0.1	<0.1	<0.1	<0.1
% float sorted		100%	100%	100%	100%	100%

Table 11.2: Charred plant macrofossils and other remains from Bronze Age pit 11033 (Area E)

Bronze Age features in Trench 11 (Tables 11.1 and 11.4)

Two pits and a gully of probable Bronze Age date were sampled. Eight samples (55 - 64, Table 11.1) are from successive fills within Pit 11090, a large feature situated on the eastern edge of the excavation and cut by a later ditch. The assemblages are all extremely small and, as is commonly seen in similar contemporary features across eastern England and the midlands, plant macrofossils are entirely absent with the exception of charcoal fragments and occasional pieces of charred root or stem. Accurate interpretation of such assemblages is extremely difficult, but it would appear most likely that the material is derived from small quantities of fuel waste, some or all of which may have been accidentally deposited within the pit fills as wind-blown detritus.

Key to Tables:
x = 1 – 10 specimens.   xx = 10 – 100 specimens.
xxx = 100+ specimens.   fg = fragment.   b = burnt

Possible industrial residues including black 'cokey' and tarry concretions and small pieces of coal are common in the upper fills of Pit 11090 but, given the date of the context, it is considered most likely that these represent intrusive material from the later ditch cut.

Single samples were taken from Pit 11215 (sample 54, Table 11.4) and Gully 29021 N (sample 4, Table 11.5). Both assemblages are extremely sparse, containing only a few small fragments of charcoal, charred root/stem and burnt organic material, and it would appear most likely that this material is derived from scattered or wind-blown refuse of uncertain origin.

Sample No.		42	43	44	45	46
Context No.		11048	11049	11050	11051	11052
Feature No.		11053	11053	11053	11053	11053
Cereals	Common name					
Avena sp. (grains)	Oat		xcf			
Cereal indet. (grain)		x				
Hordeum sp. (rachis node)	Barley			xcf		
Herbs						
Chenopodiaceae indet.				x		
Small Poaceae indet.	Grasses		x			
Other plant macrofossils						
Charcoal <2mm		xxx	xx	xxx	xxx	xxx
Charcoal >2mm		x		x	x	x
Charred root/rhizome/stem		x				
Other materials						
Black porous 'cokey' material			x	x	x	x
Black tarry material		x		x		
Burnt stone		x				x
Ferrous globules			x			
Small coal frags.		x	x			
Vitreous globules				x		
Sample volume (litres)		20	20	20	20	10
Volume of float (litres)		<0.1	<0.1	<0.1	<0.1	<0.1
% float sorted		100%	100%	100%	100%	100%

Table 11.3: Charred plant and other remains from Late Bronze Age/early Iron Age pit 11053, Group 11047 (Area E)

Sample No.		54	37	38
Context No.		11091	11045	11046
Feature		Pit 11215	Pit 11042	Pit 11042
Date		BA	BA/IA	BA/IA
Cereals	Common name			
Cereal indet. (grains)			x	
Triticum sp. (grains)	Wheat			
(spikelet bases)				
T. spelta L. (glume bases)	Spelt wheat			
Other plant macrofossils				
Charcoal <2mm		x	x	xx
Charcoal >2mm		x		x
Other materials				
Black porous 'cokey' material			x	x
Black tarry material			x	x
Eggshell				x
Sample volume (litres)		20	20	20
Volume of flot (litres)		<0.1	<0.1	<0.1
% flot sorted		100%	100%	100%

Table 11.4: Charred plant macrofossils and other remains from Bronze Age/Iron Age pit group 11138 (Area E)

Left:
Table 11.5: Charred plant macrofossils and other remains from possible Bronze Age gullies in Trench 29 (Area E)

Sample No.	4	19
Context No.	29020	29111
Context type	Gully 29021	Gully 29256
Date	BA	BA?
Other plant macrofossils		
Charcoal <2mm	xx	x
Charcoal >2mm		
Charred root/rhizome/stem	x	
Other materials		
Black porous 'cokey' material	x	
Sample volume (litres)	20	20
Volume of float (litres)	<0.1	<0.1
% float sorted	100%	100%

Below:
Table 11.6: Charred plant macrofossils and other remains from late Roman and Saxon features in Trench 29 (Area E)

Sample No.		16	26	20
Context No.		29014	29230	29218
Context type		Layer	Pit 29299	Pit 29248
Date		LROM	LROM	SAX
Cereals	Common name			
Cereal indet. (grains)		x		xfg
Triticum sp. (grains)	Wheat	x	xcf	xcf
(spikelet bases)			x	
T. spelta L. (glume bases)	Spelt wheat	xcf		
Herbs				
Chenopodiaceae indet.			x	
Galium aparine L.	Goosegrass		xx	
Malva sp.	Mallow		x	
Medicago/Trifolium/Lotus sp.	Medick/clover/trefoil		x	
Small Poaceae indet.	Grasses		x	
Rumex sp.	Dock	xcf	xcf	
Wetland plants				
Carex sp.	Sedge		x	
Other plant macrofossils				
Charcoal <2mm		xxx	xxx	xx
Charcoal >2mm		x		
Charred root/rhizome/stem			xxx	x
Indet. seeds			x	
Indet. thorn		x		
Other materials				
Black porous 'cokey' material		x	x	x
Black tarry material		x	x	
Bone		xb	xb	
Burnt/fired clay			x	
Small coal frags.		x		
Sample volume (litres)		20	70	40
Volume of float (litres)		<0.1	<0.1	<0.1
% float sorted		100%	100%	100%

Late Bronze Age/Early Iron Age pits in Trench 11 (Tables 11.2, 11.3 and 11.4)

A total of twelve samples were taken from fills within pits 11033, 11045 and 11053. As with the samples from the earlier features the assemblages are all very small, with charcoal being the principal component. However, small quantities of charred grain, chaff and weed seeds are now present, and although all are probably derived from scattered refuse, they would appear to indicate that cereal processing may have been taking place in the near vicinity.

Late Roman feature group 29247 (Table 11.6)

Two samples were taken, one (16) from Layer 29014 and one (26) from Pit 29229. Although the assemblage from sample 26 is small, the recovered material is almost certainly associated with either a cremation deposit or pyre material. Seeds of common grassland plants are moderately common and, along with numerous fragments of charred root/stem, these are probably derived from either dried grasses and grassland herbs, which were gathered for use as kindling or fuel for the cremation, or from material burnt *in situ* beneath the pyre. The few recorded cereal remains may also be related to the cremation, occurring either as an additional fuel source or as an offering to the deceased. Such deposits have numerous parallels from the prehistoric period through to early Roman times, although later Roman cremations are more unusual.

Although grains, chaff and weed seeds are present in sample 16, there is insufficient material for accurate interpretation of the deposit. However, minute fragments of burnt bone are recorded from both samples 16 and

Sample No.		2	3	4
Context No.		1003	1010	1018
Feature No.		Pit 1005	Pit 1011	Pit 1021
Cereals	**Common Name**			
Avena sp. (grains)	Oat			xcf
Cereal indet. (grains)		xfg	xfg	x
Hordeum sp. (grains)	Barley		x	x
(rachis node)				xcf
Secale cereale L. (grains)	Rye		xcf	
(rachis nodes)			xcf	
Triticum sp. (grains)	Wheat		x	x
Herbs				
Chenopodiaceae indet.			x	
Rumex sp.	Dock			x
Vicia/Lathyrus sp.	Vetch/vetchling			x
Tree/shrub macrofossils				
Corylus avellana L.	Hazel			xcf
Other plant macrofossils				
Charcoal <2mm		xxx	xxx	xxx
Charcoal >2mm		x	xx	xxx
Indet.seed		x		
Other materials				
Black porous 'cokey' material		x		
Black tarry material			x	
Bone				xb
Ferrous globule			x	
Mineralised soil concretions		xxx	xx	
Sample volume (litres)		20	20	20
Volume of flot (litres)		<0.1	<0.1	0.2
% flot sorted		100%	100%	50%

Table 11.7: Charred plant remains and other material from Saxon pits in Area C Trench 10

Sample No.	5	11	21	27	35	79
Context No.	29030	29067	29227	29245	11043	11124
Feature	Ditch 29029	Ditch 29068	Pit 29228	Gully 29246	Pit 11042	Pit 11126
Cereals						
Cereal indet. (grain)	x		x			
Weeds						
Indet.	x	x	x	x		x
Other plant macrofossils						
Charcoal	x	x	xx	x	xx	xx
Sample volume (litres)	20	20	20	20	20	20
Volume of float (litres)	<0.1	<0.1	<0.1	<0.1	<0.1	<0.1
% float sorted	100%	100%	100%	100%	100%	100%

Table 11.8: Charred plant macrofossils, supplementary sample assessment

26, and as these are the only two assemblages in which this material occurs, they may indicate that the deposits are linked.

Possible Bronze Age gullies in Trench 29 (Table 11.5)

Both assemblages are small, with charcoal being the principal component in both samples 19 (Gully 29256) and 4 (Gully 29021), while sample 20 (Pit 29217) contains rare cereal remains as well as charcoal and charred root/stem. Both are probably of prehistoric date, although presence/absence of macrofossils within an assemblage cannot necessarily be used as a means of dating when artefactual or stratigraphic evidence is absent.

Early to Middle Saxon pits, SNEL Trench 10 (Table 11.7)

Samples were taken from three small pits, which appeared to form part of a larger pit group of probable Early to Middle Saxon date. Although evidence for contemporary activities associated with these features is entirely absent, making their intended function uncertain, the composition of the plant macrofossil assemblages would appear to indicate the presence of small quantities of domestic refuse. Oat, barley, rye and wheat grains are present, along with occasional chaff and weed seeds, a possible fragment of hazel (*Corylus avellana*) nutshell and abundant charcoal fragments. Such assemblages are consistent with small deposits of domestic hearth waste, where grains have been accidentally burnt during culinary preparation over fires fuelled principally by wood/charcoal but including low levels of cereal processing waste.

Conclusions

In summary, with only rare exceptions, the recovered assemblages are all very small (i.e. <0.1 litre in volume), making accurate interpretation of the plant macrofossils extremely difficult. However, at least one sample (26) appears to be derived from a cremation deposit of probable Late Roman date, and domestic refuse may be present in the three assemblages from the Early to Middle Saxon pits recorded at SNEL Trench 10. The remaining assemblages are all probably derived from either scattered/wind-blown detritus or small deposits of refuse of uncertain origin. Small amounts of probable cereal processing waste is present in the Late Bronze Age/Early Iron Age assemblages, but at such a low density that it appears unlikely that this processing was occurring in the immediate vicinity of the site.

Supplementary samples (Table 11.8)

by Karen Deighton

Following the assessment stage a further six samples were selected for processing and rapid analysis. These were from undated or poorly dated features and it was hoped that the macrofossil assemblage would help clarify their character.

The cereal present was too fragmentary and abraded to be identified beyond wheat/barley. The weed species were fat hen (*Chenopodium album*) a ubiquitous ruderal, and cleavers (*Galium aparine*) a common crop weed. The molluscs in Sample 21 were *Ceciliodes asicula*, a burrowing species and undoubtedly intrusive.

The wood charcoals

by Rowena Gale

Introduction

An assessment of charcoal recovered from selected prehistoric, Roman and unknown contexts was undertaken to evaluate its potential to assist in the interpretation of the site.

For this report 14 samples of charcoal were looked at, mainly from CHRF Trenches 11 and 29. The samples mostly consisted of poorly preserved and very fragmented material, much of which was inadequate for identification. The assessment is based on the overall observation of the character and content of each sample and the identification of three fragments from each to indicate the general range of species present.

Methodology

The 14 samples consisted of degraded and very fragmented charcoal, much of which was contaminated with silty deposits throughout the structures. The charcoal was prepared using standard methods (Gale and Cutler 2000) and examined using incident light on a Nikon Labophot-2 compound microscope at magnifications up to x400. The taxa identified were matched to prepared reference slides of modern wood. When possible, the maturity of the wood was assessed (i.e. heartwood/ sapwood).

The taxa identified are presented in Table 11.9. Classification follows that of *Flora Europaea* (Tutin, Heywood *et al* 1964-80). Group names are given when anatomical differences between related genera are too slight to allow secure identification to genus level. These include members of the Pomoideae (*Crataegus, Malus, Pyrus* and *Sorbus*) and Salicaceae (*Salix* and *Populus*). The structure of the charcoal was consistent with the

Sample	Context	Feature	Quantity	Taxa identified	Comments
Bronze Age					
39	11064	Pit 11065 Gp 11047	x	2 x hazel (*Corylus avellana*); 1 x oak (*Quercus* sp.)	V small
75	11102	Pit 11215 Gp 11138	x	3 x oak (*Quercus* sp.)	Remainder probably oak
74	11110		xx	3 x oak (*Quercus* sp.)	V degraded and permeated with silty material
54	11091		x	3 x oak (*Quercus* sp.) h/w	V small. Oak from large wood
58	11083	Pit 11090	x	1 x hazel (*Corylus avellana*); 1 x willow (*Salix* sp.) or poplar (*Populus* sp.); 1 x hawthorn/ *Sorbus* group (Pomoideae)	V small
62	11087		x	1 x oak (*Quercus* sp.) h/w; 1 x oak (*Quercus* sp.) r/w; 1 x oak (*Quercus* sp.) s/w	V small
63	11088		xx	3 x oak (*Quercus* sp.) s/w	V comminuted. Remainder probably oak
70	11074	Pit 11060	x	3 x oak (*Quercus* sp.) h/w and knotwood	V small
47	11054	Pit 11056	x	2 x oak (*Quercus* sp.); 1 x blackthorn (*Prunus spinosa*)	V small
33	11028	Pit 11027	x	1 x oak (*Quercus* sp.), h/w; 1 x oak (*Quercus* sp.)	Small fragments. Oak from large wood.
?Bronze Age					
1	2304	Pit 2303	xx	3 x oak (*Quercus* sp.) h/w	Oak from large wood. Small frags
9	29063	Pit 29062	xx	3 x oak (*Quercus* sp.) h/w;	Oak from large wood. Mostly v comminuted.
10	29064		xx	1 x oak (*Quercus* sp.) s/w; 1 x holly (*Ilex aquifolium*)	Oak from large wood. Mostly v comminuted.
Late Roman					
16	29014	Layer	x	3 x oak (*Quercus* sp.)	Small frags

Table 11.9: The wood charcoals
Key: h/w = heartwood; r/w = roundwood; s/w = sapwood   **Quantity:** number of fragments - x = <10; xx = 11 - 50

following taxa or groups of taxa:

Aquifoliaceae. *Ilex aquifolium* L., holly
Corylaceae. *Corylus avellana* L., hazel
Fagaceae. *Quercus* sp., oak
Rosaceae. Subfamilies:
Pomoideae, which includes *Crataegus* sp., hawthorn; *Malus* sp., apple; *Pyrus* sp., pear; *Sorbus* spp., rowan, service tree and whitebeam. These taxa are anatomically similar; one or more taxa may be represented in the charcoal.
Prunoideae. *Prunus spinosa* L., blackthorn.
Salicaceae. *Salix* sp., willow, and *Populus* sp., poplar. In most respects these taxa are anatomically similar.

Results

Trench 11
Charcoal was examined from Bronze Age pits 11060, 11065, 11090 and 11215 and also from contexts 11102 and 11110 in pit 11215, which were possibly slightly later in date. In addition, charcoal was examined from prehistoric pits 11127 and 11056. The origin of the charcoal is unknown. Most of the samples contained less than 10 fragments that were suitable for identification. Oak, including heartwood, was the most frequently recorded taxon; other species present included hazel, willow/ poplar, the hawthorn group and blackthorn (Table 11.9).

Trenches 29 and 23
Charcoal was examined from context 29014, a layer dated to the 4th century AD. The sample was small and scrappy and its origin unknown. The sample included oak. Charcoal was more abundant, although very comminuted, from pits 2303 and 29062 but since dating for these features remains undetermined, further analysis would be of little value. The taxa identified included oak and holly.

Sample	Context	Feature	pH value
		topsoil	7
		subsoil	5.5
		natural substrate	5
3	29014	Late Roman layer	5.5
7	29016	Late Roman pit 29018	5.5
9	29063	?Bronze Age pit 29062	5.5
26	29230	Late Roman pit 29229	5

Table 11.11: Results of soil pH tests

Table 11.10: Animal bone summary of species present

Bos (cattle)	Ovicaprid (sheep/goat)	Sus (pig)	Avis sp (bird)	Indeterminate	Total
5	5	1	1	2	14

Environmental evidence

Although very little can be said of the environment, based on the slender evidence available, it was clear that oak was the dominant taxon in the samples, which infers that oak woodland was prevalent in the area. Most of the other species identified, i.e., hazel, blackthorn, the hawthorn group and holly, could be interpreted as either understorey (e.g. hazel and holly) or marginal woodland/ scrub. Willow/ poplar would have been common on damp or wetland.

The animal bone

by Karen Deighton

A total of 14 animal bones (484g) were recovered by hand from the excavations at CHRF and SNEL. The majority (390g) came from CHRF, with most from Trench 29. All the material was scanned to establish the species present, the state of preservation and any potential for further analysis.

Fragmentation was heavy and surface condition was very poor. The poor preservation would seem to be the result of acidic soil conditions, a factor which would account for the low numbers of bones recovered (*Soil Tests,* below). No evidence of butchery or canid gnawing was noted due to the poor bone surface condition. A single burnt bone fragment was noted from context 29117 (post-medieval ditch 29116).

The species present are restricted to a small range of common domesticates and an indeterminate bird species.

Only 209g of bone came from features which are thought to be archaeologically significant, the rest coming from superficial layers and modern features. A total 105g of bone came from the late Roman 'cremation pit' 29018. This comprised disparate fragments of cattle, sheep and pig. A further 10g of probable cattle tooth fragments came from the early Roman gully 29023. A probable Saxon pit in SNEL Trench 10 (Pit 1013) contained 94g of humerus from a large ungulate and a cattle molar.

The potential for further analysis was severely limited by the small amount of bone and its poor condition. No further work was undertaken.

Soil Tests

by Karen Deighton

The acidity of a number of soil samples was tested in the field and in the laboratory using a Hellige pH indicator. The results (Table 11.11) indicate moderately acidic conditions under a neutral topsoil.

Chapter 12: Radiocarbon dating

Three samples of charred material extracted from soil samples from Bronze Age pit 11090 were sent to the Scottish Universities Environmental Research Centre for AMS radiocarbon dating (Table 12.1).

The first two samples were cereal grains from contexts 11081 (Sample 56) and 11083 (Sample 58). The respective resulting dates of 10,080 +/- 50 BP and >47,000 BP are unreliable. The tests were kindly repeated by SUERC but the results were very similar and suggest hydrocarbon contamination of these soils. A degree of site-wide contamination is also indicated by the frequent presence of 'tar' and 'coke' in the soil samples (Fryer, Chapter 11). It is not clear where this contamination originated, but does not appear to be localised and therefore it seems likely to be related to agricultural practices.

The third sample was a fragment of probable oak charcoal from context 11063 (Sample 63), from lower down in the same pit (about 1 m below the stripped surface). The charcoal was associated with small quantities of burnt flint and Middle Bronze Age pottery. The date of 3065 +/- 35 BP, calibrated to 1420 CalBC – 1250 CalBC and 1240 CalBC – 1210 CalBC (95% probability) supports the pottery dating and is likely to be reliable (Fig. 12.1).

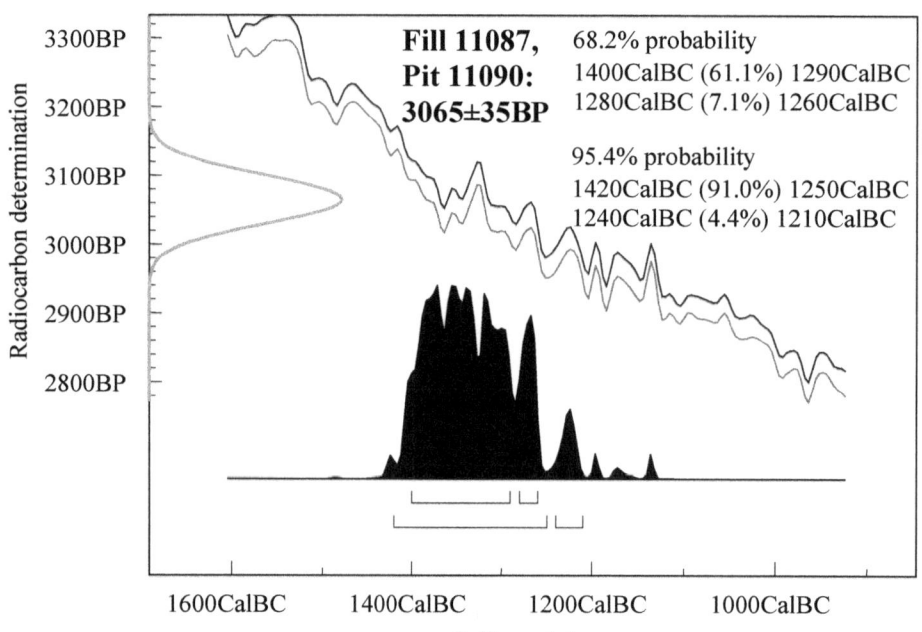

Fig. 12.1 Radiocarbon plot from charcoal in Pit 11090 (SUERC-4148)

Laboratory Number	Context	Radiocarbon Age (BP)	$d^{13}C$ per thousand	Material	Context Type	Calibrated date range. 95% confidence
SUERC-3585 (GU-12142)	11083	>47,200	-22.9	unident. charred cereal grain	lower burnt flint layer in PIt 11090	-
SUERC-3584 (GU-12141)	11081	10,080 +/- 50	-25.6	unident. charred cereal grain	upper burnt flint layer in Pit 11090	10,150-9,300 CalBC
SUERC-4144 (GU-12142)	11083	>47,200	-22.9	repeat of SUERC-3585		-
SUERC-4143 (GU-12141)	11081	10,100 +/- 60	-25.6	repeat of SUERC-3584		10,200-9,300 CalBC
SUERC-4148 (GU-12338)	11087	3065 +/- 35	-24.7	?oak charcoal	lower layer in Pit 11090	1420-1250 CalBC and 1240-1210 CalBC

Table 12.1: Radiocarbon dates (calibration using OxCal v.3.8)

Chapter 13: Discussion

Introduction

The often fragmentary archaeological evidence recovered during the course of fieldwork does not provide a secure basis for producing a synthesis of the archaeology of the region, but nonetheless, some aspects of the findings deserve to be summarised and discussed within the wider context. This chapter attempts to provide an overview of the results of the fieldwork in the light of current regional, and to some extent national, knowledge.

Pre-Bronze Age activity

Other than a few flint artefacts, probably derived from transient activity of some nature, there was no evidence for Mesolithic or Neolithic occupation in the area investigated. The absence of Mesolithic occupation confirms findings that the Kennet and Lambourn valley 'home bases' for these hunter-gatherer groups did not extend over the surrounding area. While it is likely that the local resources around Chieveley were exploited at this time and subsequently, this does not appear to have resulted in an archaeologically visible presence.

The absence of firm evidence for earlier Neolithic occupation is also perhaps unsurprising since settlement sites are normally difficult to recognise. The date at which the area started to be cleared for farming is at present unknown. While clearance and colonisation of the Berkshire Downs is thought to have started at this time (Birbeck 2000), it is not certain that the lower chalkland slopes, which are overlain extensively by Palaeocene drift deposits, should be included within this process. The pollen evidence from the mire at Snelsmore Common, about 1 km to the south-west, suggests that there was no large scale woodland clearance here until the Iron Age (690 +/- 90 BC), which is markedly later than it was elsewhere in the region (Waton 1982, 82-3). In reality, however, this pollen sequence may give disproportionate emphasis to the very local environment and its applicability to the Chieveley area must await further palaeo-environmental research of this nature.

There are few diagnostically Neolithic pieces in the assemblage of worked flint (Thorne, Chapter 8). They included a leaf-shaped arrowhead, an adze and a few blades. Several of the more carefully worked tools, cores and debitage may be later Neolithic in date, but the dominant character of the group, with its rough cores, irregular, hard-hammer struck flakes and rudimentary retouched pieces, suggests a middle to late Bronze Age technology. It is possible therefore that there was a degree of, perhaps even an increasing, utilisation of the land throughout the earlier prehistoric period, but no sustained occupation until the middle Bronze Age.

An extensive (12 ha) spread of worked flint from south of Curridge Road has been reported on as part of the archaeological investigations in connection with the Newbury Bypass (Birbeck 2000, 18-19). This has been characterised as late Neolithic and Early Bronze Age, although the absence of a description of the material in the report makes this conclusion difficult to evaluate, and a comparison with the flintwork on the current project is not possible. Also nearby, but to the north-east, a collection of flintwork from south of Ashfield's Farm is of unspecified character. There is a ring-ditch in the adjacent field which at least appears to indicate funerary activity in the early Bronze Age or later.

Bronze Age occupation

The earliest positively dated features on the site were the group of pits in Area E, Trench 11 containing Middle and Late Bronze Age pottery, together with burnt flint, worked flint and charcoal. (Soil conditions were inimical to the survival of bone.) Large sherds from a Middle Bronze Age globular urn and bucket urn also came from the subsoil or a shallow feature at the northern end of Area E, and small fragments of probable Bronze Age pottery came from other shallow features in this area. Much of the superficial flintwork would also appear to be Bronze Age in character. This material is assumed to be a by-product of domestic activities, but a funerary context cannot be entirely ruled out. The nature of these features and the occupation is examined in more detail below, but the main conclusion with regard to the site is that more sustained permanent or intensive occupation is evident from the Middle Bronze Age onward.

It is possible that this is part of a wider pattern applicable to the land away from the Chalk downlands and Kennet Valley where archaeological remains from the Early Bronze Age onward are rather more common (Birbeck 2000, 56). There is evidence from the colluvial soils in the Lambourn Valley near Bagnor of land clearance and/ or tillage from the Middle Bronze Age (Macphail & Allen 2000) and there is some indication of settlement on the Lambourn-Kennet interfluve at Bath Road at around this time (Birbeck 2000, 20). Also on the Newbury Bypass scheme, the discovery of an isolated Middle Bronze Age Globular Urn at Swilly Copse, south of Curridge Road, has an obvious and curious parallel to the pottery from TP 136, Area E on the present project. Again this vessel has been assumed to be of domestic significance (ibid, 19) and although a funerary context appears possible, it probably represents the only surviving element of an otherwise lost settlement. The character of this settlement, however, is not definable at present and may not be typical of those of the chalkland or river valleys.

Bronze Age Pits in Area E Trench 11

Origin

Although none of the shafts were excavated to a great depth and their full character was not established, it is most likely that they had their origin as solution pipes which developed in the underlying Chalk. The alternative, that they were man-made wells or shafts, cannot be disproved, but this is unlikely for the reasons examined by Healy in relation to the prehistoric shafts on Eaton Heath, Norwich (Wainwright 1973; Healy 1986). Similar shafts containing prehistoric material have been recorded at Cottage Field, Wattisfield in Suffolk (Bamford 1982), Fort Wallington in Hampshire (Hughes & ApSimon 1978), Cannon Hill, Maidenhead (Bradley *et al* 1976) and Street Farm Brampton, Norfolk (Healy 1983). The geological conditions of permeable strata (sand or gravel) overlying Chalk are common to all these sites and explain the phenomenon. Some of the geological literature is cited by Hughes and ApSimon (1978) and it is relevant to note that solution pipes were examined during the construction of the M4 motorway in Berkshire.

An anthropogenic explanation is less convincing since the excavation of narrow shafts through unstable sand (to depths of over 5m at Radnall Farm, and over 7m at Eaton Heath) would have presented enormous difficulties, and, particularly where shafts occur in quantities - there were twenty-one examined at Eaton Heath - it seems an unlikely endeavour. Shafts have also been found on Chalk geology and their origin here is more equivocal since there is no doubt that prehistoric people had the capacity to excavate deep shafts through solid geology, either to mine flint or for other purposes (shown, for example, by Grimes Graves and the Wilsford Shaft). The probably Mesolithic shaft at Fir Tree Field on Cranborne Chase has been examined with inconclusive results on this point (Green and Allen 1997). Here a natural origin is perhaps favoured in view of the enormous size of the feature (4 m in diameter and over 25m deep) which would be an unprecedented undertaking for communities at this time. At Billown, Isle of Man, at least 20 prehistoric pits and shafts have been identified, covering a wide range of dates within the area of the 'ceremonial complex', and it is possible that there are nearly 100 such features (Darvill 2000, 68). The preliminary report suggests that a number are likely to have a geomorphological origin (ibid.). The solution hollows (swallets) in the Mendips are well-known karstic features, in some cases currently active as drainage features. Several have been shown to have been receptacles for deliberate deposition in the Neolithic and Bronze Age (Lewis 2000). There is thus some evidence for the use of holes in the ground as 'natural monuments' in prehistoric times and these are likely to have been the object of special attention.

Other activity at Radnall Farm involved digging pits. These can in some cases be shown to have been subsequent to the formation of the shafts, although in other cases the evidence is simply lacking. It is possible to interpret the pits as mimicking the natural shafts. There are parallels at Eaton Heath where a number of 'shallow shafts' (1.5-2.5m deep) can be seen to have had relatively broad and more irregular profiles than the deep shafts and are arguably a distinct class of man-made feature. Similarly at Cannon Hill relatively shallow Neolithic pits were present along with the solution holes (Bradley et al 1976). A closer parallel perhaps comes from Billown where "it is clear that the larger ones [pits] involve episodic reworking and generally develop as a large hollow in the bottom of which one or more smaller pits are excavated" (Darvill 2000, 68). It is possible that artificial pits were present at some of the other sites, such as Overa Heath near East Harling in Norfolk, where some of the pits, which were associated with fire-cracked flint and Beaker pottery, were apparently related to banks (Apling 1931; Bamford 1982). At these sites it is not known whether the presence of natural solution pipes was the primary reason, or even a factor in, the occupation in the area, and it is possible that the association was fortuitous.

Chronology

At Radnall Farm there was a limited amount of dating evidence from the upper fills of these pits, but it is more problematical determining the date of origin of the shafts themselves, which were earlier and may have considerably pre-dated the deposits in the weathering cone. Even where cultural material becomes incorporated within the lower fills of the shaft it is likely to have been redeposited from upper soil layers when the sides of the shaft collapsed. This situation has been outlined in relation to the Fir Tree Field shaft on Cranborne Chase (Green and Allen 1997) where the preservation of evidence from snails, flint and pottery has enabled some analysis of the problem. A reappraisal of the Eaton Heath shafts has led to the suggestion that the radiocarbon dates show an inverted sequence due precisely to the redeposition of earlier material through slumping (Healy 1986). The Radnall Farm shafts offer no firm dating evidence at all, although it can be shown that the weathering cones were present in two instances (Pit Groups 11047 and 11138) when Bronze Age activity was current. In three other cases there are likely to have been hollows of some description to account for the digging of Pit Groups 11174, 11155 and 11213 on the probable sites of shafts. It is a matter of speculation whether there were human witnesses to the formation of any of these shafts, but the general instability of the ground is likely to have been an abiding folk memory whether or not sink holes were actively being formed during the adjacent occupation. On intrinsically unstable sandy geologies it is possible that solution holes were continually sinking rather than formed by sudden collapse, and their formation may therefore have been observable over the long term.

The fills of the weathering cones also present potential problems of sequence and dating. The soils would have been derived from the erosion of the pit sides and former land surfaces, as well as the deliberate or accidental inclusion of deposits associated with human activity. This may have taken place over a longer period than the creation of the shaft, under conditions of greater stability, but potentially includes material redeposited from the former land surface.

The deposit sequence is complicated in Pit Group 11138 by a number of smaller pits, which were, as far as can be judged, dug around the perimeter of the main shaft before very much infilling of the weathering cone. This presumably resulted in the redeposition of sand elsewhere within the feature, although there was no clear evidence of this. The chronology of this group of pits cannot be established with any accuracy. Peripheral pit 11109 appears to have been one of the earliest features since its fill lacked burnt flint which was present in the fills of central depression 11042 above the clean soil horizon 11043, as well as in the other pits. Above fill 11043 sherds of Late Bronze Age / Early Iron Age pottery were recovered from fill 11044 and Pit 11068 (on the northern side of the depression). The single sherd of Middle Bronze Age pottery from 11044 was probably residual since the layer above (11045) contained probable Late Bronze Age pottery. Other residual material includes the Palaeolithic flint from 11045 and the occasional 'early' looking flintwork. It is likely that the Roman greyware sherd from 11045 is intrusive or misascribed, although the presence of a beaded rim of Late Iron Age type from the uppermost fill, 11046, suggests that the hollow was still visible at this time and perhaps in the Roman period as well. The sequence represented by 0.8 m of accumulated sediment in Hollow 11042 might therefore have taken place over 800-1000 years from the Late Bronze Age to the Late Iron Age or Roman period. There is no suggestion, however, that the digging of peripheral pits lasted beyond the Late Bronze Age / Early Iron Age and there appears to have been little activity after this date.

The sequence in Pit Group 11047 is similar, although the dating evidence suggests that it might have infilled earlier. There were no finds from the lower fills of the weathering cone, the trace charcoal in 11143 perhaps being redeposited. Above this, the lower fill (11059) of Hollow 11060 contained only small quantities of burnt flint, while the middle fill (11058) contained mainly flint-tempered Middle Bronze Age sherds and the upper fill (11057) sandy sherds of Late Bronze Age / Iron Age date. The peripheral pits, 11056 and 11065, appeared to have been cut from the surface 11057, and so are late in the sequence. They also showed signs of re-cutting and contained occasional Late Bronze Age / Iron Age pottery, which seems to confirm this as the main period of activity here.

Of the other pits with natural origins, Pit Groups 11174 and 11213 contained no finds, which may mean that they were dug rather earlier (or later) than the dated features, or that they were simply too small and too far removed from areas of activity for any cultural material to have been deposited.

The much larger pit 11195 may have filled entirely naturally and the absence of finds, including burnt flint, from the excavated section would suggest that it was not contemporary with Pit Groups 11042 and 11138. In view of the Late Iron Age and Roman occupation in the field and the potential for redeposited material, it is perhaps more likely that the pit was earlier. A similar conclusion can be drawn about the nearby sub-rectangular pit 11110 which was 50% hand excavated and from which the shortage of finds is a more secure observation. A core rejuvenation flake (Fig. 8.10.9) and utilised blade from this feature may be earlier than the main body of flintwork from these pits.

The origin of Pit 11024 remains unclear, but the presence of pottery of exclusively Middle Bronze Age date in all its main fills suggests that it was one of the earliest features. The pit is perhaps likely to have had a natural origin perhaps forming the role of 'prototype' for the later pit-digging and related activities on the site. Burnt flint was associated with all the principal deposits in the pit.

The burnt flint was concentrated in Pit 11090, but for the reasons discussed above, most of the material in this pit appears to have been redeposited from nearby middens or occupation areas. The Iron Age dating evidence from six sherds in the lowest fill (11089) cannot be ignored and the eight sherds of Middle Bronze Age pottery from 11087, along with the burnt material in this pit would seem to have been related to earlier occupation which was cleared at a much later date. The other discrete man-made pits nearby, 11033 and 11027, would seem to relate to the general later Bronze Age period of pit digging. Gully Group 11224 are probably also of this general phase.

Purpose
The identification of groups of solution holes containing evidence of activity from the Middle Bronze Age through until the earlier Iron Age does not in itself explain the nature of the activities carried out. During this time pits of non-uniform size and distribution were dug around the periphery of two of the weathering cones, apparently when a certain amount of stability to the hollows had been reached and in some cases when the hollows had largely filled in. Other pits were dug nearby, both into filled natural shafts and away from them.

None of these pits contained items of particular significance, their contents reflecting a background scatter of burnt flint, charcoal and occasional flintwork and sherds of pottery. By their form, some of the pits could have held free-standing posts, but there was no indication of this from their fills. The purpose of any of the pits is therefore unknown.

Associated activity included the production and discard of heated flints with moderately large amounts of charcoal. This material is commonly associated with Late Bronze Age sites, sometimes as 'burnt mounds' and at other times it is simply present in notably large quantities in negative features as at Radnall Farm. The interpretation of these sites, which have been found widely in Britain and Ireland, has been the subject of much analysis and speculation (Buckley 1990, Hodder and Barfield 1991). Suggested functions include cooking, brewing, bathing and wool processing. In many cases, sites of heated stones are found next to streams, sometimes including water troughs, and where activities used hot water or steam this location would make sense. At Radnall Farm an association with water is unlikely since the supply would have been some distance away. Through a lack of any obvious alternative, it seems likely that the burnt flint was associated with a particular method of cooking which was common at the time.

No hearths or areas of scorched earth were identified and it is not clear where the flint was heated. It should be emphasised that the site of the pits was not identifiable by a surface concentration of burnt flint; on the contrary, greater concentrations of burnt flint were found elsewhere in the fieldwalking stage of investigation, both north and south of the motorway. A concentration in Area A was suggested to be the location of a ploughed out burnt mound (GGP 2000, para. 3.1.7), although this was later found not to be associated with sub-surface features. This surface flint probably represented part of a scatter of prehistoric activity (mostly likely Bronze Age), and not necessarily linked to the activities carried out in near Radnall Farm. It seems unlikely, for instance, that burnt flint produced in Area A was carried to the Radnall Farm site, a distance of over 1 km, although such a connection over a shorter distance within Area E is possible (Figs 8.4 - 6). There is therefore no reason to suspect particularly intense 'burnt mound activity' on the site and the site indeed may never have had a conspicuous mound of burnt flint nearby. The burnt flint seems to have been one aspect to the activities carried out, but perhaps not even the main or most significant one. A similar point has been made by Barber in relation to Scottish burnt mound sites where a simple four-fold classification of deposits can be seen as "a continuum which ranges from sites which are all burnt mound material and no settlement debris (class 1) to sites which are mainly settlement debris containing relatively small amounts of burnt mound material (class 4), with intermediate sites between these extremes (classes 2 and 3)" (Barber 1990, 99).

As a point of comparison, at the Green Park site in the Kennet valley near Reading the amount of burnt flint in the Late Bronze Age mound can be estimated to be 300 cubic metres (from Brossler *et al* 2004, 128). By contrast the quantity of burnt flint found in Pit 1090 at Radnall Farm is unlikely to have amounted to more than 10 cubic metres, and was probably closer to five. Although there are factors of preservation and longevity of occupation to be considered when comparing sites, it seems that burnt flint of itself is not a distinctive enough feature to enable useful site categories to be constructed. Radnall Farm need not have had a great deal in common with 'burnt mound' or 'pot-boiler' sites in other areas.

The question that remains unanswered is whether the archaeological evidence points to a particular activity undertaken in the area of Trench 11, drawn to the presence of natural hollows in the ground, or whether a background level of Bronze Age activity became more fortuitously preserved in an area where pits and hollows provided suitable receptacles for cultural debris.

Elsewhere there is a certain amount of evidence that natural and artificial shafts were used for special deposits in prehistoric Britain. Some of the best evidence comes from the Mendips where prehistoric material has been found in natural shafts in the limestone. The material from Charterhouse Warren Swallet includes human bone associated with a complete Beaker at a depth of over 15 m, and Iron Age and Roman inhumations in the upper levels. There is the clear suggestion that the hole was used for special deposition over a long period of time. Quite similar material, including human bone, Grooved Ware and a complete polished stone axe, were found in Brimble Pit Swallet (Lewis 2000). At Eaton Heath it is likely that the East Anglian Beaker, found at a depth of 3.5 m in shaft 5 was deliberately deposited (Wainwright 1973, 12). It is possible that it accompanied a burial but, as at Radnall Farm, the acidic soil did not favoured the preservation of any bone on this site. Other sherds of Neolithic and Bronze Age pottery in some of the other shafts here were considered to be unweathered and therefore perhaps deposited in open shafts, rather than being redeposited through slumping (ibid). These could also be considered deliberate deposits, although this is less clear. It can be noted that the activities associated with the shafts at Eaton Heath did not result in large numbers of objects or special deposits, at least of a kind which survived in the archaeological record, and 10 of the 21 shafts yielded no finds at all. It can be suggested that the pits at Radnall Farm were used in a similar way with few surviving signs of what was carried out.

The dating of the Radnall Farm site is somewhat later than that at Eaton Heath, although this need not preclude a similar reason for their presence or similar sorts of activities being undertaken. There is no evidence that the Radnall Farm field was a focus for activity before the Middle Bronze Age, at least for anything more than what may be characterised as transient activity which resulted in the occasional presence of early flintwork. It is possible, therefore, that occupation of any substance was attracted by the presence of natural shafts and hollows. The earliest diagnostic pottery comprises a globular urn and a bucket urn from TP136 in the northern part of the field and bucket urn fragments from Pit 11024 in the south. It seems there may have been two types of occupation, one near the pits and another in the northern part of the field 300-400m away. It is not clear whether funerary practices might have been involved since bone was not preserved. The disparate evidence of shallow gullies and pits of the Bronze Age and early Iron Age in the northern and central parts of the field is insufficient to indicate the nature of occupation here. Even the presence of bounded fields cannot be supported by evidence of this quality.

Eaton Heath revealed occupation, mainly in the form of pits, dating to the Neolithic and early Bronze Age periods, from the late 4th millennium until the late 3rd or early 2nd millennium BC. There must remain some uncertainty as to whether the deep shafts here were the primary focus of attention, although the ceramic and radiocarbon dating from them tend to cover a similar range, suggesting that such a proposition is possible. It may be worth speculating that the Bronze Age barrow cemetery later became attracted to the site for the same reason, although it is far from clear that the barrows and shafts are at all linked by anything more than co-incidence. The possibility of a direct connection, in terms of communities involved, between the East Anglian Beaker in shaft 5 and the Barbed Wire Beaker under barrow Site 9549/c4 (150m away) has been examined by Healy, but such a linkage is admitted to be tenuous (Healy 1986, 57).

It is similarly unclear whether the Fir Tree Field shaft on Cranborne Chase became a focus of ritual, since there appears to be nothing in the deposits themselves which suggests that the feature acted as more than a 'reservoir' trapping material from nearby activity. However, Beaker material from nearby man-made pits has been interpreted in terms of ritual activity late in the existence of the shaft, and perhaps even related to its closure (Green and Allen 1997, 128).

In this connection it is worth drawing attention to the later deposits within the weathering cone of the Wilsford Shaft (Ashbee et al 1989). While the Bronze Age shaft and its waterlogged deposits have received the most consideration, a small group of material was recorded from the later weathering cone. These included 134 sherds of Deverel-Rimbury, Early Iron Age and Roman pottery, some animal bone, and disarticulated human bone from a minimum of five individuals. The report states that "since there was a lack of evidence for deliberate deposition, it may be assumed that the majority of finds in the cone derive from casual events, such as weathering or possible animal activity, which would have disturbed material from the surface" (ibid, 24). This assessment, however, appears inadequate to explain all except the fragmentary and abraded Roman pottery. The Iron Age material, in particular, represents the bulk of the pottery and includes an almost complete jar. Two radiocarbon dates on human bones fell within the Iron Age. The difficulty of accounting for this material is highlighted by the absence of nearby Iron Age sites from which these 'casual losses' could have derived (ibid, 24). It seems more probable that the shaft retained some importance as a focus of deliberate deposition until well into the Iron Age, approximately a millennium after its construction.

There is therefore evidence to suggest that these kinds of features, both natural and man-made, could serve as a focus of ritual activities in prehistoric times, and indeed become objects of persistent attention long after their actual genesis. There are grounds for supposing that the Radnall Farm pits were associated with this sort of activity, but the evidence for any specific tasks carried out is lacking.

Iron Age, Roman and Saxon

With the exception of part of isolated, *in situ*, vessel from Area A, there was little of significance found dating to the Early and Middle Iron Age on the project. The occupation associated with the Bronze Age pits probably ceased in the Late Bronze Age or Early Iron Age, but thereafter there was no definable activity until the establishment of settlement in the north-western part of Area E in the Late Iron Age. This settlement, which minimal investigation suggests dates to the Late Iron Age and Early Roman periods, was designated for preservation *in situ* in the current project strategy and must remain for a future project.

The Iron Age in the region is marked by the construction of hill-forts, of which Bussock Camp, about 1 km to the west, is one. In many parts of the country there is a great increase in settlement in this period, but this does not appear to be the case locally, at least until the Late Iron Age. The much larger Newbury Bypass project also failed to locate any Iron Age sites, and there are strong grounds for suggesting settlement dislocation at this time. The Kennet valley appears to have been depopulated and it has been suggested that the population was absorbed into the hill-forts (Birbeck 2000, 56). It may be significant that the Snelsmore Common pollen diagram shows woodland clearance at about this time.

There are also grounds for proposing a reconfiguration of settlement in the Late Iron Age when more finds become apparent. This may be related to the rise of the tribal centre of *Calleva Atrebatum* (Silchester) from the 1st century BC. There is some suggestion that these settlements tended to continue into the Roman period and the site in Area E of the current project may be typical in this respect. Another potential site of this date lies to the west of Area D. Four sites of Roman date were excavated ahead of the construction of the Newbury bypass, at least two of these probably starting in the Late Iron Age (Birbeck 2000, 57).

The evidence for Roman settlement in the Newbury area and in the Kennet Valley is extensive and need not be repeated in detail here (Birbeck 2000, 57). Most Roman settlement appears to lie in the vicinity of the Roman road between Silchester and Mildenhall, which passed just north of Newbury. A probable roadside settlement (*Spinis*) lay near Speen, about 5km south-west of Radnall Farm while there was a probable small town at Thatcham Newton, about 8km to the south-east. The Chieveley area is less well known and there are doubtless more sites to be discovered. It is possible that this area, which was at a distance from any urban centres, retained a strongly native character until well into the Roman period, and this may be a factor behind the scarcity of 'stray finds' being recorded in the SMR.

Late Roman 'cremation' pits

Late Roman activity on the site is limited to two adjacent pits (29018 and 29229), a patch of scorched earth between them, and an overlying layer (29014) forming a small group of features, Group 29247. This group yielded most of the Roman material from the site - 377 sherds as well as an assortment of other finds. The pottery and other finds have been described in detail (Timby Chapter 9, Hylton Chapter 10), and although the group is quite heterogeneous there are a number of elements such as a miniature jar and the other single but broken vessels which suggest that the group is a non-domestic one. The pits have been described as 'cremation' pits, although there was just a tiny piece of calcined bone from Pit 29018, indicating that the burial rite would have involved the disposal or burial of cremated human remains elsewhere.

It is possible that the lack of cremated bone could be explained by soil conditions, but unburnt animal bone was recovered from Pit 29018 and this suggests that conditions are not as inimical to the survival of bone from the Roman period as they are for Bronze Age bone, 2000 years older. It is therefore considered likely that the general absence of cremated bone is genuine, but establishing the particular funerary rite is problematic. The nature of the evidence presents a number of difficulties of interpretation and the shortage of close parallels suggests that the rite was a rare one.

The dating of these features is provided by the pottery and coins, which indicate a date in the second half of the 4th century. A *terminus post quem* for the three coins from Pit 29018 comes out at around AD 360-70. The coins from Layer 29014 above are earlier probably resulting from longer circulation. The pottery is not dated as precisely, but it is suggested that the late Roman shelly ware might indicate the last quarter of the 4th century or beyond (Timby, Chapter 9).

Cremation burial at this time is unusual, but was present at Lankhills cemetery in Winchester (Clarke 1979). Among the seven late Roman cremations, two were in inhumation-sized pits (ibid, 129). In both cases the pyre was located next to the grave. The parallel with Radnall Farm is not exact, particularly with regard to the large numbers of 'grave goods' and the virtual absence of cremated bone at Radnall Farm. An interesting point to emerge from the Lankhills burials is the sorting of cremated material into categories before burial. Such a selection process at Radnall Farm could have excluded cremated bone from the 'grave'.

It also seems that most of the pyre debris must have been disposed of elsewhere, as only a fraction of the charcoal that would have been necessary for cremation was present in the 'grave pits'. The possible pyre site was also very clean. The grave pits contained material which may have been included as grave goods, along with fragmentary material which looks out of place in a grave. Pit 29018 contained sherds which, when joined, formed a complete small greyware dish (Fig. 9.2.11) and most of a small necked greyware jar (Fig. 9.2.13) as well as a number of semi-complete vessels and large sherds (Timby, Chapter 9). Other finds include three coins, a hobnail, and five cleats - which may have been used for re-enforcing the soles and heels of boots (Hylton, Chapter 10). These were all generally distributed throughout the fill of the pit. None of the finds from either pit, or the overlying layer 29014, appeared to have been burnt, and it does not seem that any of the finds were pyre goods.

There was a smaller collection of pottery from Pit 29229, but this included a complete miniature jar (Fig. 9.1.4) from the upper part of the fill. The largest collection of pottery came from Layer 29014, although this was more fragmented than that from the underlying pits and did not have the appearance of grave or pyre goods. The other associated items were also varied and fragmentary and none need be specifically funerary. The origin of this collection of material is enigmatic and, assuming there to have been some sort of funerary association, the rites behind its deposition remain obscure.

Late Roman to Saxon

The late Roman to early Saxon transition is an enigmatic period for which there is little archaeological evidence in the region. The presence of a small number of late Roman and early Saxon pits in Trench 29 of Area E, and early-mid Saxon pits in Area C may have a significance out of proportion to the quantity or quality of remains actually found, but how this information should be assessed is at present difficult to judge. These features appear isolated, without the context of related settlement. The Saxon material is actually poorly dated and need not be particularly early. The disposal of quern fragments apparently away from the domestic context may be related in some way to the 'domestication' of the land, perhaps related to the clearance of wood or scrub, but there are no satisfactory parallels or interpretations known to the author. The name Chieveley is thought to be derived from 'Cifa's leah', 'the clearing in the wood of Cifa', so it is possible that the area was largely wooded in the immediate post-Roman period. This receives some support from the Snelsmore Common pollen diagram which shows woodland regeneration from around AD 350 (Waton 1982, 83). Tree and shrub pollen dominates until about 1475, but this is predominantly due to local woodland. The presence of cereals and other cultivars suggests the landscape to have been a mosaic of woodland with arable clearances from the early Saxon period.

Post-medieval features

There were a number of post-medieval features encountered on both sides of the motorway which, while not particularly significant in themselves, contribute to an understanding of the development of the landscape here. These comprised mostly field boundaries in a number of areas, and in Area D a quarry. The most prominent feature was the hollow-way in Area A (Trench 16).

The hollow-way took an unexpected course in that, in its approach off the Newbury road from the south heading toward Chieveley, it made a turn of 90 degrees to join Green Lane (Fig. 7.1). The logic behind this piece of relict landscape only becomes clear in the light of early maps. The form of the hollow-way can be appreciated from the Tithe map of Snelsmore, dated 1840, reproduced here as Figure 13.1. This clearly shows that it became a field boundary for most of its length, enclosing an area of woodland or scrub. This enclosure, apparently overgrown in 1840, had been lost by the time the survey for the 1882-3 OS map was undertaken, the area having become one large field between Green Lane and the new access road to Snelsmore Farm in the intervening years.

Rocque's 1761 map (Fig. 13.2) shows this enclosure to have been an open space at the junction of the road to Chieveley village and the Newbury-Oxford road. It is not known what this space would have been used for, but the Snelsmore Tithe map suggests that it may have originated as a rectangular field to whose edge the traffic to Chieveley clung, creating a sharp bend in the road. The map further suggests that there were originally (ie. pre-1761) two separate northern routes, both somewhat irregular ones, the western from Newbury to Chieveley village along Green Lane, and the eastern along Chalky Lane toward Oxford, bypassing Chieveley itself. A new straight section of road appears to have been built linking the two existing routes and creating a new Newbury-Oxford road which bypassed the village of Chieveley. The new road cut across the rectangular field putting the peripheral trackway out of use.

This must have happened before 1761. The dating evidence from the hollow-way, which includes 18th/19th-century finds, indicates that the trackway was not abandoned much before the mid 18th century. Turnpike trusts began to proliferate in Berkshire at around this time and this may well be the context for the creation of the new stretch of road and the subsequent abandonment of the hollow-way.

Some of the field boundaries shown on the 1840 Tithe map, and lost by the 1st edition of the Ordnance Survey, correspond to ditches found in the trenches here. These include two ditches in Trench 10 respecting the hollow-way. It is also probable that the north-south ditch in Area B relates to the boundary of the rectangular enclosure here although the coincidence between map and fieldwork is not exact.

The exaggerated topography south of Radnall's Farm in Area D was shown to have been due to the excavation and dumping of material from a large quarry. This is not shown cartographically although the Chieveley enclosure award map of 1812 names the field as "Chalk Close", suggesting the reason for a former quarry here. The extraction of chalk was probably for the purpose of marling the land, most likely related to 18th-century agricultural improvements.

Conclusions

The several combined stages of archaeological work have enabled a thorough process of investigation and mitigation to be undertaken ahead of the construction of the new road junction, and have produced a modest but significant new body of archaeological information for an area of Berkshire which has hitherto received little attention. Because the work was undertaken to mitigate the construction impacts rather than being directed at specific archaeological sites, the results are perhaps inevitably fragmentary. It is notable for instance that the late Iron Age/Roman site north-west of Radnall Farm, which may have been the principal site within the area of fieldwork, was left *in situ* and as a result has not been defined with any clarity. The late Roman 'cremation' pits examined are thought likely to have been associated with, and on the margins of this settlement, but this remains a supposition. Nonetheless, a by-product of this approach has been the chance to examine the 'off-site' archaeology of the landscape – features which would probably have been missed in excavations focused solely on 'settlement' remains. There has also been the opportunity to assess the combined evidence of the various stages of archaeological work in the light of the final results, both to reach an integrated archaeological interpretation, and to evaluate the effectiveness of the strategy.

There is evidence that the Middle Bronze Age was a significant period for the intensification of activity on the site, and this may be part of a wider regional trend. It followed a more sporadic earlier prehistoric presence the sole evidence for which was contained within the ploughsoil, there being no subsurface features dating to this period. The surface finds of flintwork therefore provide the only real means of assessing this earlier activity and surface collection over ploughed fields would seem to be the most reasonable method of field investigation. The trial pitting would seem to have been less useful as well as less efficient in this case.

Most of the Middle and Late Bronze Age remains came from Area E Radnall Farm, both in association with a group of pits in the southern part of the field (Trench 11) and further north. The finds in the northern and central areas included pottery from the ploughsoil and subsoil, as well as from two shallow gullies. Much of the flintwork is likely to be of this date but it is less diagnostic. Away from the southern pits, remains of this date were therefore quite superficial and fragile. It is possible that isolated minor features were missed by the trenching strategy and in the watching brief during overburden removal.

It is instructive to note that the Bronze Age features were not predictable on the basis of the non-intrusive surveys. In particular, the location of the Trench 11 pits did not coincide with superficial concentrations of burnt flint (which lay elsewhere) and the geophysical survey also failed to identify them. The geophysical survey gave poor (but generally usable) results everywhere due to the mixed geology but it appears that excessive magnetic disturbance may have been the cause of the failure to locate the Trench 11 pits, while to the north the Bronze Age gullies were too shallow to register.

It is possible that the Bronze Age pits continued in use in the early part of the Iron Age, there being little to distinguish unfeatured Late Bronze Age from Early Iron Age sherds, but otherwise there is very little evidence of Iron Age activity. The curiously isolated pit in Area A is the only feature positively dated to this period, and its

Bronze Age, Roman and later occupation at Chieveley, West Berkshire

*Fig 13.1 Copy of part of Tithe Map for Snelsmore 1840
(Berkshire Record Office Ref. D/D1 34/3, by kind permission)*

purpose is unclear. There was some miscellaneous Iron Age pottery from the western edge of the development site (Area D Trench 1) associated with Roman material, but it is also not known what this relates to.

Occupation north-west of Radnall Farm was probably established in the late Iron Age, although this is based upon the slender evidence of pottery from topsoil in Trial Pit 139 which may be of 1st century AD date rather than much earlier. The features here are more securely early Roman but the overall size and layout of the settlement are difficult to gauge from the cropmarks or geophysical survey both of which lack clarity. The occupation site was not the subject of trial trenching except with the restricted aim of establishing its southern limit. To the east, the Roman features examined by excavation proved to be distributed sporadically and the group of 'cremation pits' were much later than the other dated features. It is curious that the fieldwalking produced no evidence at all for Roman activity in the development area. The quantity of Roman pottery from the whole site (18 g, or 0.34 g per ha) was actually smaller than the amount of prehistoric pottery (GGP 2000, 7). Roman sites are normally the type most visible of all on superficial evidence and this suggests that the focus of occupation lay further west in the unsurveyed part of the field.

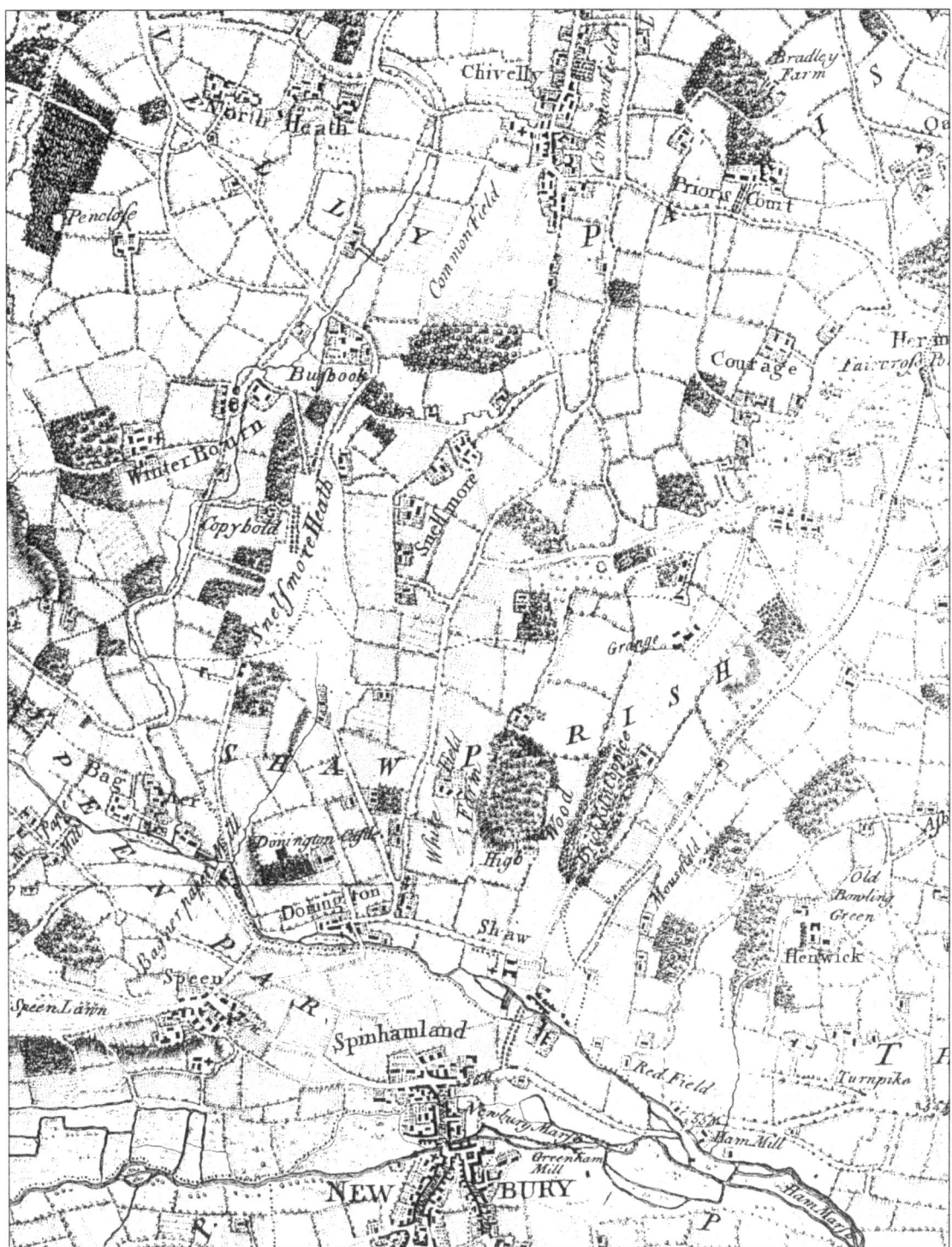

Fig 13.2 Copy of part of John Rocque's map of Berkshire c. 1761 (Berkshire Record Office, by kind permission)

The early-middle Saxon pits appear divorced from any associated settlement and were discovered fortuitously as a direct result of large scale soil stripping. Their distribution would seem to be entirely unpredictable from non-intrusive survey and it is not clear whether these kinds of features would be more commonly found in the region if more extensive excavations of this nature were to be undertaken.

There were no significant features of medieval date and the archaeological work adds little to our understanding of the area at this time. The post-medieval hollow-way in Area A is of some local interest in the context of developing communications from the 18th century. It was a less monumental feature than it initially appeared to be from the soil mark where ploughing appears to have spread ditch and bank material to produce an exaggerated effect (Plate 1). It is a feature which ought to have been identified in the desk-based assessment and targeted with evaluation at an early stage since its date and importance was not immediately apparent. The other main post-medieval feature is the quarry north of the road junction in Area D which is may well have removed archaeological remains here but whose impact in that regard it is now not possible to estimate.

Bibliography

Apling H, 1931 Bronze Age Settlements in Norfolk, *Proc. Prehist. Soc.,* XX, 365-70

Ashbee P, Bell M, and Proudfoot E, 1989 *Wilsford Shaft: excavations 1960-2*, English Heritage Archaeol. Report, 11

Bamford H M, 1982 *Beaker and Domestic Sites in the Fen Edge and East Anglia,* East Anglian Archaeol., 16, 38-9

Barber J, 1990 'Scottish Burnt Mounds: variations on a theme', in Buckley, 98-101

Birbeck V, 2000 *Archaeological Investigations on the A34 Newbury Bypass, Berkshire/ Hampshire, 1991-7,* Wessex Archaeology 2000 on behalf of Highways Agency

Borrill H, 1981 'The Casket Burials', in Partridge 1981, 304-321

Bradley R, Over L, Startin D W A, and Weng R, 1976 The excavation of a Neolithic site at Cannon Hill, Maidenhead, Berks 1974-5, *Berks Archaeol. J.* XX, 5-19

Brossler A, Early R, and Allen C, 2004 *Green Park (Reading Business Park. Phase 2 Excavations 1995 – Neolithic and Bronze Age sites.* Oxford Archaeology Thames Valley Monog., 19

Bradley P, 2004 'Worked Flint' in Brossler, Early and Allen, 45-57

Buckley V, 1990 *Burnt Offerings: International Contributions to Burnt Mound Archaeology*, Wordwell, Dublin

Clarke G, 1979 *Pre-Roman & Roman Winchester. Part II. The Roman cemetery at Lankhills*, Winchester Studies 3

Clarke G, 1979 'Hobnails and Footwear' in Clarke G, *Pre-Roman and Roman Winchester. Part II: The Roman Cemetery at Lankhills,* Winchester Studies 3, Oxford, Clarendon Press, 322-325

Cramp K, 2002 'Lithics', in Oxford Archaeology 2002, 9-10 and Appendix 3, 24-29

Crummy N, 1983 *The Roman small finds from excavations in Colchester*, Colchester Archaeol. Rep., 2

Darvill T, 2000 *Billown Neolithic landscape Project, Isle of Man. Fifth Report 1999,* Bournemouth University School of Conservation Science Res. Rep., 7, Bournemouth & Douglas

EH 1991 *Management of Archaeological Projects,* English Heritage

Gale R, and Cutler D, 2000 *Plants in Archaeology,* Westbury and Royal Botanic Gardens, Kew

GGP 1999 *Chieveley A34-M4 Junction Archaeological Desk-Based Assessment,* Gifford Graham & Partners, Report No. B2221A.R01A, Aug. 1999

GGP 2000 *Chieveley A34-M4 Junction Archaeological Field-Walking survey*, Gifford Graham & Partners, Report No. B2221E.RO1, Aug. 2000

Green M, and Allen M J, 1997 An Early Prehistoric Shaft on Cranborne Chase, *Oxf. J of Archaeol.,* 16 (2), 121-131

Hall M, 1992 'The Prehistoric pottery', in Moore J and Jennings D, *Reading Business Park: a Bronze Age landscape*, Thames Valley Landscapes: the Kennet Valley, Vol 1, Oxford, 62-71

Healy F, 1983 Neolithic and la ter material from a shaft at Brampton, *Norfolk Archaeol.,* xxxviii (iii), 363-374

Healy F, 1986 'The excavation of two early Bronze Age round barrows on Eaton Heath, Norwich 1969-70', in Lawson A J *Barrow Excavations in Norfolk, 1950-82,* East Anglian Archaeol., 29, 50-8

Hodder M A, and Barfield L H, (eds) 1991 *Burnt Mounds and Hot Stone Technology,* Papers from the Second Inernational Burnt Mound Conference Sandwell, 12th-14th October 1990, Sandwell Metropolitan Borough Council

Hughes M, and ApSimon A, 1978 A Mesolithic Flint Working Site on the South Coast Motorway (M27): Near Fort Wallington, Fareham, Hampshire, 1972, *Proc. Hampshire Field Club Archaeol. Soc.,* 34, 23-35

Lewis J, 2000, Upwards at 45 degrees: the use of vertical cavers during the Neolithic and early Bronze Age on Mendip, Somerset, *Capra* 2 available at http://www.shef.ac.uk/~capra/2/upwards.html

Lyne M A B, and Jefferies R S, 1979 *The Alice Holt/ Farnham Roman pottery industry,* CBA Res. Rep., 30, London

Macphail R I, and Allen M J, 2000 'Evaluation of the soil sequence at the Lambourn Valley site', in Birbeck 2000, Technical Reports, 8-10

Manning W H, 1974 'Objects of iron' in Neal 1974, 157-187

Manning W H, 1985 *Catalogue of Romano-British Iron tools, Fittings and Weapons in the British Museum*, British Museum

NA 2003 *A34 Chieveley / M4 Junction 13 Road Improvement: Archaeological Design and Mitigation Strategy,* Northamptonshire Archaeology, March 2003

NA 2004 *A34 Chieveley / M4 Junction 13 Road Improvement: Archaeological Assessment and Updated Project Design,* Northamptonshire Archaeology, March 2004

Neal D S, 1974 *The Excavation of the Roman Villa in Gadebridge Park, Hemel Hempstead 1963-8,* Society of Antiquaries, London

Oxford Archaeology, 2002 *A34/M4 Junction 13 Improvement Scheme Chieveley West Berkshire Trial Pitting Survey,* OA Job No. 1350

Partridge C, 1981 *Skeleton Green: A late Iron Age and Romano-British Site,* Britannia Monog. Ser., 2

PCRG, 1992 *Prehistoric Ceramics Research Group: The study of Later Prehistoric pottery: guidelines for analysis and publication,* Occ. Paper, 2, Oxford

Pitt-Rivers A H L, 1887 *Excavations on Cranborne Chase,* I

Rahzt P, and Meeson R, 1992 *An Anglo-Saxon Mill at Tamworth, Excavations inn the Bolebridge Street area of Tamworth, Staffordshire in 1971 and 1978,* CBA Research Rep. 83

Richards J, 1978 *The archaeology of the Berkshire Downs: an introductory survey,* Reading: The Berkshire Archaeological Committee Publication No. 3

Stace C, 1997 *New Flora of the British Isles.* Second edition. Cambridge University Press

Stratascan, 2002 *A report for Gifford and Partners Ltd. on a Geophysical Survey carried out at A34/M4 Junction 13 Improvement Scheme, Chieveley, West Berks. May-September 2002,* Job Ref. No. 1670

Tomber R, and Dore J, 1998 *The National Roman Fabric Reference Collection,* MoLAS. English Heritage/British Museum

Tutin T G, Heywood V H, *et al,* 1964-80 *Flora Europaea,* 1-5, Cambridge

Vince A, 1997 'Pottery', in Vince A G, Lobb S J, Richards J C and Mepham L, *Excavations in Newbury, Berkshire 1979-1990,* Wessex Archaeology Rep. No. 13, 45-68

Wainwright G, 1973 The Excavation of Prehistoric and Romano-British Settlements at Eaton Heath, Norwich, *Archaeol. J,* 130, 2-42

Waton P V, 1982 'Late Devensian and Early Flandrian vegetation changes in southern England', in Bell M and Limbrey S (eds) *Archaeological Aspects of Woodland Ecology,* BAR Brit. Ser., 146, 75-92

Wright S M, 1992 'Millstones', in Rahzt and Meeson 1992, 70-79

Young C J, 1977 *Oxfordshire Roman pottery,* BAR Brit. Ser., 43, Oxford